101 Commonsense Rules for Making Things Happen

How to Make Plans and Implement Projects

John R. Brinkerhoff

STACKPOLE
BOOKS

Published by
STACKPOLE BOOKS
5067 Ritter Road
Mechanicsburg, PA 17055

Cover design by Tracy Patterson with Steve Bernard
Illustrations by Durf McJoynt

Printed in the United States of America

First Edition

10 9 8 7 6 5 4 3 2 1

Library of Congress Cataloging-in-Publication Data

Brinkerhoff, John R.
    101 commonsense rules for making things happen : how to make plans and implement projects / John R. Brinkerhoff. — 1st ed.
        p.   cm.
    ISBN 0-8117-2419-0 :
    1. Strategic planning.   2. Time management.   I. Title.   II. Title: One hundred and one commonsense rules for making things happen.
    HD30.28.B754   1993
    658.4'012—dc20   93-1215
                                                                    CIP

Contents

4. Data 44

5. Time 60

6. Measures 74

7. Simple Conceptual Planning Tools   86

8. Resources 108

9. Costs 123

Introduction

Human beings want to make things happen. Our lives are filled with purposeful activities—things we have to do or want to do—and there is little time for purposeless living. Life is more complicated, perhaps, than before (although that tends to be irrelevant because we are living now), and it seems we have to try harder simply to keep up. Sometimes it seems that we have no choice but to make things happen.

Making things happen involves planning, preparing, and implementing. This book is roughly 80 percent about planning, 10 percent about preparing, and 10 percent about implementing. The basic thought behind the book is summed up in the following five Ps:

Proper Planning Prevents Poor Performance.*

Humans habitually plan and prepare, many times without even realizing it. When we arise in the morning, we make things happen as part of our ritual: wash, shave, get dressed, make coffee, eat breakfast, and either go to work or do other things as is our wont. Implementing even these routine activities benefits from planning and preparing,

---

* The agile alliterist will be able to add additional "P" words to his or her delight and to the consternation of others. I have seen this thought stated with an elegant expression of nine "P" words. See what you can do to match that!

for we have to have the resources—the soap, shaving cream, towels, coffee, coffee machine, bread, jam, milk, cereal, car, gasoline—with which to perform the routine, and we have to set aside time for these activities, and we have to impel our bodies along the way. So even our most basic routines require planning and preparing, albeit of a rudimentary sort.

We have to plan deliberately and prepare prudently for more complicated or unusual activities. Going to work may be planned so well that we don't even have to think about the route but can essentially let the car drive itself, but when we have a special meeting away from the office, we have to plan by checking the timetable and perhaps leaving a half hour earlier than usual or, if we are lucky, a half hour later. So we do have to plan for differences from our routines.

At the other extreme, when it comes to major projects, such as building a bridge or a new office building or deploying a half million troops to the Persian Gulf, everyone sees the necessity of planning. Most of us, however, will not be involved in these major kinds of projects and will have to be content merely to accomplish projects that are only somewhat more than routine.

This brings us to the reason why knowing how to plan, prepare, and implement is so important. The need for planning and preparing to implement nonroutine minor projects is neither obvious nor sustained by habit, so making these ordinary sorts of things happen often causes trouble for many of you. By learning the basics of planning, preparing, and implementing, you can make things happen without calling on the services of professional planners.

Planning is ubiquitous in human experience, and the ability to plan and prepare may be as much of the essence of humanity as the ability to communicate. But my experience as a practitioner and student of planning indicates that not all humans are particularly good at it. For one thing, planning is not taught in schools, *per se*. We learn some of the elements of planning, but individually and not as a unified process. We learn about goals, about costs, about money, about measuring, about scheduling, and about other particular subjects, but usually these topics are not assembled into a single system. If you are an engineer, soldier, or businessperson, you will have learned enough about planning and preparing to do your job, but many people simply don't have an opportunity to put it all together. This book will help you do just that.

The 101 rules in this book are designed to feed you bite-size chunks of an overall process for planning, preparing, and implementing so you can digest it a little bit at a time. The order of presentation ranges from the simple to the complicated, and follows the logical path of a plan from goals to costs to preparing and implementation. The first fourteen chapters deal with planning, chapter 15 is devoted to preparing, chapter 16 to implementing, and chapter 17 to a bit of homespun philosophy. This organizational scheme is an artificial device to make the process easier to understand; planning, preparing, and implementing often overlap and may even occur simultaneously. The book is comprehensive and introduces you to many different topics and planning tools, but it does not aspire to provide thorough, detailed coverage of any single topic. If you want to learn more about a particular part of the planning and preparing process, there are a great many other books that will help.

By way of illustration, I have applied the planning process to two common cases—project planning and business planning—but the rules herein are also useful for planning and preparing for vacations, holidays, weddings, parties, home improvements, making purchases, and just plain living. This book about making things happen can be applied to any project or set of goals you want to pursue.

1 Getting Started

The hardest part of planning, as with many other human endeavors, is getting started. Simply putting the first brick in place, the first word on paper, or the first number in the calculator seems to be a very difficult proposition. Once the start is made, most people are able to proceed at reasonable speed. But that very first entry has some emotional block associated with it that makes it hard, hard, hard. Because of this, I am devoting the first chapter to some really basic rules designed to make it easier for you to start the planning process.

You must understand, however, that all the rules in the world, no matter how very commonsense they are, will not substitute for the desire to accomplish something. In business it is the desire for profit—or at least a decent living—that makes the difference between success and failure. In athletics, the desire to win can make it possible for any team in the National Football League to win the big game. In life it is drive that counts. It is your desire to attain some goal that must drive you. There is no reason to plan just for the sake of planning. So unless you really want to learn how to make things happen, don't go any farther. Put this book on your shelf and wait until you really want to learn, for it is an aid and not a panacea.

The four rules of this chapter are intended to help you decide what you really want to do, visualize how you are going to do it, and then put it down on paper. These first steps provide the essential foundation for all of the planning and preparing to follow.

Rule 1: Decide What You Want to Make Happen

The most important part of making a plan is to figure out what it is you want to do. This is your goal. There is no point in having a plan without a goal, for there is no way to measure progress or detect success unless there is one.

This sounds simple but, like so many things in life, is not. Discovering what we want to do is a real problem for all of us at one time or another, and it is a big problem for some of us almost all of the time.

A goal may be simple or it may be complex, but it always has to contain three basic elements: result, time, and feasibility.

A result is what most people think of when they contemplate a goal. The result is what you want to happen, and the more concrete the result, the better for your planning. Your goal might be to graduate from college, backpack across Europe, buy a car, build a house, become a partner, or catch a fish. You may think it strange even to contemplate a plan without a goal, but that happens sometimes, and often the stated goal is not the real goal or even a realistic one.

There is a great deal of difference, for example, between a goal of having a Cadillac or that of simply having ground transportation. If the goal truly is to have a Cadillac, the cost is already pretty well defined and there will be few alternatives. This goal already includes numerous assumptions and preliminary decisions. If the goal really is to have ground transportation, there are more alternatives—including in some circumstances not owning a car at all. So the result intended in the plan needs to be considered carefully at the outset.

Time is always a factor in goals, either explicitly or, more likely, implicitly. When you want to achieve a result, you really have to say when you want that result to occur. If you leave out the time element, the goal is too indefinite to serve as the basis for a plan. You want to graduate from college in four years or five years, but not just "sometime." You want to buy your car now, or next week, or a year from now. You want to become a partner in the next five years. You want to catch a fish next Wednesday afternoon. If you are going to plan to achieve the result, you will have to include a time frame or deadline for the achievement. Many plans include a definite time frame in the goal statement, but some only imply a time frame. "I want to ski in the Alps while I'm still young" might not include a specific deadline, but it is understood that time is a factor. It is always best to state a time by which to achieve the goal.

Feasibility is the third element of a goal. It usually does not make sense to have a goal that cannot be achieved. A plan to fly to Mars is not a useful basis for planning for an individual or even for a small company. It might be feasible, however, for NASA, which already reached its goal of placing a man on the moon. The planner needs to make certain that the goals are attainable within the reasonable constraints of time and expense. There is no use planning for the impossible or the improbable.

Some goals may stretch the limits of feasibility, however. The poet Robert Browning said correctly that "a man's reach should exceed his grasp. . . ." Nothing could have been more inspiring than President Kennedy's goal of putting a man on the moon by 1960. At the time he set that goal for the United States, it was strictly speaking not feasible, but having the goal and the will to work on it made it feasible. Thus in some cases, just setting the goal makes the result feasible.

On the other hand, it will not do to make silly goals. Some mothers are doing that for their children. They set goals for their sons to be lawyers and their daughters to get married to rich, young, good men. Today those goals might very well be reversed, and the daughters are to become doctors and lawyers while the sons marry rich, young, good women. Whatever. The point is that mothers who set these goals often do so without the slightest chance that they will really come true. It is just fantasy in their minds. The fact that the goals are infeasible, of course, does not stop a lot of planning and activity to achieve them. One of life's realities is that children most often do what they want despite their parents' desires.

Goal setting is an iterative process. You set a goal or goals, you consider them, and then you revise them in light of other considerations. It is foolish to refuse to change goals when circumstances change.

Rule 2: Visualize Your Goals

One of your first iterations in the planning process ought to be done right at this point, before you set your goals in concrete. Conduct a feedback loop at this point by visualizing your goals, comparing the results with your first ideas, making the appropriate adjustments, and then moving along in the process. A feedback loop adds new information to a previous part of the process. Planning involves a lot of feedback loops, so you might just as well get used to the idea.

Visualizing is not the same thing as deciding, for it is both less definite and more thorough. Deciding is goal oriented, while visualizing is more of an abstract rumination on what could, might, might not, should, or should not take place.

The way to visualize what you want to make happen is to dream about it, reducing the sharp edges of your initial goals to fuzzy sets of things that shimmer and glisten. Take away definite thoughts and bring in some indefinite ones in a kind of purposeful daydream in which you peer into the nooks and crannies of your goals from outside. It is sort of an extracorporeal experience.

The best time to visualize your goals and plans is at odd moments when you are not caught up with anything else to do. Some people might be able to set a definite time for this kind of thinking. I cannot. I have to let it occur when the spirit strikes. A good place to do this kind of thinking is when you are resting in your bed just waiting to go to sleep and have nothing else to worry about. I like to visualize and explore things while driving my car on the Beltway around Washington, D.C. While the active part of my mind is alert to the dangers of northern Virginia drivers, my subconscious fusses around with the next project. Waiting, which is otherwise sheer torment for impatient people, can be put to good use by using the time to visualize.

Visualization is an art. It requires the ability to create an image or images of the projects—goals, plans, timing, and all of the other complexities. It requires imagination and discipline at the same time. I believe that everyone can visualize but that many have never allowed themselves simply to think in this loose way about what they want to do.

Just let the ideas float around in your mind. Explore one avenue of possibilities to its logical conclusion. Then do another. Connect unlikely events. Disconnect firm pairs. Let the things move and join and separate and flow of their own accord. Just visualize it all as a *gestalt.**

This is not a waste of time. It will give you a feel for the overall dimensions of the project. It will help you to test the feasibility of the goals. It will help you to check the sanity of the course of action implicit in those goals. It will point out unintended consequences and unforeseen connections. It may prevent a blunder. It will certainly not hurt, and it might even help.

Once you have visualized what you want to do, you may want to go back and adjust your goals. Repeat this process as many times as necessary. At some point your goals will be clear and definite enough to warrant proceeding to the next step in the planning process. At this point, freeze the goals and move out smartly.

Rule 3: Think about How You Want to Make It Happen

The next step is to consider ends and means. You have thought about what you want to make happen, and you have spent some idle moments visualizing exactly what that entails. Now you have to think again, but this time think about how you are going to achieve your goal—how you will proceed to make it happen. Means may influence ends by being infeasible, tainted, costly, or leading to a different end. Means are never easy.

Infeasible. One of the purposes in thinking about the means at the start of the process is to check again to see if the project is feasible—that is, can it be done at all? We all can think up and dream up a lot of goals, but they are just wishes until the "how" has been considered. Looking at the "how" often indicates that the goals simply are not attainable—sometimes not attainable at all, and sometimes not in a desired time frame. A feasibility test should be

---

* This is an expression from psychology that implies an integrated structure with properties different from and more than those of its parts.

done early so that resources (including time) are not wasted in chasing a goal that cannot be achieved. Very often the first step in planning a major project is a formal feasibility study. The object of the feasibility study is primarily to see if the project can be done at all, but in the course of the feasibility study many valuable lessons also can be learned about the best way to accomplish the work.

Tainted. Sometimes a look at how you can attain your goal indicates that the means necessary to do so are tainted: wrong, immoral, unethical, or illegal. In this case you will have to consider whether the ends justify the means. This is an age-old dilemma for planners of all sorts. Once you determine what you have to do to get the job done, you may wish to call the whole thing off. Or you may make a value judgment that achieving the goal is more important than your honor, your reputation, or even avoiding a criminal record.

Costly. All means are costly, but cost is relevant only in relation to the ends sought. One of the things you should think about up front is whether achieving the goal will be worth the expense. While you are thinking about how the goal can be attained, come up with a rough estimate of the costs involved—not only the monetary costs, although they are important, but also the costs of diversion from other work, of stress, of impact on familial or group relationships or on your reputation. What is it going to cost you and the others involved in the plan to make it happen?

Leading to a Different End. Most often, even if one or more of the other cases do not apply, you will find that how you have to proceed will influence what you can do. Life is not often as simple as setting goals and then just doing them. Most often the means influence not only the path you will take but also the goal itself. Thinking about this possibility at the start will help you to avoid disappointment when your achieved result does not match your planned goal. You should also consider if the goal as modified by the means is really what you want to make happen.

You will find it useful to execute another feedback loop at this time. Now that you have thought about the how-to—the means to the end—go back and rethink your goals with the new information you have gained. Almost always, your original goal will be modified.

Sometimes you will give up on part or all of the goal because it will have been proven to be infeasible. In other cases the goal will have been shown to be unattainable except by means that you find distasteful. Many times the goal will prove to be too costly even to contemplate seriously. In these cases, your next step will be either to abandon the goals completely and stop this particular planning process, or to change your goals because of what you have learned in thinking about the means.

Incidentally, this goals-means feedback loop should occur constantly throughout the planning process. Don't just do it the one time up front; do it all of the time. As each task or subtask is defined, consider the goals and the means implied. Modify the means to serve your purposes: Keep costs down; keep the means right; keep them on track for what you want to make happen.

Rule 4: Think about It Again

You are probably getting tired of thinking. The first three rules for planning involved a lot of thinking, and now I am suggesting even more thinking. What a bore!

But it is better to think a bit more now than to be very sorry later when something does not work out. This is the idea behind the old saw "A stitch in time saves nine." Or is it? Think about it.

You have now conceived a goal, visualized it, checked how you would achieve it, and revised it to account for the means. You are ready to start the plan. Wait! Is there anything you have forgotten? Think again. And again. And again.

When I was a lad, my father taught me a lesson about thinking again that has stood me and my family in very good stead over the years. In those days (the 1940s and '50s), we did a lot of driving for fun. Can you believe it? The roads were still open and the cars were not so powerful. So our family would get into the sedan and drive to the beach or the mountains or just anywhere. On these trips the means (riding in the car) were just as important as the end (getting somewhere). But we also had a lot of gear to take along—sweaters, raincoats, pillows, food, toys, maps, money, house keys, and the usual impedimenta of automobile touring. It was quite a deal just to get the car loaded and everyone inside. Then my father would get in the car and make ready to start on the trip. He would put the key into the ignition and start the car, shift the gears into reverse, and pull halfway out of the driveway. Then he would stop, put the gears in neutral, and say, "Has anyone forgotten anything?"

Invariably, someone had. Mother or my sister, Carrol, would return to the house for the forgotten food, sweater, or whatever. That habit my father taught me about thinking again before starting the trip has stayed with me through the years, and I generally try to do it consciously. It is a lot easier to get the forgotten items from the driveway than it is from the interstate fifty miles away.

Once I failed to make my last-minute check, and I really messed up. I was about to fly on business, and I left the tickets at home. Those of you who have flown the skies lately realize that buying a ticket at the airport is one of the most expensive acts possible. Even more expensive than buying a golf club. The tickets I had left at home were at a special fare rate, but I had to buy an airline ticket at the full price. Imagine! It ruined my whole trip, and I wished that I had taken the time to think about what I was doing before I did it.

Now is your chance in the planning process to do just that.

Once you are in the hurly-burly of the planning process itself, it will be difficult to step back and take an objective view of what you are doing. The more effort and ego you put into the plan, the bigger the emotional investment you will have made in it. Once you have set some tent poles in concrete, you will be less willing to change, and of course, it will not be very easy to change. So now is the time to think it all over.

Rule 5: Write a Concept Paper

Once you have decided on what you want done and have figured out generally how you will go about doing it, the next step is to write it down.

I can hear you now, moaning about paperwork and the extra effort involved. But except for the most humdrum of daily tasks, such as shaving or brushing your teeth, it is worthwhile to write a concept paper. This is the first comprehensive sanity check on your plan. If you have a good concept, you will have a good concept paper. If you cannot write down in simple words what you intend to do and how you are going to do it, you have a serious problem—your goals and approach may be flaky.

Writing a concept paper is useful for such commonplace events as trips, weddings, and parties, but it is essential for construction projects and business deals. Even the smallest things in life get complicated, as anyone who lives today understands. The primary task in planning is to keep it simple enough so that it can be done. The concept paper is the key to this.

A concept paper is short—usually one page, and no more than three pages, even for a big project. It forces you planners to sit down and put on paper what you have been thinking about and visualizing mentally. The act of expressing your ideas in words and setting them down on paper usually does one or more of these things:

- Reveals serious logical flaws and inconsistencies.
- Shows clearly the gap between ends and means, if there is one.
- Forces you to shed your myths and half-formed dreams and get specific.
- Cuts through all of the nonsense and helps make the plan conform to reality.

A concept paper usually has to be rewritten at least once. Few of us can visualize things in concrete terms or hook things together logically without writing them out. This is true even for verbal people. You really don't know what you have until you convert your ideas and even your words into prose.

Start with a clear statement of the goal or purpose of the plan. Then you might simply write a paragraph about how you are going to achieve your purpose. The next part might be a treatment of the basic assumptions upon which your concept is based; then some problems or constraints; and finally, some consideration of costs or resources needed to accomplish the plan. The concept paper is very general, but it should be comprehensive in the sense that it covers all angles of the proposed project.

My advice is to sit down with your writing tool—computer, word processor, typewriter, pen and writing pad, or whatever—and write out the whole concept from start to finish without pausing for agonizing reappraisals. Don't worry if it doesn't hang together. It would be nice if all plans gelled up front, but that is not their nature. Get complete coverage, let the concept paper rest for a while, then pick it up, revise it, and check it out with your original ideas. Modify it again, and then decide: go or no-go.

If you decide to go ahead, the concept paper will have significant value. It can serve as the starting point for the plan itself, for you can expand the concept paper into a topical outline. It can serve as a means of selling the project to others before you go to all the trouble of making a detailed plan. Finally, it is possible (though not certain) that you will be able to use it later as the executive summary.

If you decide not to go ahead, writing the concept paper will have saved you from a blunder.

2   Basic Planning Concepts

The eight rules in this chapter are intended to provide you with some basic concepts that underlie all planning. Planning is a commonplace activity, but there can be good or bad planning. This chapter presents some principles of good planning.

Even good plans do not guarantee good results or even attaining your goal, however, for it is possible for an excellent plan to fail in the implementation. On the other hand, it is possible to have a plan that is only fair and still attain your goals. Even a poor plan vigorously implemented is better than either a good plan implemented weakly or no plan at all.

There are a large number of possible rules for planning, so it may seem arbitrary to designate eight as "basic." The selection actually is arbitrary, but that does not mean it is not useful. Planning is in itself a humongous subject and, as suggested in Rule 6, needs to be eaten one bite at a time.

As you will soon note, many of these basic rules merely lay a foundation for more difficult rules to follow. So let us proceed a rule at a time to eat this elephant.

Rule 6: Take One Bite at a Time

This is the Elephant Rule. The late Gen. Creighton W. Abrams, U.S. Army, was a great man, and he was also eminently quotable. One of the best sayings attributed to him, in my view, is the following:

"When eating an elephant, take one bite at a time."

This is a profound thought. Many of life's projects are so immense and so complex that the mere thought of actually trying to do them can be overwhelming. Imagine trying to build the great pyramids of Egypt, or the Panama Canal, or the Empire State Building. Imagine fighting a global war against Germany and Japan, or putting a man on the moon, or conquering poliomyelitis. All of these things are big, but all of them got done—a bite at a time.

The same philosophy applies on a lesser scale. Just imagine even getting your homework done, or getting through final exams, or simply existing for a whole first year at college. Just think about the wedding, the honeymoon, and the marriage to follow. Just think about how you are going to cope with a new baby, or with the fifth baby. How are you going to get that proposal done, write that report, and also see that the boss is briefed—all in one day? How are you going to have the whole family over for turkey on Thanksgiving, then host the big Christmas party that everyone expects you to give? How can you get any of these complex things done—always with limited time and resources? One bite at a time!

All large projects or processes can and must be broken down into successively smaller projects or processes until the work can no longer be divided and is simple enough for an individual or a small team to accomplish. These ultimate jobs are called "primitive tasks," and this part of the planning process is called "task identification," or "job breakdown." It is an essential procedure.

Primitive tasks are those that can be described in finite terms and that produce a definite product or service. Primitive tasks are accomplished by an individual or a small team of people working together. A small team is one in which the leader can exercise direct personal control over all of the members. Despite the marvels of telecommunications, this means in practical terms that the team is working together in close physical proximity. A team is often called a "work center" in planning terminology. The work may be singular in that a unique product is created each time, but more often the work is repetitive and the task is done over and over again. A primitive task in building a house might be to toenail a stud into the footer board. Another might be to nail a brace to two studs. A third might be to nail the header to the studs.

Primitive tasks for many areas of planning are habitually aggregated into larger tasks well understood by the practitioners. Thus, using the examples above, the several primitive tasks involved in erecting studs for the typical wood frame house construction process would be described collectively as "framing the house." This task is often treated as a primitive task itself, but in reality it consists of several smaller tasks. Custom, training, and experience allow carpenters to integrate these tasks into the larger task and thus simplify the work planning and scheduling process.

If you ever try to eat an elephant, you will soon discover that simply taking bites at random may be very messy and not the best way to do it. You need to consider the location of the first bite, the size of the bites, and the order of biting to consume the elephant with the greatest dispatch and the least effort. In short, you need an elephant-eating plan—a work breakdown.

There are two ways to approach work breakdown. One is from the top down, and the other—not surprisingly—is from the bottom up. Most work breakdown is accomplished from the top down because that is the way most plans are made. But sometimes it is possible to use the bottom-up approach very effectively, particularly if one has been planning the same kind of activity repetitively for a long time. Both approaches to work breakdown are good, but they do not always give the same answers. One really great way to do a thorough job in work breakdown is to go both ways—one team or individual working top down and another bottom up. The idea is to see if the two methods meet in the middle like two tunneling teams working toward each other from opposite sides of the river.

The top-down approach breaks the entire mammoth project into several subordinate major tasks. Then each of these major tasks is broken down into subordinate tasks. Then each subordinate task is in turn broken down into another set of sub-subordinate tasks. And so on until the primitive tasks are reached for each of the downward paths. This sounds simple, but in practice it can get very complicated. As in any disaggregation process, there are choices to be made, so there are a number of different planning solutions depending on these choices. Since the most important choices have to be made at the start of the process before much experience is available, some of the work breakdown solutions can be pretty weird when the fifth or sixth level of subordinate tasks is reached. As with other processes of this nature, the solution is to begin the breakdown over again, avoiding the problems that appeared in the first trial.

The bottom-up approach starts with primitive tasks and assembles them into logical subtasks that in turn are grouped into major tasks and finally into the overall plan. The advantage of bottom-up planning is that it is rooted in the reality of what can be done at the primitive-task level. The disadvantage is that some pushing and pulling may be necessary to aggregate the tasks into the overall plan. Bottom-up planning is most useful for planners who are very experienced in a particular field and understand how the primitive tasks and subtasks should fit together logically. In our terms, bottom-up planning works for people who already know a lot about the internal composition of elephants.

So if the job is tough and big, try to cut it down to size and do it a bite at a time. If you can get more help, assign separate jobs to each member of your team so that the individual tasks add up to the completion of a larger task. Plan so that the cumulative effect of all of the tasks will produce what you want to make happen.

Rule 7: Define the Terms

> "'When I use a word,' Humpty Dumpty said in a rather
> scornful tone, 'it means just what I choose it to mean,
> —neither more nor less.'"*

One of the fun things about planning is that you get to be like Humpty Dumpty. Oh, I don't mean you have to fall off a wall and get all broken up about it. I mean you get to choose the meanings of the words you use. In planning jargon, this is called "defining the terms," and it is both acceptable and accepted practice. It is also necessary, particularly in some of the more exotic planning realms.

Defining one's terms is necessary to ensure that each word you use has only one specific meaning, at least in the context and duration of your plan.

We are not talking about consistency of word usage. It should go without saying that you should use a word to mean the same thing throughout your entire plan. This should go without saying, but it cannot. Some planners do attach variable meanings to words: In part I, a blivet is five pounds, but in part IV, it is ten. Or at the start of the plan, a "category" means a group of people, but by the end of the plan, a "category" means a group of ideas. That kind of inconsistency is at least bad form and at most terribly confusing. Things are going to be confusing enough, so don't compound the confusion by being inconsistent.

A far more serious problem, however, is that you may use a word to mean something quite different from the meaning that some or all of those reading your plans will attach to it. If so, your message will not be understood. It is not the message you transmit that counts, but what other people receive. You may send out clear signals, but if they are misunderstood, you will not have communicated well, making it more difficult to achieve your goal. Reasons for being misunderstood are static, or background noise; different value systems or cultures; and different meanings for words.

---

* Lewis Carroll, *Through the Looking Glass,* chapter 6.

Static,* or background noise, is prevalent in society, and we will just have to live with it while being aware that it distorts our messages. You can try to reduce static by emphasizing the important content of your communications and avoiding side issues that detract from it.

Cultural differences often distort messages so that the whole thought you are trying to convey means something quite different to the other person—even if there is agreement on the words. This is often a problem for American businesspersons dealing with businesspersons from another country. It is beyond the scope of this book to tell you how to appreciate a completely alien viewpoint enough to communicate well. But you should be aware that this kind of problem exists.

American English is one of the most exasperating languages, while it is also one of the most useful. The reason for both conditions is the same: The use of words is very flexible. There are many words that mean the same thing, or almost the same thing, and often many meanings can be applied to the same word. So the American language is very flexible. But it also can be very exact. That is important for planning.

Clearly defined terms are important in every discipline. Science, for example, cannot proceed with sloppy word usage, and scientific progress depends on everyone knowing exactly what every word means. Groups of professionals, such as engineers, lawyers, doctors, and philosophers, each have vocabularies that consist of words with exact, precise meanings. The set of words used by a particular set of professionals is called "jargon," and it is one of the features of a professional group. Jargon enables communication within the group to be both quick and exact and to be capable of conveying subtle shades of meaning. The big disadvantage is that jargon is incomprehensible to anyone not a member of the "in group." Despite this, it is still useful even for outsiders if care is taken to provide meanings for the more arcane terms.

You will find it advantageous to use the standard or customary terminology of the group you are addressing in your planning. If

---

* Strictly speaking, static is electrical interference with radio transmissions, but I am using the word in a broader sense to mean all of the noise that occurs constantly in the background and interferes with the signals we are trying to send.

you are planning a trip, you can use the standard terms adopted by the travel industry. If you are planning a party, the catering industry also uses standard terms. If you are planning to build a house, the construction industry has words already defined and commonly understood. If you are planning a small business start-up operation, the accountants and lawyers and bureaucrats will provide you a ready-made lexicon of terms with standard meanings. So most of the terms you will use are understood well enough that your audience will understand them without your having to provide special definitions up front.

If you are going to use words in your plan that you know have variable meanings, however, or if you are going to attach to words meanings that are other than the normal usage (not recommended), you will have to define your terms at the outset of your planning process.

In some cases, you might want to invent special words for special concepts or special artifacts that are of your own creation or are particularly important to your plan. You might say, for example, that for the purposes of your plan, the word "xesis" means a six-sided, regular polygonal structure. Who is to gainsay you on that kind of thing? In one sense, inventing your own terms makes it more difficult to communicate, but in another sense, it facilitates precise communication. Inventing new words is common practice in advertising and marketing. Many of the names of automobiles (e.g., Lexus) and numerous corporate names (e.g., Exxon) are invented words given explicit, unique meaning by their creators.

Identify the terms whose meanings are so variable or of such importance to your concept that they need to be defined specifically. There also may be other words that are relatively obscure but that you intend to emphasize. Include definitions for these terms in the introduction of the plan, or add a glossary or an appendix.

If you have only a few key words or phrases to define, it is usual to note those in the introduction. This allows the reader to get your definitions before plowing through the rest of the work, and it is a low-key way to do it. You could say, "In this plan, the term *polliwog* is used to mean a young frog." Or, "All references to year are to the calendar year." These kinds of simple, up-front definitions could assist materially in the presentation of your plan to others.

If several (five to twenty-five) key words and phrases need to be defined, you can list them with their meanings in a glossary. The glossary is a separate part of the plan document, and it is listed in and usually immediately follows the table of contents. The inclusion of a glossary alerts the reader that certain words have specific meanings in your plan.

If many terms must be defined, you may list them with their definitions in an appendix. Mention the appendix in the introduction, noting that you have defined the terms so that everyone will understand what they mean in the context of your plan. If you have to define more than twenty-five terms for your plan, however, you are probably going to have difficulty getting your message across, and I suggest you go back and try to use more standard, accepted words and meanings.

You are going to have a hard time with some people when you insist on using words strictly. Inevitably someone will say during an argument over terminology, "Oh, that's just semantics," or "Let's not argue semantics." These people do not appreciate that semantics is the science of communication and promotes understanding of the differences among subtle shades of meaning. They are really saying that they find no merit in exact meanings—especially if those meanings lead to conclusions other than their own preconceived views. I believe that conveying exact meanings is the essence of communicating well.

Rule 8: Set the Counting Rules

Setting up the counting rules is closely related to defining the terms, except that it deals with quantities instead of concepts or qualities. If your plan has any numbers in it—and almost all plans do—you will need to consider some counting rules.

Counting rules are the procedures for establishing how many of what kinds of critters you are going to deal with in the plan. They are the rules for aggregating like items into groups and for enumerating or establishing how many of the items are to be considered. This sounds simple, but it is not.

One of the obstacles to negotiating arms-control agreements between the U.S.A. and the U.S.S.R. during the Cold War was establishing the counting rules. The negotiating teams spent weeks arguing over which strategic nuclear weapons were included in the coverage of the agreement, whether manned bombers were in or out, and if old submarines with cruise missiles were within the suggested limits. Days were spent on the definition and number of "intermediate-range missiles" on each side. As progress was made, the counting rules became even more complicated. Do missiles in the overhaul process count? How about submarines in for extended maintenance? How about missiles not in Europe but in the western U.S.S.R.? These disputes over the counting rules, of course, were not mere exercises, but were in reality the heart of the agreements that were being hammered out.

Arguments over what counts and what doesn't count can even seem ludicrous at times. I once attended a seminar at the prestigious Brookings Institution during which high-level defense officials and defense intellectuals spent the whole afternoon arguing over what should be counted in a "six hundred ship navy." My conclusion was that if you can't figure out what is included in a number, there is nothing magic about the number.

One aspect of the problem is that counting has to do with numbers, and many people simply are uncomfortable with numbers, which makes it even more necessary to establish counting rules in advance. Numbers people don't mind a bit of ambiguity in counting rules, for they believe they can manipulate the numbers to their own advantage better without such rules. But most of us are not numbers people. We want two plus two to equal four—always. So it is useful to lay out in advance what counts, how things are bundled together into groups, and how the process of estimating or enumerating the quantities will take place. Counting rules are particularly important in business deals.

Rule 9: Consider What You Need to Know

One of the steps in the planning process is to gather the information necessary for formulating the plan. Before you gather the information, it is useful to consider what you actually need to know for the plan, for three reasons. First, collecting information is expensive and time-consuming. You will drive your costs up unless you have a good idea of what you need to know and what you don't need to know. Second, the process of obtaining information will be much more efficient if you think about it in advance. And third, you will have a basis for the research- or data-collection plan you are going to use in accordance with Rule 19.

Let's consider for a moment just what you do need to know for planning in general. There are five categories: people, things, time, locations, and methods.

People are involved in every plan, even if you are the only person. So one of the things you should consider are the people who will be involved in the planning and in the implementation of the plan. Rule 38 tells you more about how to make a list of the actors in the drama you are about to produce.

Things—inanimate objects—will play a part in your plan, primarily as resources to be used, but also as points of reference. You will probably need to know something about at least some of these things: vehicles, machinery, houses, offices, factories, churches, food, clothing, furniture, appliances, publications, and knick-knacks. The origin, utility, cost, and location of these things are information you might need in order to facilitate the planning process.

Time is a very important kind of data, and an entire chapter is devoted to its subtleties and nuances. You will have to consider the time factor in almost every plan. The most important thing you need to know about time is how much of it you will have available. That is, is there a deadline before which you have to achieve your goal? If so, you have a major element of your plan in place already; if not, then you need to learn more about how to view time to set your own schedule.

Locations are involved in every plan. You are either going from one location to another or staying in the same location. Either way, you need to know the characteristics of all of the locations likely to be relevant to the plan so that you can determine the degree and nature of the relevance. One way to find out about locations is to establish their spatial relationships by studying maps, and this can be augmented by reading books and watching videos about the places you will consider.

Methods are also important. Methods are simply ways to do things, and there are many available to you. You will use one or more methods of operation in your plan, and it is good to learn about various methods so you can determine which are useful and available for your plan.

You will probably need information about other areas for your plan. These might include intangibles, such as the political environment, recent advances in technology, or even the weather. You need to think about these things beforehand so that you can learn what you need to make your plan a good one.

Once you have considered and made lists of the kinds of information you would like to have, you have the basis for collecting and organizing the data you need for your plan. Additional advice on this topic is provided in chapter 4.

Rule 10: Make Assumptions

As you will find to your chagrin, you will never have enough information. Some information does not exist, some is highly unreliable, some is unavailable, and some is too hard or too expensive to get. For these reasons you need to insert into your plan some make-believe facts to compensate for the information that is lacking. These artificial facts are called assumptions.

Assumptions are essential to every plan, and as with many other things, they can be good or bad. The trick is to know in advance which is which. Good assumptions are based on sound logic. They are merely helpful rather than decisive, so that if they are wrong the entire plan does not fail. Assumptions that are so crucial that the success of the plan depends on them are bad, even if they are based on some logic. And, of course, some assumptions are simply foolish.

Assuming what will happen in the future is tricky business. No matter how you try, you will never be able to predict the future exactly. Yet in order to simplify your planning process, you will be tempted to pretend you know what will happen. If you assume, for example, that you will have a certain period of time before a competitor will do something, you are likely to be wrong, for you cannot control what the adversary does. You may barely be able to control what you do. So assumptions about the future are problematical, and you should fashion your plan so that it is not completely dependent on events beyond your control.

Assumptions are guesses. These are common in the planning business, and, in fact, degrees of guesses have been hallowed in planning folklore. A WAG (wild-ass guess) is simply that—something you have pulled out of your left ear with no basis other than intuition. These are dangerous but also are sometimes brilliant. A SWAG (scientific wild-ass guess) is somewhat better: The assumption is based on some general knowledge and reasoning, although the specific application is murky. SWAGs are made a lot, but then so are WAGs. Some advice on converting WAGs to SWAGs, and possibly to IWAGs (informed wild-ass guesses), is provided in Rule 79. The trick is never to confuse any kind of guess with cold, hard facts.

One basic rule is to limit assumptions to the minimum required for the plan. Build as much of your plan as possible on facts, and use only those assumptions absolutely necessary to make progress. Avoid any unnecessary assumptions. Another basic rule is to improve your assumptions as you obtain better information later in the planning process.

You can use historical records as the basis for some assumptions. If your project needs good weather, you need to assume what percentage of the time the weather will be good. This calls for a reasonable assumption about the weather based on previous weather. You look up the weather records for the appropriate time of the year, and you assume that the future will resemble the past. This is the most common way of predicting the future, and most of the time it is good enough, particularly for natural phenomena such as weather. If it has rained every April for the past 100 years, it is reasonable to assume that it will rain again next April.

You can predict other aspects of the future based on trend lines. If sales of an item have increased 10 percent each year for the previous five years, it is reasonable to assume that they will increase 10 percent each year for the next two years. This kind of trend projection is not nearly as good as that for natural phenomena, however, for there is no real assurance that the trend will continue. The broader the variable that is being predicted, the better will be the trend projections. That is, you will be able to predict sales for an industry or a factory better than for a specific item. You will be able to predict overall inflation rates better than the increase in prices for a particular commodity. There is a trade-off between specificity and validity: The more specific, the less valid.

It is dangerous to try to assume specific behavior by a particular individual, for human beings are notoriously unpredictable. Gambling is based on odds and personality. Successful gamblers play the odds and avoid outguessing the opponents. Poor gamblers ignore the odds and try to outguess the opponents. Great gamblers do both. But you probably won't want to gamble with your plan by making unwarranted or unnecessary assumptions.

Rule 11: Challenge Your Assumptions

Once you have made the assumptions upon which your plan is based, you must challenge them or arrange to have some trusted associate challenge them.

Admit it! You did not take seriously the advice in Rule 10. You have included in your plan assumptions that simplify your problem and make it appear easy for you to make something happen. You have built into your assumptions your own worldview, biases, and preconceived notions. In short, you have probably made some unrealistic assumptions. Don't be alarmed; this is normal. But you must not let these assumptions go unchallenged.

Set aside time to go over the assumptions and try to destroy them. If you cannot do this yourself, get someone else to do it for you. It is quite possible that you lack the objectivity or intellectual

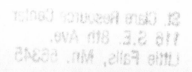

rigor to attack the assumptions you have spent some time formulating. That is normal but not very helpful. If someone else challenges your assumptions for you, you have to be able to stand the vicissitudes of the process. Few people can really react well when their cherished ideas are being attacked. For that reason, few of us really get honest opinions from others. Subordinates are afraid to give their real opinions, and peers seldom intrude on others' domains. Only bosses will provide honest criticism, and even they won't do it all of the time for a variety of reasons. The key person is you—the planner. Get someone to challenge your assumptions and then have the fortitude to learn from it rather than resist it. You should be interested in why people disagree with what you thought were self-evident truths.

One common mistake is to assume away the problem. You look at the situation and see instinctively a major roadblock to what you want to do, and your response is to assume that the roadblock is nonexistent. Suppose you are a planner for the school board and you want to construct a new school in a period of fiscal austerity. In this case you may very well make as your number one assumption that sufficient funds will be available to build the school. Making this assumption allows you to proceed to design the school you want, but unless your assumption of essentially unlimited funding is really going to be true, you could find yourself with a faulty plan on your hands when the funding turns out to be unavailable.

Similarly, if a key element of your plan depends on obtaining the support of another group, you may find it very attractive to assume that you will obtain the necessary support. It would be better to challenge this kind of assumption and replace it with a fact based on discussions with that group.

It is not uncommon for planners to insert at the outset of their process some assumptions of questionable validity. This is often done in a sincere but misguided effort to get the process under way. Sometimes, however, it is done in an effort to wish away unpleasant realities, and this is certain to lead to disaster when implementing the plan. The only way to avoid faulty assumptions is to assure that someone makes a vigorous, honest challenge to them.

Rule 12: Consider Unintended Consequences

Another very important thing is to consider the unintended consequences of your plan. All solutions create more problems, most of the time ones the planner never even dreamed of. Some of this is the difference between short-range and long-range planning: Some solutions that looked good in the short range turn out to be poor in the long range.

When vehicles powered by internal-combustion engines were introduced, they provided (among other things) a solution to a tremendous environmental pollution problem. The large numbers of horses used to power vehicles generated immense quantities of horse manure, which had to be cleaned up and disposed of. Horse manure was a tremendous public health problem, and it stank. Replacement of horses by engines using gasoline ended the horse manure problem, but it created another, new problem of environmental pollution from the exhaust fumes of the internal-combustion engines. The short-range solution caused a long-range problem.

It is not customary to think about unintended consequences, because the planner concentrates on thinking about the intended consequences. Your entire attention is focused on what you want to make happen, so you are unlikely to be emotionally ready to poke at your plan to see what else it might cause to happen—particularly if bad results could foil your own goals.

Most unintended consequences are also unexpected—people just didn't realize that what they were doing was going to have that result. Some unintended consequences, however, are foreseen but simply ignored. The fact that burning coal and oil caused pollutants to enter the atmosphere was known and certainly expected, but the intended consequences of industrial production and electrical power for the masses were so good that the bad consequences of pollution were never a factor at that time. We never intended to foul the atmosphere and bring smog to the cities, even though we had enough knowledge to foresee that that was going to happen.

This is not a matter of intentions. Almost all of the bad consequences of earlier projects were brought about by well-meaning people who lacked either the ability or the tools to recognize the unintended consequences of their actions. One primary cause of unintended consequences is simply that the planners of a time did not have access to later knowledge, so they operated within a framework that precluded them from knowing fully what they were doing. History is full of things that seemed like a good idea at the time but later turned out to have bad consequences. The accompanying figure summarizes some of these.

Some Illustrations of Unintended Consequences

Things We Did	Original Goals	Unintended Results
Used DDT	Crop Enhancement	Toxic Effects on Animals
Built Large Dams	Flood Control	Downstream Erosion
Created Suburbs	Better Living	Inner-City Decay

So you need to take a good look at what you want to make happen to see what else will happen. What have you overlooked regarding the consequences of your plan? As with challenging assumptions, this may be hard for planners to do themselves because they are close to the problem, have too much emotional investment in their plan, or are too intent on making something happen to see clearly what else could result.

In that case, it is advisable to call in outside people to look at large and complicated plans and bring to bear a new and presumably less biased viewpoint that may be able to find obvious faults or results overlooked by the planners. There is no certain way to find all unintended consequences, because some of them are simply beyond the state of the art in science, technology, or human understanding at the time. It is wise, however, to take a few minutes to reflect, "What will happen if I do this?" or to ask a friend, "George, are any bad things going to happen if I do this?"

Just because there are some bad consequences does not necessarily mean that you will stop your original project. Nothing is going to be an unalloyed benefit, but it is better to recognize all of the results of a plan before you put it into motion. It is the *unintended* part of the consequences that needs to be done away with. If you can foresee the consequences of your plan, then you can weigh the good against the not so good or the bad and consider whether on balance the project should proceed, be modified, or simply not proceed.

Incidentally, all plans have unintended consequences, so don't be too righteous about yours. My advice is to give this some serious thought at the outset, and once you have done that, forge ahead.

Rule 13: Plan Backward

This sounds like peculiar advice, but it isn't. There are two ways to approach the time dimension. You can start now and work forward, which is "forward planning." Or you can start at some future instant of time and work backward, which is "backward planning." You do backward planning all the time without realizing it.

I confess that I myself did not really appreciate the value of backward planning until I learned about airborne operations at the Army Command and General Staff College. In planning an airborne operation in which thousands of paratroopers jump out of airplanes with their weapons, gear, supplies, and even vehicles and cannon, it is necessary to ensure that all of the many elements involved will do their own tasks at exactly the right times. So airborne planners formalized backward planning by setting a time that they were to seize the objective, then working backward from that time to synchronize the actions of all of the aircraft, airborne units, support personnel, radar, and every other element involved in the operation. By subtracting time, they set the time of the parachute jump, the time each aircraft would have to take off from each airfield, the time each airborne unit would have to be at each airfield to board the aircraft, the time the units would have to depart from their bases to arrive at the airfields on time, and so on backward until the time the paratroopers would have to get up that morning. In this way, each element would appear simultaneously in the skies over the objective.

Planning backward for an airborne operation is a big thing, but the principles are the same for little things as well. Take going to

work, for example. You know when you have to arrive at the office
in the morning, so you plan backward from that point to determine
what time you have to get up to make it to work. Let's say you have
to be at the office at 8:15 A.M. You estimate that it takes forty-five
minutes to drive from your house to the parking garage and ten
minutes to find a parking place, park the car, and walk to the elevator
to go up to your office. Subtracting the total of fifty-five minutes from
8:15, you find that you have to leave your house in your car at 7:20 A.M.
Allowing five minutes for unexpected delays, you set your departure
time at 7:15. Now you have to estimate how long it takes for you to
eat breakfast, get out to the garage, and warm up the car before you
can drive off. Say that takes on the average thirty-five minutes. You
have to be at the breakfast table at 6:40 A.M. You then estimate that it
takes you forty minutes to get up, shower, shave, get dressed, and
get to the breakfast table. If so, that means you have to get up at
6:00 A.M. to get to the office at 8:15. Backward planning establishes
an end time, checkpoints along the way, and a start time. As you gain
experience or as factors change, you may adjust the plan accordingly.
If you have to start making your own breakfast, you might need to
add fifteen to twenty minutes, so you get up earlier. If you find a
shortcut to the office that saves ten minutes of travel time, you can get
up later. As you have probably noted, there is nothing very sophisticated about this. It is really just common sense.

We plan backward frequently in our daily routines and for trips
and outings. We sometimes fail to understand the process of planning
backward, so we find it hard to apply those same commonsense
principles to more complicated plans.

Failing to appreciate how to plan backward often results in late
delivery of the product or service. This is common in the house-
building industry, where it is essential that each subtask be performed
in a particular sequence that is well understood by (most) contractors.
That is, you have to build the foundation first and put in the walls
before you paint them. The process is really more complicated than
that, and I will comment on it in more detail later, but the point is
that contractors too often plan from the start date and think forward
instead of starting with the occupancy date and working backward.

The two different approaches often yield dramatically different results. Commonly, the contractor takes the start point and estimates how long it will take for each subcontractor to come in and perform his tasks. Adding up this time provides an estimated completion date— which is usually too optimistic.

I maintain that if hitting a specific completion time on the nose is important, mere addition of estimated time durations from a start point is not as effective as planning backward. Planning forward makes the completion date a variable, with all that implies. Planning backward forces a solution that tries at least to provide a result at a particular time. Here, the variable is the starting point, and it may become necessary to adjust the time periods within the plan to hit the desired completion date. The difference is in the mental outlook of the planner or contractor.

Backward planning can be and is used for almost any kind of a plan. Since it requires a high degree of discipline within the plan itself, planning backward is not necessarily the best approach for all projects. It would not be very useful, for example, in planning an archaeological dig in which the end point could not be predicted and the time spent on any one task depended on what happened during that task. So you don't have to use this method, but you should at least be aware of what backward planning means and what it can do for you as a planning approach. My advice is to use backward planning for those cases for which it is important to achieve a particular result by a specific time.

3 Key Distinctions

Making things happen is both simple and complicated. The best way to make complicated things seem simple is by being very careful how you plan and prepare. Planning and preparing are simple activities, because they can be broken down into basic ideas, and they are also sophisticated activities, because they require you to make some fundamental choices between ideas that appear to be similar but in reality are quite different. It is important, therefore, that you appreciate these distinctions and make good use of them.

A great scientist—I think it was Isaac Asimov—defined intelligence as the ability to distinguish between similar objects.* The five rules in this chapter each point out a basic distinction that affects how you approach planning and preparing. Making things happen is easier if you make these distinctions.

Rule 14: Planning versus Preparing

There is a distinction between planning and preparing. You can plan without preparing, but you can't prepare without a plan. You also can plan and prepare without ever implementing the plan.

Planning is figuring out what you want to do and how you

---

* See the *Foundation* series. OK, so Asimov is a great science fiction writer, not a scientist. See how important it is to make subtle distinctions?

want to do it and what it will take to go about doing it. Planning is a mental exercise, and the product is the plan. When you have finished the plan, you have figured out a way to make something happen, but you have not yet done anything about making it happen.

Preparing involves taking some concrete actions to get ready to implement the plan. It is not implementing the plan, but it may be considered (to make a subtle distinction) implementing certain selected parts of the plan. The parts of the plan selected for early or even premature implementation are those that would make it faster and easier to implement the plan if you have to or want to carry it through to completion. When planning to respond to events that occur suddenly, such as hurricanes, implementing part of the response plan in advance is crucial to being able to implement the entire plan swiftly. When planning for a goal that is remote or strictly voluntary, implementation of part of the plan in advance may be done to save money or to get key resources nailed down.

There is a distinct difference in the relative cost of planning versus the cost of preparing. Planning is a lot cheaper, because it involves only the cost of the labor to do the planning—including data gathering and supporting analyses—and the clerical and support structure to put the plan in the computer and down on paper. Thus, the cost of the planning itself is very low compared with the cost of the project—typically only a small fraction.* On the other hand, preparedness does involve spending money to buy real things, and the costs of preparedness can be substantial depending on just how prepared you want to be.

If, for example, you are thinking about building a vacation home, you can do the planning quite cheaply. Planning would involve deciding on a location, finding some land, deciding on the style of structure, finding out about local laws and rules, establishing some costs, laying out a time line, and checking for fiscal feasibility. This would be a bare-bones plan costing little except your own labor and perhaps some money in obtaining data about the prospective

---

* This is not meant to imply that planning is inexpensive, for merely planning some large projects can cost many millions of dollars.

location. If you wanted to do a more complete plan (and run up your planning costs), you could hire an architect to draw up the plans and specifications for your vacation home. At the end of this process, you have a plan, but you haven't done anything about implementing it. That is where preparedness starts.

You could prepare for implementing your plan for a vacation home in several ways. One way would be to start a savings program to defray the initial costs, such as a down payment on the land. You could start buying the kind of furniture you want and store it away until you put it into the house. Or you could buy the land and hold it until you are ready to build the house itself. These preparedness actions could be taken a long time in advance or just before you start implementation. Buying the land in advance might make sense if you believe prices will go up or the right parcel of land will be unavailable when you want to build the house. You might also take such administrative actions as obtaining rezoning or building permits.

Admittedly, the boundaries among planning, preparing, and implementing are fuzzy. We might just as well have considered hiring an architect to be a preparedness measure instead of a planning action. Or we could have considered buying the land to be implementation instead of preparedness. The exact classification, however, is not as important as understanding the real nature of what you are doing to make that particular thing happen.

Planning is a neutral event connoting a willingness to think about the goal, but preparing indicates a strong but still tentative commitment to achieving the goal. I feel that it is useful to make a distinction between planning and preparing. You should have a general idea of this distinction before you plow too deeply into planning. Chapter 15 deals with preparing in more detail.

Rule 15: Strategy versus Tactics

Strategy and tactics are different and have different applications at each level of planning.

These terms originate with military planning and operations. Strategy derives from the Greek *strategos* and refers to the art of the general, while tactics refers to the way in which troops organize and conduct the actual fighting. Military officers today use three planning levels: tactics, operational art, and strategy. Tactics pertains to military operations on the battlefield of units up to a division of 15,000 personnel. Operational art pertains to military operations within a theater of operations and deals with larger organizations, such as corps and field armies, of up to several hundred thousand personnel. Strategy pertains to the allocation of military forces among theaters of war. In a press conference near the end of Operation Desert Storm, Gen. H. Norman Schwarzkopf used these three planning levels to describe vividly his opinion of Saddam Hussein's capability as a military leader:

> Ha! He is neither a strategist, nor is he schooled in the operational art, nor is he a tactician, nor is he a general, nor is he a soldier. Other than that, he's a great military man. I want you to know that.*

The terms are also applied in planning for other than military objectives, and just two levels—strategy and tactics—are usually sufficient.

There has been a lot of discussion over the years about the nature of and differences between strategy and tactics in business planning. There is general agreement that strategy is an aggregated, higher-level view of the planning problem, while tactics is a detailed, lower-level view. Another approach is that strategy is a general statement of what you want to make happen, while tactics is a detailed statement of how you are going to make it happen. Enough! I'm getting confused.

Let's use a football analogy to illustrate the difference. The game plan is the strategy. The offensive and defensive plays are the tactics. The game plan sets forth the general way that the team plans to defeat the opponents, including such high-level objectives as establishing the running game early, throwing enough passes to keep the linebackers deep, and if leading in the final quarter, preventing

---

* Otto Friedrich, ed., *Desert Storm: The War in the Persian Gulf* (Time Warner Publishing, 1991), 123.

long passes or runs by the opponents. Tactics involve such procedures as blitzing the opposing quarterback, blocking two on one, pulling a guard to lead the run, and conducting a proper goal-line stand. Both are necessary to win the game, and both need to work together in a complementary sense.

You will need to apply both strategic thinking and tactical skill in your planning.

Rule 16: Objectives versus Capabilities

You will have to decide whether your plan is to be based on capabilities or objectives. This is an important distinction, particularly on complex or costly projects.

Objectives planning, or requirements planning, starts with the goal and determines what resources have to be made available to achieve that goal. Capabilities planning starts with existing, available resources and does the best that can be done to achieve the goal. These are two fundamentally different views of the world.

Much government planning is the objectives kind, which starts with a goal to be attained, figures out how to achieve that goal, and estimates the costs necessary to do that. Often the goals are established by Congress and the Executive Branch working together and stated in terms of what is to be done. The defense budget is an objectives plan based on a national security strategy with foreign policy goals, estimates of military forces to support that strategy, detailed lists of resources to support the military forces, and, finally, the amount of money needed to pay for it all. This is probably the only way that governments can plan, because their revenues depend on programs, which have to come first.

The drawback of objectives planning is that it depends on having a certain amount of money, which may or not be available. This is often the case in governmental planning, because the planners who set objectives are not the same people who provide the funding. Thus, there is often a gap between promise and performance. In defense planning, for example, the objectives planning process meant for many years that the nation had a military strategy not fully supported by defense budgets and, therefore, not capable of being implemented effectively.

Despite this drawback, objectives planning is useful. Since the whole point of the planning process is to figure out a way to make something happen, we have to start at least in the objectives mode by stating the goals and estimating how much effort, resources, and money it would take to achieve them. Then we can decide to pay for it all or select some lesser amount. This is particularly good for initial feasibility studies. If the amount we are willing to spend is less than that required to achieve our goals, we have to cut back on our goals or impose on ourselves a gap between ends and means.

Capabilities planning is useful if funds are fixed at a certain level. Military planners do capabilities planning when preparing contingency plans for potential military operations. They list the military forces and resources available, state the military mission, and figure out how to accomplish the mission with the available forces. If the mission can be accomplished by the available forces and resources, the result is acceptable. If the mission cannot be accomplished by available forces and resources, the planners have the basis for asking for additional forces or scaling back the mission to fit the capability at hand.

For everyday planning, the capabilities approach has much to commend it. Say you want to buy a car. Instead of establishing a goal of buying a Jaguar and then discovering that you don't want to spend the $50,000 it would take to do that, it would be more efficient to decide initially how much money you want to spend for ground transportation and then look for a car in your price range. Most of us do this instinctively when purchasing clothing or household items, but few realize that it is capabilities planning.

You will be using both kinds of planning for your projects. Just remember to keep in mind whether you are basing your goals on your resources (capabilities planning) or your aspirations (objectives planning).

Rule 17: Analysis versus Design

There is a difference between design and analysis. Planning is essentially a design process—creating something. Analysis is used in the planning process to allow you to understand something. Design is much more difficult than analysis, both conceptually and practically. You should appreciate the distinction between the two ways of thinking so you can incorporate them into your planning process appropriately.

Analysis is the process of understanding a phenomenon or a particular set of phenomena. It starts with a concrete set of data describing the phenomena and proceeds to take the phenomena apart in order to understand the internal structure and relationships among the various elements.

Design, on the other hand, starts with a goal and proceeds to describe the parts, steps, or elements required to accomplish the goal. The design process establishes the appearance, composition, output, and procedures of the product. Design starts with a nebulous concept and proceeds to make it a concrete reality.

When I studied civil engineering, we had a course on structural analysis. It consisted of finding the load capacity of a railroad bridge. We were provided the specifications of the bridge (the data set) and told to proceed systematically through the bridge structure until we found the critical part that was the weakest. The strength of that weakest part would be the strength of the entire bridge. We worked for a whole semester, going through that bridge truss by truss, member by member, abutment by abutment, and pin by pin. We calculated the strength of each steel beam, each truss, and each pin holding beams together. Finally, on the day before the course ended, we found that the two pins connecting the north side of the bridge structure to the abutment (ground foundation) were the weakest parts and the critical members of the bridge. During this process we made no decisions on how to construct the bridge or what strengths the various parts ought to be; we only determined the actual strengths using standard methods. The process was complex but straightforward, and the answer was achieved by grinding the numbers day after day. There was only one correct answer to the bridge analysis problem.

Later I took a course in structural design. It was quite different. We were given a goal of crossing a river and were told the vehicle loadings the bridge would be built to withstand and a cost ceiling.

From that start point we were to design a bridge. While each step in the analysis problem had required rating a particular component of the bridge, each step in the design process required a decision. We had to decide on the type of bridge, the kind and size of the foundations for the abutments, the size of the beams or trusses, the kinds of materials (steel, wood, reinforced concrete), the lateral bracing scheme, the kind of decking, and many other details. Each decision required a selection from among several choices, and the decisions often were based as much on artistic merit as on engineering criteria. The design process was messy because there was no certain route that, if followed, would provide the correct answer. There were many correct solutions to the design problem and quite possibly no best solution.

Even the way costs are counted differs between the two approaches. In an analysis, the cost is definite and is defined by the thing being analyzed. Estimating the cost may be difficult, but there is a single cost that is correct. In the design process, however, cost is a variable that depends on the selections made at each decision point. If a more expensive mode of construction is chosen at an initial step, it is likely to require expensive choices thereafter. So the designer has to keep cost in mind while meeting the technical or performance requirements and satisfying the intangible preferences of the client or sponsor as well.

It is true, of course, that some analysis is very complicated and requires the use of very sophisticated tools and methods, but that is because the thing being broken down and rated is itself very complicated. Design is much harder than analysis and requires the application of more than simple technical judgments.

Analysis is still a valuable skill for a planner, because it allows you to appreciate better how to make the best choices among alternative ways to achieve your goals.

Planning is more like design than like analysis, because the planner at each point in the process has to make decisions that foreclose forever the possibility of making other decisions at those points.

Rule 18: Supply versus Demand

Every plan has two basic parts: supply and demand. My general advice is to keep them separate in the planning process. This is difficult, because the two are so closely interrelated that you will have to deal with them at the same time continuously, and that makes it easy to confuse them. I have seen a lot of plans in which supply and demand got so mixed up that it was hard to tell which was the driving force in the outcome.

You will recall from Rule 16 that there are two basic kinds of plans: objectives plans and capabilities plans. Objectives plans are driven by demand, while capabilities plans are driven by supply. This rule deals with how to recognize the two and keep them apart.

Both supply and demand pertain to resources, including tangible items, time, and energy or effort. If one believes that money is a resource, it applies also to money (see Rule 77). Mostly, I use the term *resource* to apply to tangible goods and real services, such as steel, lumber, airline tickets, food, and dry cleaning.

Supply is the amount of a resource available for use at a particular time and place. There are two elements of supply: inventory and production. Resources stocked in inventory are on hand and available instantly to meet demand. Resources not yet produced but in the production process or planned to be produced may also be available to meet demand if the plan works. So the only part of supply that is absolutely certain are the resources already produced and held in inventory—provided, of course, that the resources in inventory are the appropriate make and model to match the demand.

Demand is the amount of a resource the planner would like to have available for use at a particular time and place. Some organizations (particularly government organizations) use the term "require-ment" instead, which, in my opinion, implies that the resources *have* to be there—or some unstated dire consequence will result. Require-ments are often regarded as sacred, particularly by the persons stating the requirement. Thus, requirements tend to be regarded as fixed and not even subject to question. This, of course, is a completely unrealistic approach and often leads to unworkable plans.

I was present at a Pentagon meeting that provided convincing evidence that the supply of military health-care professionals was insufficient to meet the requirement to support the armed forces in the short term. There was no way that the supply could be increased to meet the requirement, but my suggestion to revise the requirement to bring it more in line with the supply was met with emotional resistance. The representative of the health affairs office (which had dreamed up the requirement in the first place) informed me that the requirement had been approved by the assistant secretary, was engraved in stone, and could not be changed. Needless to say, the gap between the sacred requirement and the insufficient supply was not solved that day.

"Demand" has more flexible connotations, implying that you want or even need the resource, but you recognize that you might have to change it to match the supply when it comes to a crunch. In the real world, where things actually have to get built, shipped, or otherwise accomplished, there is never a gap between demand and supply.

It is essential to compare supply and demand always along the time line. Supply meets demand only when it is there on time.

The general rule is that a later supply cannot meet an earlier demand. To a man starving in the desert, even a seven-course meal is to no avail if he dies before it arrives. If you need a truckload of lumber today, it is unsatisfactory if it arrives next week. On the other hand, an earlier supply can meet a later demand, and this is the basis for stocking resources ahead of the need. Many planners miss this point entirely by simply adding up supply and demand over a long period of time and saying that because the totals match, there is no problem.

This was the case when I worked in the 1970s on military manpower for national mobilization. The total supply of trained military manpower in the first six months of a mobilization exceeded the total demand for the same period of time, so people were saying there was no problem. When we broke the supply and demand down into ten-day increments, however, we were able to show that there was insufficient supply in the first two months but excess supply in the last two months of the six-month period. After learning that, we took steps to move some supply forward in time and stretch out the demand so that supply matched demand for each ten-day period.

The spatial distribution of supply and demand also enters into the planning process. Food on the docks of New York City or even Mogadishu will not meet a demand for food to feed starving people in Somalia. To assure that the supplies will be in the proper location at the desired time, it is necessary to allow in the plan for the lead times, money, and transportation resources to move supplies from where they are to where they are wanted

The original point of this rule was to keep the two concepts—supply and demand—separate. This remains valid. I find it very helpful to set up two schedules, one for supply and another for demand. Even the terms applied to the two concepts may differ.

Staffing an organization involves establishing the demand for jobs (manpower function) and supplying people to fill those jobs (personnel function). The numbers and kinds of jobs for a work center depend on what has to be done, and it is possible to apply experience or industrial-engineering techniques to figure that out. Once the jobs have been described, the manpower office translates them into authorized positions (spaces, billets), stating the skill and grade or experience an applicant should have to perform the work. The personnel office then supplies people (faces) to fill the job vacancies. Demand is expressed in authorized strength or approved staffing basis; supply is expressed in on-hand or present-for-duty strength. One of the major problems in large organizations is failure to recognize the difference between the manpower and personnel functions, so that in many cases the supply of employees fails to match the demand for work.

You will discover many opportunities to confuse supply and demand or to create rigid "requirements" that cannot be met. My advice is to resist all temptation and simply keep supply and demand apart in the planning process until they have to meet to accomplish work.

4   **Data**

In order to plan, you will have to have data. Data are the basic facts upon which you will build your plan.

If you are following the steps suggested in this book, you will already have considered what information you need to know in order to plan. This is the first step in the data compilation process. The next steps are to get the data, organize them, and check them.

Wait a minute—it is not as easy as it sounds!

There is a surfeit of data in the world, but a deficit of information. Data are facts. Information is data placed into context and processed to apply to your own particular problem or plan. So while you are obtaining data for your plan, you have to keep in mind that you also will be processing them into information. This can be an expensive process in terms of time, money, and frustration. So it is also important to obtain your data carefully, and this requires a plan—a data-gathering plan, or research plan. Once you have the plan, you compile or gather the data. Then you have to organize them so that they are useful to you and can be applied to your planning process. The next several rules are designed to help you deal with data.

Rule 19: Make a Research Plan

The first thing to do when starting to obtain the data for your plan is to make another, more specialized plan to obtain the kind and amount of data you want. There are a lot of data out there, and simply going out and randomly catching some is unlikely to provide you what you need to know for your plan. So you need to prepare a research plan.

Social scientists have turned the concept of a research plan into a monstrous thing with elaborate schemes and many sophisticated and subtle points. This kind of elaborate and intricately designed research plan is probably necessary for these social scientists to ensure that their conclusions are not biased by their data. They build into the design of their entire experiment the exact data they need. But a complicated research plan useful for scientific research projects is likely to be too complicated for everyday planning.

Your research plan should start with what you need to know as discussed in Rule 9. List these items and then expand on them as to exactly what data are needed to answer the questions. Then establish the attributes of the data and likely sources. You don't need an elaborate scheme, but it helps to do some preparatory thinking in an organized way about data. If you are starting a small business, you would want to know something about the market, the competition, the products or services you intend to sell, and the rules and regulations for small businesses in your locality. Taking these as the main points in your research plan, you could define each topic in more detail until the plan serves as a useful guide for answering your information needs.

The basic attributes of data are kind, quantity, and sources. The kind of data pertains to the phenomena the data describe or measure. The quantity of data is the number of data points or separate data items needed to prepare a good plan. The source of the data is simply where you can find what you want.

The kind of data you need for your plan is linked directly to the goal of your plan. If you are planning a war to defend Kuwait against Iraqi aggression, you need to know lots and lots of things from a wide variety of sources. Most of us don't have to plan that kind of project, but we still need to have a plan. If you are building a house, you need data on sources, costs, and availability of building materials. If you are throwing a party, you need data on food, drink, and maybe even caterers. If you are driving to another city, you need data on distance and direction. If you are trimming the Christmas tree, you need to know where you stored the ornaments and decorative lights after last year's New Year's Eve party.

The amount of data depends on your experience, your desires, and your budget. If you are experienced in the house-construction business, you will be able to infer additional information from basic data. That is, you can tell generally where and how to obtain the data from your previous construction projects. Unless there is a change, you will be able to plan on doing the same kinds of things and using the same kinds of data. Personal disposition has a lot to do with the amount of data you need. If you are a confident cross-country driver, you may want to know only the route numbers of the interstate highways from Washington, D.C., to Albuquerque, New Mexico. If you are a novice and want to make certain that you will not get lost, you will want a lot more data than that. While it is possible to drown in data, my advice is to get too much rather than too little. You can always discard unnecessary data, but it is often too late to get data you don't have when you need them. Finally, data are costly. You have to weigh in your research plan how much time and how much money you are willing to spend to get the data.

Once you have dealt with kind and quantity of data, you should think a bit about sources, then put it all together into a plan to compile, record, organize, and utilize the data. Your research plan can range from an idea to a one-page outline to a thirty-page detailed listing of data items. It all depends on the complexity of the basic plan. A good research plan lists each data item, specifies the amount of each, and provides some idea of where it can be found.

There is nothing mysterious or magic about data, and I want to take particular pains to make that clear. Data are simply the facts that you need to have to make your decisions and prepare and implement your plan. Once you have decided in your research plan on what kind of data and how much you want, you need to go out and get them, and that process is called compilation.

Rule 20: Compile the Data

Now that you have figured out what you need to know, the next thing to do is to go out and compile the data, which means "to collect from different sources and put into a new form."*

One thing you should appreciate at this stage is that compiling data is not easy. It sounds easy, but it is really the hardest part of any planning or analytical effort. Operations research analysts say that their work is 90 percent compiling the data and 10 percent analyzing them. You will note that this sort of parallels the engineers' saying that invention is 90 percent perspiration and 10 percent inspiration, except that operations research analysts don't sweat.

The world is full of data compiled neatly into innumerable data bases,** which are sets of data already compiled by some other planner. A primary characteristic of data bases is that none of them will fit your own particular needs.

The end product of the data compilation stage is information. You process the data into information by putting them into the specific context of your concept and plan. It is important to appreciate the difference between data and information. Today we are drowning in data, but we still have insufficient information.

Billions have been spent on data compilation, data base creation, and computers. Computers are, in fact, the reason why we have so much data. The old ways of storing data on stone tablets, papyrus scrolls, parchment sheets, books, encyclopedias, and the backs of old envelopes have given way to storing data via computers. Stacks of paper with data inscribed thereon strewn around the room have given way to stacks of floppy or not-so-floppy disks with data inscribed thereon strewn around the room. We have achieved a monstrous increase in our ability to compile data. We have more data than ever before. Just by yourself, you can have in your own library of computer disks more data than Archimedes, Galileo, Newton, Einstein, or Edison.

---

* *Webster's New Universal Unabridged Dictionary,* Second Edition, 1983.

**The older term "data bank" has fallen into disrepute among the cognoscenti of data, who resent its frankly fiscal implications. I once had a senior person chew me out royally for referring to a data bank. This person said that a bank was for money, and his numbers were more important than that!

You can even buy the stuff from data purveyors. Large corporations have large computer systems stuffed with data. The government has many gigantic systems, all stuffed with data. So there are lots of data, but most of the time, if you want an answer, you will still have to find it on the back of an envelope somewhere.

But this meander through the backwaters of information theory will not help you plan to achieve your goals. You are going to have to compile the data you need to have as the basis for your plan. As I said before, this will not be easy, even though the principles are easy.

Remember in high school English class when you went on the compulsory trip to learn how to use the library? You had to put up with it all as the librarian told you how to find a title in the card file, look up a book in the stacks, use the reference room, and consult the index of periodicals. Grim stuff! Later, you had to write research papers with (ugh!) footnotes and a bibliography. You had to learn how to take notes down on a three-by-five or five-by-seven-inch card, depending on how affluent your school district was. You had to learn how to collect the results of your reading and research into usable form. You then had to consult your notes while writing the paper. Surprise! All of this elementary stuff you learned in school is just right for compiling data. The teachers taught you something really useful, and you will be doing the same thing over and over again throughout life as you compile data for your plans.

The four steps in data compilation are as follows:

1. Find the sources.

2. Get the data from the sources.

3. Record the data into usable form.

4. Organize the data.

Finding sources of data is easy. Finding the right sources for your purpose may not be so easy. The obvious places to turn for data are the library, trade associations, the yellow pages, newspapers, magazines, professional societies, friends, and colleagues.

Unless you have a lot of experience, the best place to start is in your own home. For most household planning, the telephone directory of businesses and services is a good place to obtain basic information on data sources. If you are planning to add a deck in the backyard, look up contractors. If you are planning to start a new small business, look up business consultants or associations and call them for advice on how to start.

The next logical place is the library. Besides the Library of Congress, which has a copy of just about everything, there are libraries in practically every county, city, and suburb of the United States. Universities have libraries, as do professional associations, corporations, and many other groups. Some of the libraries specialize in particular types of information, while others are more general in their holdings. All libraries, however, have one important thing in common: They are eager to help you find what you want to know. Librarians are injected with a special serum that gives them an overwhelming desire to assist you in finding the book, periodical, reference, or citation that you request. Simply make your needs known to them.

Don't overlook the government as a source of data. The U.S. Government puts out large masses of data, ranging from the census to a gigantic statistical abstract of all kinds of wonderful stuff. The government's information services are so huge that special catalogues are published listing the books, brochures, and reports available from various agencies. Much government information may be obtained free for the asking, but some of it will cost a nominal amount. All kinds of wonderful things can be purchased from the Government Printing Office in Washington, D.C. The Congress puts out a lot of information in the form of hearing transcripts, General Accounting Office reports, and copies of bills. Sometimes you can get a free copy of a new report by asking the office responsible for the action.

There are many associations in the U.S.—so many, in fact, that there are associations of associations. There are even private companies that earn their money by managing associations too small to afford their own administrative staffs. Associations are groups of people or groups of groups that band together to—guess what—trade data. They are in the business of compiling and distributing data, and if your interest overlaps with theirs, they normally will provide you with lots of data for your own planning.

Getting the data from the sources will involve a great deal of physical effort and possibly travel. It may be possible to get data you need by connecting your computer to one of the large numbers of data bases selling their services. Or you can hook up with a bulletin board and obtain data from many different sources.

Getting data is not the easiest thing, however. Recently I was starting to prepare a paper on an aspect of national security, and I wanted some data on the population of the United States. That sounds like a simple thing, right? Well, it turned out not to be so simple.

All I wanted was a list of the population of the United States for each year from 1900 to 2000. I followed my own advice and started making a data search plan. My first reference work was *The World Almanac* for 1992. I found population data in the book, but they were inconsistent for the early years because the counting rules changed, and the list ended at 1989. *The World Almanac* had some of the data but not everything I needed to know.

Then I decided to use my contacts to get the real numbers. I called a colleague in the Department of Labor. This man was the expert on the U.S. Labor Force, and he was a number person too. I called him and asked him about getting the numbers. He referred me to the Census Bureau. I called Census, and they promised to send some information, which they did. I got a statistical abstract and went through it. I went to the Government Printing Office to purchase additional tables I located in their catalogue. Although I could not obtain all the population data I sought from one source, I managed to piece it together from multiple sources. This will be typical for you as well, because the data you need are always going to be special and hard to get—no matter what you are looking for.

My advice is to stick to the steps I have outlined in this rule, and persevere until you get the data you need for your plan.

Rule 21: Record and Organize the Data

Now that you have compiled some data, you have to take the time to record them and organize them so they will be useful. Data are raw material—like iron ore. They need to be processed to extract the value—the iron—from them. This can be complicated, but it consists essentially of just two actions: recording and organizing.

Recording is the process of writing down the essential characteristics of each piece (item) of data. The characteristics may include, but are not limited to, the following: name or title; source; key words describing the content of the data; and some assessment of the reliability and value of the data. This listing of each data element is necessary for two reasons. First, it is an essential step before you can organize the data and then use them. Second, it is necessary to provide proof that you have the data.

One of the most familiar data records is a bibliography—a listing of books or articles used as sources for a written paper. A bibliography may also be compiled to provide hints to readers on conducting research in a particular field. The bibliography lists the author(s), title, publication date, publisher, and location at which the book was published. An annotated bibliography may contain additional information on the content of the book and perhaps some evaluation of the book. So a bibliography is a record of data, but since it lists sources already published, it is a record of what are called secondary sources.

Once the data are recorded for future use, it is time to give some attention to organizing. Actually, it was time to think about organizing the data before you collected them, for the way in which data can or should be organized is highly influential in what is collected, how it is collected, and what sources are to be consulted.

Data are organized by listing the items in groups or sets along with similar data so that analysis can be performed. Analysis of data seeks to define differences and similarities among different data sets in order to draw conclusions on cause and effect. Different sets of data may be compared to see how changes in one data set affect another data set. There are a lot of different ways to compare and contrast data sets, so the best kind of data organization is one that is flexible.

The easiest way to organize data is to just write the items down under the right headings. The trick is to get the right headings. Most of the time, the headings for data organization will be the same as the original topics designating what you need to know to achieve your goal. Sometimes you will have modified these original questions as a result of the planning process, so you will have made changes.

If you are organizing data about a new business, you might want to have headings for revenue estimates, cost of supplies, labor costs, insurance premiums, taxes, rent, and other overhead costs. If you are planning that vacation home, you might want to organize data under headings for opportunities for use, rental opportunities, initial costs, and annual maintenance costs.

Suppose you are planning some changes in your work force. The logical starting point would be the existing work force. You compile the data on the work force, which consists of the characteristics of the people in the work force: name, gender, age, hair color, eye color, ethnic background, religion, time on the job, job title, skills, and possibly an evaluation or rating of performance. These kinds of data usually are organized by individual, with a file containing these and other attributes of each individual.

In order to find out all about a single person, that is a good method of organizing the data. All you have to do is to pull the individual's file and read all about him or her. But if you are trying to understand the nature of your work force and do some analysis for planning, that kind of organization is inefficient. In order to obtain, for example, an idea of the age distribution of your work force, you would have to pull each individual file, note the age of that individual, write it down, and then arrange the ages in some kind of order (generally numerical) so that you can understand the distribution of ages. If you anticipate that you or the boss will want that kind of information from the basic data, you can have someone do that tabulation of ages in advance so that the information will be available at all times. Again, however, this is not a good solution, because the list of ages will change each time an employee leaves or joins, and keeping it current will be a problem. Actually, until the advent of the computer, this is the way we had to organize the data.

The computer makes it possible to organize the data and retrieve information quickly and flexibly. The computer alone does not guarantee that capability, because simply putting data into a computer does not guarantee either speed or specificity in getting the data back organized the way you want. Recognizing this problem, the software developers have been creating programs for data base management since the computer was invented. These programs have improved with the size and speed of the computers, and they are truly awesome these days. Most computer data bases will allow you to retrieve data in any combination you have built into the data base when you set it up. That is the rub: You have to organize your data in order to set up your data base.

In the personnel work force example noted above, we could set up a data base organized to list each individual and the attributes of each individual in separate fields. The power of the data base is that it allows the user to select a particular attribute of interest and sort the data in that field. This means the computer can search each file and note the age of each individual in the data base, then sort all of the ages numerically, or in specified age classes, or any which way. This ability to retrieve the attributes selectively and relate them to one or more other attributes is a powerful tool in understanding the nature of the data in the data base. It would be possible to show how the ages of the people in your work force related to their skills, so you could detect if the oldest group was in a particular set of skills, such as production, or sales, or personnel. You could find out the distribution of ethnic groups by skill, the distribution of blue-eyed people by age, or any other combination of attributes. Whether these combinations all make sense is another question.

The computer data base allows you to organize the data as you want in order to do your planning. It is another way to base your plan on solid facts.

Rule 22: See for Yourself

One of the best things to do while you are preparing a plan is to make a personal reconnaissance of the intended area of operations: Go see for yourself if you can.

Nothing is more comfortable than knowing what to expect. And there is no better way to know what to expect than having done it before. This means making a personal visit or a personal trip or a personal inspection. The key word is *personal*.

My own reaction to the unknown is fear, even when the circumstances are not themselves frightening. This may be irrational, but I bet I am not alone.

A personal reconnaissance is nothing more than a trip to see firsthand what the roads look like, what the terrain provides, what the amenities are, or what the room is like.

Few would marry someone sight unseen. Few would purchase a car without having at least seen it and more likely having already test-driven it. Most of us like to sample things before buying. This involves making a personal inspection or personal test.

When I am expected to go to a certain place for a business meeting or to make a presentation, I prefer to know the layout and location of that place in advance. If time permits, I will make a personal reconnaissance so that when I have to go to that place for the real thing, I know where I am going and will not get lost or be late. When I cannot make a personal reconnaissance, I allow extra time for myself to get lost or make a wrong turn, or in case I have simply underestimated the time it will take. This extra time allowance usually means that I am early, but several times it has been the margin for error in simply getting to a meeting on time.

One of the best aspects of living in the same place for a long time is that you become familiar with the streets, the stores, the landmarks, and the lay of the land. I have lived in the northern Virginia—Washington, D.C., area now for almost thirty years, and I know it pretty well. So when I have to go somewhere, I have confidence that I know how to proceed and avoid the possible pitfalls. Even with my knowledge and familiarity, however, I consult a map most of the time. It is a great comfort to have a vision in my head of the roads, the routes, and the peculiarities of this place—my hometown area—when I have to drive around or take the bus or subway. Simply knowing is great, and it saves time while allowing me to concentrate on other aspects of my business.

The value of a personal visit is enhanced by training and preparation. Training involves knowing in general what to look for. If you are planning a party, you will need to know how to estimate the number of people a party room can hold. If you are planning a construction project, you will need training in what to look for at a potential construction site. If you are planning a trip, you need to be familiar with the idiosyncracies of air, sea, rail, or motor transportation systems. When the infantry commander makes his personal reconnaissance of the route for tomorrow morning's attack, he brings into play his schooling and previous experience so that he knows what to look for and how to interpret what he sees. The same is true for all other occupations and kinds of plans.

Preparation is learning about the specific object of the visit in advance. Since personal visits or inspections often are limited in time and scope, you can obtain the best results by preparing carefully in advance. Look at the map, read the reports, scan the photographs. Do what you can to make your visit as profitable as possible. Know in advance what to look for and what you are looking at. The importance of preparation is particularly high when you have time for only one visit. The initial visit to a new place is invariably confusing and difficult, even if you are well trained and well prepared. So careful preparation is very important. Don't be afraid to do the work to make your reconnaissance as useful as possible.

If you cannot make a personal visit, it will be necessary to rely on reports, photographs, maps, and other surrogates for the real thing. Sometimes you simply don't have time to see for yourself. Sometimes you don't have the money to pay for the trip. Sometimes, as in the case of a battlefield commander, you can't gain access to the place you intend to visit—or attack. So you may have to rely on information about the place rather than on your own eyes.

I make it a rule to visit any room where I have to make an oral presentation for a personal inspection of the facilities before I go there for the real thing. It is always good to visit in advance the place where you have to preside or speak, because this allows you to visualize how the speaker's position relates to the audience and how the room is laid out. For me, this knowledge is valuable as I begin my psychological preparation to speak. In several instances, my personal reconnaissance has prevented disaster. I have discovered public-address systems that did not work, vu-graph machines that were missing or inoperative, and even rooms that were too small for the groups. Most of the time my personal visit made it possible for the faults to be corrected before the event. Some people might feel that insisting on making a personal inspection is a sign of lack of confidence or nervousness about speaking, but to me it is a sign of the true professional. Every professional golfer plays a few practice rounds on the course before he or she plays it during the tournament. Every professional tennis player likes to try out the surface of the courts before the tournament begins. Why shouldn't you try out the room and the equipment before you have to speak?

There is a great temptation simply to ignore this step. Going to an area or scouting out a route takes time and energy. You actually have to get up from behind your desk or easy chair and leave the office or house and go somewhere foreign and strange. This takes resolution, and a lot of people find it easier not to go. They prefer to sit back and rely either on secondhand information or no information at all. These people are ill-advised. It is better to make the effort up front when it doesn't count than to make mistakes on the real thing. Going into new territory is always scary, but it is better to do it in a scouting mode than in an operational mode. As in so many of life's choices, it is better to choose the harder but correct path.

A personal visit ought to be part of your planning process. If you are going to buy a house, you want to look at it. If you are going to build a house, you had better look at the land before you design it or hire an architect. If you are going to furnish a house, you had better look at the furniture stores. There are limits, however—if you are going on a vacation trip, it is probably going to be hard to make a personal visit just to get ready for the real trip!

Not doing a personal visit is generally tantamount to buying a pig in a poke—not a great idea for any planner.

Rule 23: Check the Facts

One of my great friends and mentors, Harold C. Chase, a constitutional law professor and Marine Reserve general, used to delight in reminding critics that they were entitled to their own opinions but not to their own facts. He would then proceed to use the facts to change their opinions. Hal Chase, of course, was right in the sense that facts are facts, but he also knew that what are considered to be facts are often variable. In truth, many people do have their own "facts," as the arguments over the Kennedy assassination demonstrate. So you have to be careful in what you call "the facts."

Facts are very important to the planning process, so a great deal of effort needs to be made to validate them. You can make several possible errors with respect to facts:

- Your "facts" may be opinions.
- You may have the wrong facts for your plan.
- You may be interpreting the facts incorrectly or using them improperly.
- The "facts" may be in doubt.

Some people give or write their opinions as facts, when they are not. They do this believing that opinions repeated often enough magically turn into facts. They are wrong. Nevertheless, it is true that opinions stated frequently, loudly, and vigorously sometimes attain the status of pseudo-facts, commonly believed but erroneous nonetheless. TV "documentaries" commonly assert the opinions of the producers and directors as historical facts, and most people watching the shows have neither the know-how nor the inclination to check them out and catch the TV people up on the distortions. This approach to fact-making attained its zenith under Joseph Goebbels, the propaganda minister for Adolf Hitler who proclaimed that if a big lie were repeated often enough, people would believe it. This "big lie" technique is something you especially have to watch out for if your plan involves controversial political issues. If you were planning to start up a family-counseling service, for example, your "facts" would be different if you got them from a pro-choice group as opposed to a pro-life group.

Sometimes your facts are correct but irrelevant to your plan. In that case, you have the wrong facts. This indicates a defect in your research plan. If you are planning to travel from Chicago to Anchorage, Alaska, overland on the Alaska Highway, even the most complete and correct facts about Caribbean cruises are not helpful. Although this may seem to be an obvious kind of mistake, do not be deceived.

Many people simply accept the facts they can get easily whether they are applicable to the plan or not. Don't be one of this kind; test your facts against your needs. When the differences are not as obvious as confusing the Caribbean with Alaska, it may be hard to test for relevance. For example, a complete set of facts about the highways in Washington state might be correct, but those facts would not be relevant to going from Chicago to the Alaska Highway, which starts at Edmonton, Alberta. The direct route would be to proceed from Chicago to Edmonton via North Dakota or Montana. Unless one had other reasons, it would not be necessary to travel through Washington. Remember, a very large number of facts are out there, but only a few apply to your problem.

Sometimes the facts are technically correct but used improperly. This error is a cousin to the use of irrelevant facts, but more subtle. When I was an Army officer, I once worked for a fine general officer, Donn Starry, who would react to a new fact by asking, "Yes, but is that good or bad?" This was a good question, for many people simply seized new facts and ran with them without questioning what they meant. Even true facts that are relevant can be misleading if they are held to be good when bad or vice versa, or if they are inserted in the wrong part of the puzzle.

Sometimes the actual facts are in doubt—sincere people cannot agree on the truth. I once watched in awe as two Civil War buffs spent four hours arguing about the Battle of Antietam (Sharpsburg). These two experts knew all about the battle, but each had a different picture of the events and the facts. They were not really so much interested in the outcome of the battle as in their different interpretations. The argument was fierce and, like the battle, was a draw. History is often a puzzle, and you have to watch out for so-called "facts." I was in the history business for a while, and I can tell you that no one knows for certain the number of troops on hand or the casualties suffered by the armies on either side at the Battle of Antietam. Many people put forth "facts," and groups exist for the sole purpose of defending a certain set of "facts." But in many of these cases, the simple fact is that no one really knows what happened. If your plan depends on a fact that is in doubt, convert it into an assumption so that you will reduce appropriately the extent of your reliance on it.

Therefore, never take "facts" for granted; even truths that seem self-evident need to be checked for relevance and accuracy.

5   Time

Time is always one of the fundamental elements of a plan. Time is the fourth dimension (the other three are spatial dimensions—height, width, and breadth or latitude, longitude, and elevation). Time is a mysterious natural phenomenon that has engaged the minds of philosophers and scientists throughout the ages. For one thing, time appears to be irreversible and to flow continuously from now toward the future. There has been much speculation about being able to reverse or transcend the onward flow of time, such as in the hit *Back to the Future* movies and the earlier and more elegant T. S. White book, *The Once and Future King,* in which Merlin the magician and mentor of King Arthur is born old and gets progressively younger with the years. Despite these fictional attempts to transcend time, we ordinary mortals have to put up with the simple truth that time flows onward and there is nothing we can do about it—except use it to our advantage in planning.

Time has two aspects: instant and duration. An instant refers to one particular point on the stream of time. That is, 3:30 P.M., Eastern Standard Time, 22 December 1992, is a particular point or instant in time. There are many different ways to designate particular instants, all of them arbitrary and none of them particularly meritorious.* We measure time with a day having 24 hours, each of which has 60 minutes, each of which has 60 seconds. That system, which has only commensurability to commend it, is inherited from the Babylonians, who had a thing about the number 12. If we took our time-measuring system from the Romans, we would probably use 20 hours, 100 minutes, and 100 seconds instead. (The Romans had a hard time writing 12 in their awkward system of numerals.) The day is based on the time it takes the earth to rotate once on its axis, the month on the time it takes the moon to revolve about the earth, and the year on the time it takes the earth to revolve about the sun. These basic concepts are valid for our particular system, even though there are definitional subtleties that allow a month to vary from 28 to 31 days or so. The actual calendar we use is arbitrary and was imposed by a pope who had absolute authority at the time. Never mind! The system we have is good enough for planning.

Duration of time is the difference between two instants of time. In a sense, duration expresses the concept of passage of time from one event to another. We speak of a period of time in terms of two dates or as so many time units. The phrase "four hours" expresses a period of time lasting that long from start to finish.

In planning we use time in both senses: as instants to denote particular points along our planning time line and as duration to denote how long we believe it will take to accomplish something.

Many philosophers consider time to be relative and variable instead of absolute and fixed. Both views are probably correct. When you are on vacation, time appears to flow more slowly than when you are caught up in a busy, hectic business schedule. And sometimes when you have to get a briefing done quickly, time appears to slow down to let you do the work. These varying views of time occur because of changes in mental attitude. While variable time

---

* Some of the other ways to designate that particular instant in time are 3:30 P.M. December 22, 1992 (civilian usage in the United States); 1530 22 December 1992 (military time); 9212221530 (typical computer time); 3:30 P.M. 12/22/92; 3:30 P.M. 22/12/92; 8:30 P.M., Greenwich Mean Time, December 22, 1992; or 12:30 P.M., Pacific Standard Time, December 22, 1992.

may be interesting, it is time as a fixed, unvarying flow that is very useful for planning purposes: A minute is a minute is a minute—and always will be!

Because we need to look at time as a tool, however, the first rule regarding time treats it somewhat as a variable, and you need to draw back to determine how to use it in your plan.

Rule 24: Set Your Planning Horizon

The first thing you have to decide about time is how far in the future you want your plan to cover. The period of time from now to the point at which your plan will culminate in results (you hope) is called your "planning horizon." Four general time spans are adopted for planning horizons: immediate, short-range, mid-range, and long-range. Sometimes the word "term" is used instead of range, as in "short-term." People disagree, however, about the exact time lengths each includes, and what is meant by these terms varies considerably. The accompanying figure gives a general range of time for each horizon.

General Ranges for Planning Horizons

Horizon	Time Span
Immediate	Minutes or a few days
Short-range	Several days to a year
Mid-range	Two to ten years
Long-range	Generally ten to twenty years or more

Immediate planning is done for immediate ends. The results are wanted right away, and time is perceived in short periods. This includes what is commonly called "operational planning," which is intended to guide day-to-day matters; here, implementation may occur while the planning is still taking place.

Short-range planning is the most common planning horizon for government and business. For federal, state, and local levels of government, the common planning horizon is one year, because that is the budget period and the budget determines what can actually be done. So the primary planning effort is focused on preparing, justifying, obtaining approval, and spending the annual budget. Since most of the content of organizational budgets is governed by inertia or by what happened before, the marginal changes to the previous year's budget are the really important things to budgeteers. Influencing these annual budget changes absorbs most of the attention of large organizations, often to the practical exclusion of attention to long-range planning and only grudging acceptance of mid-range planning.

Generally speaking, immediate and short-range planning tend to drive out mid-range and long-range planning. The pressure to produce for immediate satisfaction occurs among adults and organizations, as well as children. Bosses want results, and they usually want results that will benefit the organization or themselves *now*—so that they can benefit personally.

Mid-range, or strategic, planning is a modern phenomenon. Until recently, U.S. businesses were caught up in short-range planning, and this has been identified by some economists as one reason for the country's industrial decline. The government pioneered in mid-range planning, notably with the introduction of the Five-Year Defense Program in the Department of Defense (DOD) in the 1960s, and has at least made an effort to conduct long-range planning. Following the lead of the DOD, the entire federal government and many state and local governments have pushed their planning horizons out to five years or so. This movement to mid-range planning has had some good effects in providing at least a basis for consistent policies and programs over a multi-year period, but short-range politics and interest groups continue to exert pressure for short-range changes.

Long-range planning is the most difficult because of the problems of forecasting the future. As current trends are projected forward into the future, the chances for error are increased dramatically. It would be credible to forecast tomorrow's weather based on today's, but not to forecast the weather ten years from now based on that same data. As we project farther and farther into time, the likelihood that current trends will continue unchanged diminishes. Planning today to achieve results in ten or twenty or fifty years is very difficult indeed. Nevertheless, it is very important, for we know from historical studies that many things occurring now were in fact caused by forces unleashed and actions taken much earlier. Many, if not most, of the really important events that shaped the future were not even recognized by the people at the time, including those people who were involved in the critical events. Rule 84 provides more information on long-range planning, and Rule 12 discusses consideration of unintended consequences.

It takes real vision and selflessness to sponsor and support long-range planning, and that is why there is so little of it. The government tries to project ten to twenty years or more into the future, but the work generally is done by small groups of planners huddled into the "long-range plans branch" and communicating primarily with each other. The connection between long-range plans and what is actually done in the short range or formalized as mid-range plans is tenuous.

All this is by way of background so that you will understand the importance of selecting a planning horizon for your own project. Most of your plans will have an immediate planning horizon, and almost all of the rest will be short-range plans. Unless you are planning for an organization, you most likely will not be involved in formal mid-range or long-range planning. Still, even an individual or a family can benefit from doing some mid-range or long-range planning. Such decisions as buying a house should be made with a long view, and even a decision on whether to refinance an existing mortgage has to be done in the context of the four to six years it might take to save enough on monthly payments to offset the closing costs and points.

I used to ask my children, "What do you want to be in thirty years?" or "What do you expect to be doing in thirty years?" My intent was to get them to do some backward planning (Rule 13) to appreciate that what they were doing as teenagers or young adults would influence their future lives. Most of the time I received blank stares in response to these questions, for young people seldom visualize themselves as old people. My children started mid-range planning only as they started having responsibilities of their own. One of the ironies of life is that one's personal planning horizon tends to extend farther into the future just as one's ability to live farther into the future is being diminished. If only we could persuade the young to think ahead!

Rule 25: Pick Your Time Scale

Once you have set your planning horizon in terms of a number of days, months, or years, you need to establish the time scale you will use in your plan. Obviously, these two decisions are related: There is no point in using seconds as a time scale for a long-range plan designed to extend over twenty years. Within a planning horizon, however, many choices are possible.

The time scales that seem most appropriate for each planning horizon are indicated in the accompanying figure, but only as approximate suggestions.

Time Scales for Planning Horizons

Planning Horizon	Range of Time Scales
Immediate	Hours, days
Short-range	Weeks, months, quarters
Mid-range	Months, quarters, years
Long-range	Years

The selection of a time scale depends on more than merely the planning horizon. For example, if you want to plan annual events over a period of many years, both years and months need to be specified. A major factor in establishing a time scale is the precision of the data that will be used in the planning process. There is no use in having a time scale in days if the data are only available in quarterly or annual form.

For immediate planning, hours or days provide a good time scale. Even seconds or minutes may be useful for some really short-term plans.

Short-range planning tends to be measured in months or quarters, although for project type planning (as opposed to fiscal planning), weeks are a convenient time scale since a week is a definite time period during all of the year and is a customary work period of five days' (forty hours') duration. Because there are numerous holidays, however, even weeks tend to vary in the number of workdays and thus in the output that can be planned. No time scale available provides a work period that is constant for an entire year. You will just have to work around it. (By the way, the standard work year has 260 days, or 2,080 hours. The U.S. government uses a standard work year of 2,088 hours for reasons that are obscure but probably explicable in fairly reasonable terms.)

Mid-range planning commonly uses years because annual goals are convenient and tie in with so many other aspects of planning. If more detail is needed, quarters can be used, but these tend to be awkward in terminology. Quarters are particularly useful in fiscal or other planning tied to some budget cycle, because budget people and programmers customarily use quarters in their plans. Months might be used if particularly fine detail were needed for the plan.

Long-range planning commonly uses years, although it would be useful to adopt a five-year scale to extend over twenty years, and for very long-range planning, decades might be better.

It is often useful to use some multiple of a time unit for your planning. You might adopt a biennial (every other year) or a biannual (every half year) time scale. You might even have two time scales: one for major tasks in your plan and another to provide more detail for the breakdown of tasks into subtasks. There are many possibilities, and they depend on your particular needs.

The time scale you select will be the basis for your schedules.

Rule 26: Set Up a Schedule

The next step in your planning is to set up a schedule or schedules. A schedule is a time-phased array of tasks and subtasks to be accomplished. Using your desired time scale, assign a particular time to each task, subtask, and event to be done in the plan.

In the text of plans, it is common to array time vertically so that

it flows from early to late or from now toward the future. A typical
plan for a businessperson's day might be as follows:

    8:15 A.M.:   Arrive at office

    8:30 A.M.:   Staff meeting

  11:00 A.M.:   Meet with Client X to pick slogan

  12:30 P.M.:   Lunch with Ed

    2:30 P.M.:   Pick up photographs at studio

    5:00 P.M.:   Meet George to discuss contract

On this schedule each appointment is noted and defined in
time exactly.

There are two different ways to specify the time of day. The
normal U.S. method, used in the sample schedule above, separates
the day into two twelve-hour periods, distinguishing these with the use
of A.M. or P.M. The international, or European, method uses a twenty-
four-hour clock. International time is the same as U.S. time until noon;
then it continues on to 13 hours, 14 hours, and so on up to 24 hours.
The exact hours are denoted as 0800 or 1500 (the equivalents of 8 A.M.
and 3 P.M.), and the minutes are added with a colon (8:20 or 15:30) or
without (0820 or 1530). International time is easier to use, less likely
to confuse, and familiar around most of the world. I commend it to
you, for like the metric system of measurements, it ultimately will
prevail because of its simplicity and logic.

A mid-range schedule expressed in years could be as follows:

  1992:   Start planning for new subway system extension

  1994:   Obtain approval of plans and cost estimates

  1996:   Obtain funding for extension

  1997:   Start work on extension

  2000:   Subway system extension open

Sometimes you will not know the exact starting time for your schedule, as when plans are to be prepared and then held for implementation upon approval or in response to some future event. In this case, a common practice is to employ some code name to designate the starting point. The most famous such code name is "D-Day." A useful starting code for planning purposes may be devised to fit the project. W-Day could refer to a wedding, P-Day to a party, C-Day to the date a contract starts, and Ex-Hour to a meeting with the divorce lawyer (ouch!). In these cases, you specify time in your schedule as it relates to the start time (which has not yet been identified with a real time). Such a schedule would look as follows:

B-Day:	Start construction
B+10 days:	Foundation completed
B+22 days:	Framing completed
B+32 days:	Walls up and roof on
B+48 days:	Plumbing and wiring done
B+72 days:	Wallboard up, puttied, and painted
B+90 days:	House completed and ready for occupancy

While the vertical presentation of a schedule is useful in a text document for planning complex projects, it is easier to apply the time dimension horizontally along the X axis of a rectangular coordinate system. This horizontal axis is the time line. The time scale you have selected is marked out along the time line, and events, costs, quantities, and results may be indicated along the vertical Y axis. Each point on this kind of diagram is defined exactly in time and for whatever dimension has been applied to the Y axis. Some sample time lines are shown in the accompanying illustration.

These time lines may be based on hours, days, months, or years. You may show each unit of time, or you may include several days or years in one period. A time line may be absolute by indicating instants in real time, or it may be relative by indicating periods from your code-named start point.

Sample Time Lines

1993	1994	1995	1996	1997	1998	1999	2000

Jan	Feb	Mar	Apr	May	Jun	Jul	Aug	Sep	Oct	Nov	Dec

Mon	Tue	Wed	Thu	Fri	Sat	Sun

8:00	9:00	10:00 A.M.	11:00	12:00	1:00	2:00	3:00 P.M.	4:00	5:00

Schedules are basic to planning and to living. We all use schedules all of the time. In one sense, plans are really schedules.

Rule 27: Keep a Calendar

A calendar is a method for keeping track of the various units of time. Normally a calendar arranges the days of each month by week, but other arrangements are possible, such as simply listing the days in sequence from January 1 of a given year.

My advice is to keep a personal calendar for the things you want to do or have to do in the future. Such a calendar is invaluable in an increasingly complex world, allowing you to keep track of dates and times of appointments and meetings, tasks you want to accomplish by certain dates, and errands and chores you plan to do each day.

The utility of calendars is widely recognized, and a wide variety is available, including preprinted calendars ranging from very loose and simple to very structured and detailed, planning calendars with blank spaces for each day, and computer software that allows you to prepare your own, tailored calendars. Calendars are big business and worth it! Computer programs allow you to produce calendars tailored to your special needs and eccentricities, including special recurring events, such as birthdays of loved ones.

Some calendar systems offer preprinted forms designed to provide both a calendar and a schedule of events for each day. My own personal calendar consists of booklets covering two months each, with a printed page for each day of the month. I carry the current booklet in a leather wallet in my inside coat pocket or briefcase. I use only one page per day, but there are options to use two pages or a half page per day. The space on each page is for noting appointments, things to do, things done, expenses incurred, and probably a lot of other items as well. Each booklet also includes blank planning calendars for the two months of the daily pages and two additional months as well, plus extra space to mark down items beyond those months. I have used this personal calendar system for more than twenty-five years, and I love it.

Rule 28: Consider Sequence

Effective planning requires understanding the relationships of events along the time line. One event may occur later than, earlier than, or at the same time as another event. These temporal relationships may become complicated, and the time line is a tool to help you simplify and understand them.

As long as there are no conflicts among tasks, the relative time positions of events do not cause problems. Unfortunately, however, there often are these kinds of conflicts. Basically, there are two difficult time-dependent relationships that must be mastered if planning is to be effective. The first problem is that of sequence, and the second is that of simultaneity (addressed in Rule 29).

Sequence implies that one event precedes or follows another event. In the forward-planning sense, one event is thus a prerequisite for another event: Task A must be completed before Task B can be started, or Task X must be started before Task Y can be completed. These temporal relationships among events complicate the planning process a great deal, and they have to be dealt with systematically or the plan will not work. Often the time dependency is based on physical realities, but sometimes temporal relationships are simply human-devised rules, mostly but not always based on some rational considerations.

Most people are probably familiar with course prerequisites in high schools and colleges. This is the practice of admitting to

Philosophy 102 only those students who have successfully completed Philosophy 101. The idea is that the course is really part of a sequence in which each part builds on the previous part, and it would be difficult if not impossible to deal with 102 without first learning what was covered in 101. This makes good sense, and a lot of things in life seem to be built in this manner.

House construction is a good example of sequence based on physical realities. In building a house, the various parts have to be accomplished in a strict sequence in order to do the work with minimum effort at minimum cost. Builders know this, and they spend a lot of time scheduling the various subcontractors working on their housing projects. If the subcontractors do their work out of sequence, something has to be done over or the results will be poor.

For a house, it is easy to visualize the correct sequence. The foundation has to be built before the rest of the house can be started. Then comes the framing, the roof, the walls, the painting, and the finishing. At the proper times during the schedule of major tasks, the other systems, such as electricity, plumbing, telephone, and heating and air conditioning, will be built. For plumbing, for example, several visits will be needed in order to fit the work in easily and efficiently.. The plumbers will first work on the house during the foundation stage, when connections to the water and sewage lines will be installed. Then they will return to "rough in" the pipes when the framing has been furnished but before the wallboard is installed. When the walls have been finished, the plumbers will return to install the sinks, showers, tubs, and toilets. The same kind of in-and-out scheduling is used by the electricians, the heating and cooling people, and other specialized subcontractors.

Dealing with sequence is not always easy, for life appears to present us multiple time dependencies that can be hard to visualize. The proper sequence of events for your project may not be as obvious as for building a house. You will need to constantly consider the sequence of events as you carry out the planning process. As we shall see in chapters 7 and 11, some of the more sophisticated planning tools have been devised just to help you do this.

Rule 29: Consider Simultaneity

Another important aspect of time in planning is that two or more events frequently overlap in time, so that at a given instant several project activities may be occurring. This is good news in the sense that you can plan to do more than one thing at a time, but it is a complicating factor because you have to be able to detect and avoid conflicts for resources, attention, or space. You have to be able to plan without in effect putting two things at the same time-space coordinate.

Simultaneity is the general term used when two or more events or phenomena occur at the same time. There are some finer distinctions, however, as the following example involving three events, A, B, and C, illustrates.

Cases of Simultaneity

```
A    xxxxxxxxxxxxxxxxxxxxx

B    xxxxxxxxxxxxxxxxxxxxxxxxxxxxxxxxxxxxxxxxxxxx

C        xxxxxxxxxxxxxxxxxxxxxxxxxxxx
     0    1    2    3    4    5    6    7    8    9
```

Events A and B start at the same time and are said to occur simultaneously. Here the emphasis is on the start points, and so the fact that B continues after A stops is lost in the usage of the term. Events A and C also occur simultaneously, but since they start at different times the effect is different. Two events that occur at the same time but start at different times are sometimes called concurrent events.

It is important to consider the overlapping of events in time if the resources needed to start up and carry on a task or activity are the same as those needed for other tasks. If you have only one front-loader, you can dig only one foundation at a time, and your schedule had better not count on doing three at the same time. (Unless you plan to rent two more front-loaders for that critical event.) You can schedule your construction concurrently, however, and still have three houses going at the same time, but starting at different points to allow your one front-loader to dig three foundations successively.

Since it generally is advantageous to plan to do work in several parallel paths, you will most likely have to deal with events that overlap in time. Simultaneity carries with it the idea that there is competition for the same resources, while concurrency implies that the events are more or less independent and do not rely on the same resources. These general definitions are not commonly adhered to, however, and you need to define the dependency of overlapping events in specific terms for each case.

As with sequence, simultaneity can be very complicated when you are dealing with three or more separate time lines and event paths. Fortunately, you will be able to take advantage of some of the planning tools described in chapters 7 and 11 to deal with both of these time-based phenomena.

6   **Measures**

Any planning process involves measuring things. Measurement entails placing a value on a particular dimension or amount. You have to measure time, money, resources, length, breadth, width, height, and depth, as well as any other items that need to be defined in terms of quantity, space, or weight. It is not an easy thing to do, and there are some basic rules that will help you.

Measuring is not the same as describing. Simply describing something involves telling *what* it is, while measuring something involves in addition telling *how much* of it there is. While this simple distinction has a very fuzzy boundary, it remains valid and you should keep it in mind. Often you will be tempted to seek a measure of something, when what you really want is a description—sufficient to allow the item or phenomenon to be recognized but not enough to allow it to be sized or costed.

All of us have measured things—the heights of our children as they were growing up, the area of the dining room in the new house, the length of the driveway—and in performing these measurements, we probably used a graduated tape, a yardstick, or a ruler. These measuring instruments are often used to establish the size of things. But it is essential that you understand that measuring something is not very straightforward at all.

Once I taught a class on elementary measurement and I illustrated the problem by asking each of my fifteen students to measure the length of a table in the classroom using a tape measure. Then we performed some simple analysis on the results. We listed all of the measurements on a blackboard and noted some interesting things. First, no two students had exactly the same figure for the length of that table. Second, some students had simply given the length in terms of feet and whole inches, while others had stated the length in terms of feet, inches, and fractions of inches. Third, all of the answers were close. The experiment demonstrated that measurement is as much of an art as a science, and that it is not as simple as it might seem.

The five rules in this chapter are designed to help you deal with measures and measurements in your planning.

Rule 30: Don't Mistake Precision for Accuracy

A common mistake made by planners and others is to mistake precision for accuracy. These two words are not interchangeable. Precision is the amount of detail with which a measurement is described, while accuracy is the extent to which a measurement varies from the truth. Precision is denoted by the number of significant figures used. Significant figures are the numerals used to express a number ahead of a string of zeros. The number "100,000,000" has only one significant figure, while the number "103,000,000" has three, and the number "103,219,505" has nine.

An example from the table-measuring exercise will serve to illustrate the two terms. For the purposes of the illustration, let us assume that the table is exactly 6.25 feet long. A measurement of 6.25 feet would be entirely accurate and sufficiently precise. A measurement of 4.589643215 feet would be very precise because it is stated with ten significant figures, but it would not be accurate. The wrong answer is given in great detail, which is a common mistake by people who do not understand the difference between precision and accuracy.

A measurement of 6 feet would be less precise but more accurate than the previous number (although not completely accurate), while a measurement of 6.24902167345283 feet would be very precise and quite accurate. In this last case, however, the increase in precision (from three to fifteen significant figures) does not lead to any increase in accuracy.

The difference between precision and accuracy is quite important in planning.

Precision does not assure accuracy. Just because a table of numbers is presented in many significant figures or the estimates are given to the sixth decimal point does not make them accurate. The use of many significant figures indicates only that the measurement has been accomplished at a fine level of detail. Some people try to give an impression of accuracy by stating quantities and measurements with great precision, but they are fooling you and, perhaps, themselves.

My advice to you when you are presenting quantitative data is to reduce the degree of precision for numbers that you know are merely estimates. That is, round off your estimates to the nearest mile, nearest thousand dollars, or nearest million kilowatts in order to convey exactly the degree of precision warranted by the way in which you obtain the numbers. If you are making a guess or an assumption on a measurement, it is misleading to state that guess with ten significant figures. The accompanying example illustrates the difference.

Estimated Costs of the New (Big) Doghouse

Overly Precise		Roughly Right	
Lumber:	$4,633.65	Lumber:	$4,600
Nails:	762.65	Nails:	800
Paint:	1,087.25	Paint:	1,100
Total:	$6,483.55	Total:	$6,500

The overly precise table conveys a false image of accuracy, while the roughly right table, in which the costs are rounded off to the nearest hundred dollars, conveys correctly the sense that these are rough estimates to be used for planning purposes. After the materials are purchased, the bill for payment may well be presented to the nearest cent, but such precision is not warranted before that.

There are some differences of opinion among serious people about accuracy. Some hold that accuracy is an absolute and that a measurement is either accurate or inaccurate, with no other possibilities. Others say that there may be degrees of accuracy. While I understand and have some sympathy for the view that something is either accurate or inaccurate, the other usage is better for practical planning.

I suggest that we can have a range of accuracy from completely accurate to very accurate to somewhat accurate and then on to wildly inaccurate. This permits us to distinguish between data we provide as good representations of the truth and data we guarantee only to be somewhat in the ballpark. As long as we have some idea of the difference between truth and measurements, we can live with a degree of inaccuracy. We should not ever try, however, to portray somewhat inaccurate data falsely by giving them a misleading degree of precision.

Remember again, it is better to be roughly right than precisely wrong. Of course, it is best to be precisely right.

Rule 31: Establish Your Units

One of the things you should do at the outset of your planning process is to establish the units of measurement you will use throughout the process.

There are four basic quantities to measure in our world: distance, weight, volume, and time. We have a fairly easy system for measuring time (see chapter 5), but the systems for distance, weight, and volume are messy, and there are many different units of measurement for these quantities. Distance can be stated in terms of inches, furlongs, meters, miles, fathoms, and microns. Weight can be stated in terms of pounds, grams, stones, carats, and tons. Volume can be stated in terms of pints, gills, liters, gallons (two varieties), barrels, and hogsheads.

Some of these units of measurement were derived originally from a readily available standard, such as a foot being compared to the length of a human foot. The disadvantages of using a unit of measurement that varied according to the size of someone's feet became apparent to traders and manufacturers, and so arbitrary standards have been established for units of measurement.

A meter, for example, used to be defined as the length of a platinum-iridium bar kept under sterile conditions in France, but in 1960 the standard for the length of a meter was changed to become 1,650,763.73 wavelengths of the orange-red line in the spectrum of the Krypton-86 atom under specified conditions.* All of the other instruments designed to measure things for distance—meter sticks, tape measures—are calibrated by reference to the standard.

Many units of measurement apply almost entirely to a particular field of endeavor. A fathom is equal to six feet and is used for boating purposes, mostly as a way to show how nautical the user really is. A gill used to have great application in the whiskey-drinking business. These peculiar units of measure persist but are more and more relegated to specialties, while most of us use either the English or the metric system.

The English system of measurement units is used extensively today only in the United States. Even the English have given it up. The basic units of the English system are as follows:

Distance: inch, foot, yard, mile

Weight: ounce, pound, short ton, long ton

Volume: ounce, pint, quart, gallon

The English system persists only because of the reluctance of people in the United States to adopt the "foreign" metric system. So we put up with the basic lack of systematic relationships that makes the English system hard to use. There are 12 inches in a foot, but 3 feet in a yard, and 1,760 yards in a mile. Why? Was it invented to give schoolchildren fits doing word problems in arithmetic? Similarly, there are twelve ounces in a pound of weight, but eight ounces in a pint of volume. The lack of a systematic approach in the English system is

---

* Thanks, *Encyclopaedia Britannica, Micropaedia,* Vol. VI, 15th ed., 1973, p. 842. I needed that!

a distinct disadvantage, and its continued use can only be characterized as a triumph of nostalgia over utility.

The metric system is used almost everywhere in the world except the United States of America. It is designed so that measurements are related by factors of ten at each level, and handy prefixes are used to denote the level. This is convenient in the modern age, because our numbering system is built on the base of ten. The units of the metric system are as follows:

Distance: millimeter, centimeter, meter, kilometer

Weight: milligram, centigram, gram, kilogram

Volume: milliliter, centiliter, liter, kiloliter

Milli- is the prefix for a thousandth of the base unit, centi- is the prefix for a hundredth of the base unit, and kilo- is the prefix for 1,000 times the base unit. The system is neat and makes sense, and it is easy to use.

Actually, many of our measurements in the United States have already gone metric. We measure our wine in metric terms, and that is important. We perform a lot of our manufacturing using metric units, and that lets us export products to other nations that use the metric system. Despite the obvious advantages of having the whole earth use the same units of measurement, the United States has been slow to convert to the metric system.

My advice is to pick whichever major system you prefer at the outset of your planning process, keeping in mind that the standard practice for the area in which you are planning will be important. If you are buying lumber, the key unit is the board-foot (the volume of a piece of wood one foot by one foot by one inch thick). If you are planning a big party, the key unit is the shot (1.5 ounces of hard liquor). You should also decide, depending on the size of the quantities you will be dealing with, whether to adopt units at a high level of aggregation (miles, tons, barrels), a low level of aggregation (inches, ounces, pints), or somewhere in between. Once you have picked the units of measurement for your plan, convert all quantities into these units habitually and comprehensively, so that your tables and your calculations will be consistent.

Rule 32: Select Your Measures of Merit

Another important measure you need to establish has nothing to do with the size, weight, or location of the resources you need. It deals instead with what you want to accomplish.

A measure of merit is a quantitative expression of success. It allows you to determine at any time just how well you are doing at achieving your goals. You probably expressed your goals, at first at least, in terms of some qualitative, fairly fuzzy ideas, such as become wealthy, buy a new house, or hold a wedding. That is fine for getting started, but qualitative statements of goals are not very useful in calculating costs, benefits, schedules, and above all, success. You need a measure of how well your plan meets your goals—and later, how well the plan implementation measures up to the plan.

A measure of merit may be a single number, or it may be a composite number made up of several different elements. The proper measure of merit may be obvious, but in many instances it is not, and the selection of the best measure of merit is in itself an art not to be taken lightly, for the measure of merit affects all of the analysis and planning.

Let's start with some obvious measures of merit. If you want to get rich, the measure of merit is your net worth. If you want to graduate from college, your measure of merit is your grade-point average, which may be a minimum to be exceeded if your goal is just to graduate or a number to be maximized if your goal is to be first in the class.

If you want to build a house, you may have as a measure of merit the cost, but using that measure alone could reward a plan that calls for cheap materials and a small house. A better measure of merit might be the cost per square foot of living space, which would not be influenced by the size of the house but would provide an indication of cost. If you choose to track cost per square foot, you need neither minimize your number nor maximize it but could settle instead for a range that suits both your pocketbook and your lifestyle aspirations. (Total cost of the house, however, can be used as the measure of merit if you already have a fixed floor plan.)

In business planning, the measure of merit could be net worth, but that is a static number that does not reveal how you are doing. A better measure of merit for a small business operated by the owner is probably net income after expenses and taxes, which would be the equivalent of a salary if you worked for someone else. There are many possible measures of merit for a corporation: return on invest-ment, return on sales, price of a share of common stock, dividends to the shareholders, or quarterly profits. Selection of the measure of merit influences operations. Critics of U.S. corporate management say that focusing on maximizing short-term profits as the measure of merit causes managements to ignore long-term survival. Some critics say that selection of share price as the measure of merit for corporate management leads to actions that detract from good business sense. Without taking a position on these arcane matters, it is easy to see why selecting the measure of merit in a business can have great influence on what you plan to do and how you do it.

Once you have established a measure of merit, you can use it to see how well you are doing at meeting your goal. You are probably familiar with the typical charitable fund-raising activity. Sooner or later someone will post a sign showing how the organization is doing. The measure of merit is the number of dollars contributed to the cause, and the progress of the campaign is shown relatively easily but quite effectively as the percentage of the goal that has been met. The goal itself is selected somewhat arbitrarily, probably based on last year's goal with some amount added in the name of progress and inflation. The campaign is judged a success when the goal is attained or surpassed. During the campaign, the managers responsible for it can see how well they are doing and put on more pressure if the progress indicated by the dollars contributed versus the dollars desired is too slow to ensure success by the end of the campaign period.

My advice is to select one or a few measures of merit so that you will be able to see clearly what your plan has to accomplish and later how well the implementation of the plan is succeeding. If you can find a single measure that really represents what you are trying to do, that is good. Often, however, you will be forced to have several measures of merit. They may be independent or even conflicting. If you have several measures of merit, you will have to exercise judgment to determine the mix of these numbers that best represents progress and then success or failure.

Rule 33: Establish Your Tolerances for Error

Since measurements are inexact, it is necessary to make allowances that establish your tolerance for error—the range of error you are willing to put up with.

Tolerances are expressed as a desired measurement and an indication of the amount of error that can be accepted and still have the plan work. A tolerance that specifies an acceptable error of "10 meters plus or minus 1 millimeter" calls for a length ranging from 9.99 meters to 10.01 meters. A tolerance that specifies an acceptable error of "10 meters plus 2 millimeters" calls for a length ranging from 10.00 meters to 10.02 meters. A tolerance that specifies an acceptable error of "10 meters minus 2 millimeters" calls for a length ranging from 9.98 meters to 10.00 meters. In each example the total allowable error is 2 millimeters, but the application differs according to the plan requirements.

One of the major applications of tolerances is in the manufacture of automobiles, in which many parts are made separately in many plants and then assembled in a single plant. These parts have to fit together in accordance with the design and plans for the automobile, so they have to be the size specified. There is little margin for error, so the tolerances are small. In fact, in one sense the progress of manufacturing has been the story of decreasing tolerances. In the early days of industrial production, each part was made individually by hand and the measurements varied a great deal. These parts had to be cut, filed, or forced to fit together. This took a lot of time and effort, and thus manufactured items were costly and scarce. As tools and materials got better, it became possible to reduce the tolerances so that all items of a particular part became interchangeable. This made it easier to put them together into an automobile, refrigerator, or television set, and allowed quality to go up and cost to go down.

Tolerances apply not only to physical measurements but to time schedules as well. Take flying on commercial airlines, for example. There are few direct flights these days, and each airline routes its flights through one or more hubs, so the air traveler usually has to go on one flight from the start point to a hub at which to connect to another flight to the final destination. For example, when I travel to Albuquerque from Washington, D.C., I land at Dallas–Fort Worth to catch another flight. This means that there is a certain time period between the arrival of the first flight and the departure of the second flight. It is a good idea to arrive at the hub with enough time to deplane and get to the new gate for the second flight, and this means you have to establish the time tolerance for making the connection. The amount of time it takes to go from the arrival gate to the departure gate depends on their distance apart and the general configuration of the airport. If you are connecting on the same airline, the gates usually are close together, but not always. And you will not know the arrival or departure gate until just before or after you land (sometimes this information is provided just before you land to speed up the connection process). Of course, if the first flight is delayed, your time to make the connection is reduced. Nevertheless, when making the reservations for the flights, you have to make some judgments about the amount of time you believe will be sufficient to assure that you will not miss the connecting flight. Thus, you are establishing the tolerances in your travel itinerary.

Cost is a factor in specifying tolerances. Generally, it costs money to reduce error, and the smaller the tolerance, the higher the price for an item. As with so many other aspects of planning, there is a definite trade-off between high quality and low cost.

My advice is to recognize that you need to specify the tolerances you are willing to accept for your schedules and for the resources you need for your plan. Many—perhaps most—of these tolerances will be set already by commercial, industrial, or government groups, and for these all you need to do is pick the tolerances acceptable for your plan. If your plan involves putting things together, think ahead of time about the amount of error you are willing to tolerate.

Rule 34: Decide on Safety Factors

It is prudent to build into your plans some safety factors just in case you have made some mistakes. It is inevitable that you will make mistakes in the planning process. Your assumptions will be wrong, your data will be slightly inaccurate, your analysis flawed, so you will find that you need more of this and less of that than you had figured. That is just during the planning. Once you start implementing the plan, it gets worse, for Murphy's Law kicks in with all of its variety of things that can go wrong. Remember, if something can go wrong, it will.

When things do go wrong, it is really great to have a bit extra to cover the shortage or to have an alternative already figured out to work around an unexpected bottleneck. It is also great planning. Inserting some extras—resources, money, effort, time—into the plan all falls under the heading of safety factors.

Originally, safety factors were used by engineers to cover their ignorance. Lacking exact knowledge of how strong their materials were, they made certain there would be few failures by doubling or tripling the strength provided. When the Brooklyn Bridge was built, little was known about the tensile strength of the iron members used to create the span, and so the engineers built into the design a good safety factor. Later, as understanding of iron and steel improved, it was possible to provide the same load capacity for less material— and less cost. By modern standards, the Brooklyn Bridge was probably overdesigned by a factor of four or five, but that is better than failing to provide a safety factor and having the bridge fail.

Safety factors are a hedge against an uncertain future. I learned the importance of inserting a safety factor early in my career as an engineer. I had just reported to the 808th Engineer Battalion on Okinawa in 1950, and I was put in charge of building some hardstands for B-29 aircraft at Kadena Air Force Base. This was my first construction job, and I really didn't know much about what I was doing, but I had experienced troops working for me and it was going all right. Then one day the battalion operations officer visited the site and asked me when the project would be completed. I calculated in my head the work to be done and, without adding a safety factor, told him seven days. Well, you know what happened. Two of the dozers broke down; the surveying team was called to another project; and it rained two straight days. As a result, I found myself facing an impossible deadline that I myself had set. The battalion operations officer was a crusty soul and did not take kindly to my being late. Too late I realized that I should have inserted a safety factor to have had some extra time when things went wrong. If I had told him ten days, I would have made the deadline despite the equipment problems, the surveyor diversion, and the rain. I might even have finished ahead of the deadline and reaped some reward for good management. I learned my lesson from that and have taken care ever since to insert a safety factor in estimates of job completion and of resource requirements.

There is a down side to safety factors, of course, and that is cost. If you put three times as much steel into the bridge as your calculations show you need, you are not only decreasing the probability that it will fail but also increasing its cost by the same factor. So the necessity to control costs acts as an effective constraint on large safety factors. Generally, safety factors of 10 to 20 percent are still used in construction, but improved knowledge of materials, building practices, and quality control allows these to be reduced, with consequent savings.

Nevertheless, even sizable safety factors can be justified when the consequences of failure are considered. In planning, most attention is placed on the benefits of success, but some attention also should be placed on the consequences of failure. This is particularly true of small business, where hope often overwhelms reality. The insertion of a significant safety factor can prevent catastrophic failure, which could incur costs far more damaging than the extra cost for the safety factor would have been in the first place. You should always look at the down-side potential.

My advice is to insert appropriate safety factors in your plans, if for no other reason than to ensure that you don't suffer catastrophic failures from unexpected events. Always make these safety factors an explicit item in your calculations. They are a legitimate entry, and hiding them would make them appear to be underhanded.

7 Simple Conceptual Planning Tools

Just as with any other job, you need the right tools to do your planning. A carpenter needs a saw, hammer, and screwdriver; a plumber needs a pipe wrench; an electrician needs pliers. A planner needs as a minimum some paper and a pen, but there are many other tools available. Some of these tools are hardware, such as computers, calculators, and cameras, and some are software programs, such as calendars, project schedules, and accounting systems. The planning tools discussed in this chapter are conceptual.

Conceptual planning tools are models or procedures that allow the planners to visualize and understand what is to happen more clearly. The ability of the human mind to visualize intangible things is limited. Some people are better at it than others—nuclear physicists, for example, seem to be blessed with an inordinate ability to visualize abstractions—but all of us are limited. We just find it hard to think about fuzzy things such as schedules, shapes, relative locations, and relationships. We generally can cope with two or three variables, but when the scope of the effort gets more complicated than that, we need help. That help comes from conceptual tools, which are designed to enable planners to make abstract ideas more concrete and allow a few variables to represent the entire complicated thing.

The planning tools discussed in this chapter are relatively simple, but they are important. They can be done manually or using the latest high technology available, but in either case they will make it easier for you to perform the planning process. Some additional, more complicated planning concepts are discussed in chapter 11, following the chapters on resources, costs, and money.

As when approaching any other toolbox, it is wise to select the right tool for the job. Using a common screwdriver for a Phillips head screw is bad form, and using a scheduling program to help you visualize spatial relationships is equally bad form. Neither will do the job for you, so you have to know about a lot of tools and pick the right one for your job.

Rule 35: Draw a Picture

The first planning tool is the best and easiest. It requires only a piece of paper and a pencil or pen, and it will help a lot.

When you have trouble grasping how the various pieces of your planning puzzle relate, when it is not clear when things should be done, when the whole thing is hard to understand, the first thing you should do is draw a picture.

The picture need not be a work of art; a simple sketch on the back of an envelope is sufficient in some cases, and a pencil drawing on notepaper is usually adequate. Pictures are particularly good for establishing spatial relationships, considering the time line and sequence, and solving arithmetic problems.

Drawing a picture is very helpful in establishing the spatial relationships of different objects, such as furniture in a house, cities on a tour, the layout of an office, or the location of food dishes at a buffet dinner. When furnishing a house, it is really a good idea to sketch a floor plan of the house and draw furniture in various locations before buying it and having it delivered. When planning a day's activities on a trip, it is useful to sketch the locations of the places you want to visit or mark them on your map. When setting up a production line for a document, it is helpful to draw the office layout and assign people to stations in the processing flow. In preparing for a dinner party, a sketch of the buffet table would help you to know where to put each food item when you lay out the buffet dinner.

Drawing the time line and putting the various events on it at the moments they are scheduled to occur can help you get the sequence of events straight. On the drawing, conflicts and overlaps will be readily apparent. These kinds of pictures are called project schedules, and one is discussed in Rule 37.

Solving arithmetic problems is always helped by a drawing. When I was taking algebra and we had all of those horrible word problems to solve, my life (and my algebra grade) was saved by a teacher who insisted that we draw a picture of the problem as the first step in solving it. We clutched our pencils and our rulers as we uncomprehendingly read the word problem:

> If two trains started d miles apart at the same time traveling x and y miles per hour respectively, how much time would it take for them to meet?

For me, drawing a picture showing the basic spatial relationships—or the geometry of the situation—did make it clearer. For this problem, I would draw a line and indicate Train 1 at Point A and Train 2 at Point B at a distance of d miles away, as shown in the accompanying illustration.

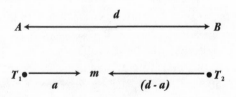

This simple picture illustrates the basic layout of the problem. Since the total travel distance has to be d, if one train travels a distance we call *a*, the distance the other train travels is *d-a*, and they will meet at some point, *m*. Since both trains travel the same amount of time, *t*, the basic equations are as follows:

$$1.\ a = xt \qquad \text{(Train 1)}$$
$$2.\ d - a = yt \qquad \text{(Train 2)}$$

Substituting *xt* for *a* in equation 2 gives us the following:

$$d - xt = yt, \text{ or } d = xt + yt$$

$$\frac{d}{\quad}$$

Solving for *t*: $t = (x + y)$ which is the solution.*

If you had trouble with this, look again at the picture and see how the different quantities relate. If you still have trouble, get out the old math book and review your high school algebra, or even take a night-school course in business mathematics. You will find that knowledge of basic mathematics will help your ability to plan.

Line Diagram

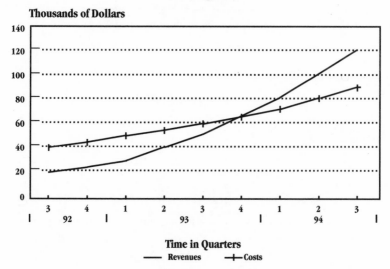

Thousands of Dollars

Time in Quarters
— Revenues   —+—Costs

---

* Check for the solution: If *d* = 10 miles, *x* = 2 mph, and *y* = 6 mph, the time for the trains to meet is 10 ÷ (2 + 6) = 1.25 hours. Train 1 travels 2 x 1.25 = 2.5 miles, and Train 2 travels 6 x 1.25 = 7.5 miles. The distances add to 10.0 miles, so the answer checks.

Another kind of picture that helps is to draw rectangular coordinate axes and plot equations or projections on them to get a feel for their shape and behavior. If your planning involves mathematics, this should become routine. The line diagram on the previous page shows planned revenues and costs for a business over time. This helps you visualize how the business will go in the first few years.

Pictures are used routinely in construction of buildings, where they are known as plans. Construction plans are drawings showing how the house is to be constructed and how the pieces fit together. It would be extremely difficult to build a house without construction plans.

The following diagram is a simple floor plan of a doghouse—a big doghouse—to help you figure out how to build it.

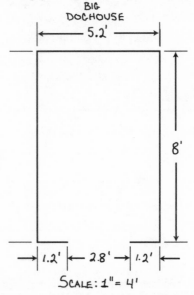

This floor plan can be drawn by hand using a straightedge ruler and a ballpoint pen. The drawing is to scale so that one inch on the drawing equals four feet in reality. The dimensions help you figure out how much lumber to buy and how long to cut the pieces. Obviously, it would be good to have another drawing showing the height of the doghouse. There are computer programs that help you do this kind of thing, but you really don't need one for simple projects. You don't even need a straightedge—a freehand sketch will suffice for most of the things you want to do. The point is that even a simple drawing helps.

My advice is to draw a picture to help crystallize in your mind the spatial or time relationships of the objects or events in your plan.

Rule 36: Make a Model

Another tool you can use to assist you in the planning process is a model of the thing you are trying to build or accomplish.

A model is a representation of reality. It is not the reality, for it forgoes some fidelity to achieve other advantages. Models are useful to see how large structures will look and fit into their environment before you build them. They are useful for seeing how complicated systems work that would be too costly to re-create in full size or reality. They are essential to understanding processes, such as combat, that cannot be re-created in reality and occur relatively infrequently of their own accord.

There are many different types of models. They run the gamut from very simple to very complex and range from pure mathematical models to physical analog models, which duplicate the real thing on a smaller scale. An equation, such as $F = ma$, which represents the mechanics of motion, is a model. The picture the last rule advised you to draw to improve your understanding of the project is also a model. A small-scale replica of a proposed house or office building is a model. A computer program that simulates the operation of a street lighting system is a model. And a massive computer program that replicates combat by firing each weapon on both sides of an engagement and assessing losses using probabilities of hit and kill is also a model.

Models are used because they are convenient. The planners are willing to trade a loss of accuracy in order to save time or money. Models of traffic systems are faster and cheaper than observing the actual systems themselves. Perhaps the ultimate in this kind of model is a scale model of the Mississippi River constructed by the

U.S. Army Corps of Engineers at Vicksburg, Mississippi, that is used to predict flood surges on the river. The widths and depths of the model are scaled according to hydraulic formulas and allow the engineers to predict flood stages downstream days before they occur in reality. Small-scale physical models of ship hulls and aircraft bodies are used in water basins and wind tunnels to check out the operating characteristics and make changes before going to the expense of building the full-scale ships and aircraft bodies. Models of housing developments and office buildings are made to show prospective purchasers how the buildings are laid out, in order to save their time and give them an overall viewpoint not easily attained from the ground.

An analog model is one that replicates on a small scale the behavior of a system, subsystem, or phenomenon. A model of a house is an analog model, as is a watch that presents the hour hand in the timely position on a twelve-hour dial.

A digital model is one in which the data have been reduced to numbers that can be manipulated mathematically. A watch that shows the time by numbers calculated by a computer and displayed on a screen is a digital model. Digital models have been really useful only since computers have become available in large numbers.

Models are also used to represent phenomena or systems that are too expensive to re-create completely or that occur infrequently in nature. Wars are phenomena that occur too infrequently to be available for systematic study and must be investigated using models. We could not schedule a war simply to test out some new weapons and tactics, although we do use training exercises for that purpose. Much of the time, however, we use models and try to learn from them. We also would not want to create natural disasters for study purposes even if we could, so we rely on models to learn about the disasters and how to plan to manage them.

There are three uses of models: training, operations, and predictions. Models are particularly good in training people to operate equipment that is expensive to acquire and operate. The Department of Defense saves a lot of money by using inexpensive aircraft simulators for a lot of pilot training instead of expensive aircraft. Similarly, tank crews can learn to shoot simulated electrical bullets before going on a firing range to shoot expensive real bullets from their tank guns. Models of air-traffic problems can help new air-traffic controllers to learn their jobs without the risk of accidents. Models can be programmed to be self-teaching and self-developing, so that students can play around and absorb the principles of operations of many complicated systems.

Models are also used to screen out a lot of distracting "noise" from some complicated systems and allow the operators to focus only on critically important things. An operating model of a traffic-control system can be used by the operators to change the timing and sequence of traffic lights in the real system.

The least reliable use of models is to predict the future. The future is essentially unknowable, but we persist in making predictions based on the assumption that what we observe happening in the past will be reflected in the future. So we project present trends into the future and use them as the basis for making decisions that will affect the future. This is risky business, made more so by the credibility automatically attached to any product of a computer. Computer models that predict the future are not really much better than crystal balls in the hands of experienced seers, but they appear to be better— which makes them dangerous.

I have been in the modeling business and have both created and used models. My belief is that no models are any good, but they can be useful if employed properly. This statement disconcerts people who fail to appreciate the distinction between goodness and utility and who want to believe the models. My view is that outputs from models should not be taken as the answer to a question or the solution to a problem, but only as another input to be integrated with other facts, judgments, and hunches to answer a question or solve a problem. Modelers say that the real output of a model is insight—added appreciation for the reality being modeled. Insight is not a very tangible product and is not valued very much by customers, who want concrete results in a hard-copy printout, but insight remains the only real product of a model.

My advice is to use models to save time and money or to study phenomena that cannot be reproduced easily, and use the outputs of the models to gain additional insight into your planning problem.

Like fire, a powerful force for bad or good depending on usage, models can be powerful tools for bad if you take them literally but for good if you use them to improve your understanding.

Rule 37: Use a Gantt Chart

The time schedules of large projects become complicated very rapidly, and some systematic approaches have been devised to help you keep track of all that has happened, is happening, or is supposed to happen. These tools are called project schedules, and there are several different types and many variations. All project schedules display tasks on one axis and time on the other axis.

The first and still the most basic project-scheduling system is the Gantt Chart, named after the inventor Henry L. Gantt, a pioneer in the field of project scheduling. A Gantt Chart lists events or tasks down the left side. The start time, duration, and end time of each event or task is shown from left to right opposite the task. A Gantt Chart can show when one task is dependent on another as a prerequisite and may also display the costs and labor effort for each task. This kind of chart allows you to project all of the tasks in your plan and see how they relate. You may adjust the chart when your inspection reveals inconsistencies and lack of workable sequence. I produced the following simple Gantt

Daily Schedule in Gantt Chart Format

Events	Time of Day						
	0800	1000	1200	1400	1600	1800	2000
	•	•	•	•	•	•	•
Get dressed	xx						
Breakfast	xx						
Travel	xxxx						
Staff meeting		xxxxx					
Lunch			xxxx				
Client meeting A				xxxx			
Client meeting B				xxxx			
Travel						xxxx	
Dinner							xxxxx

Big Doghouse Schedule

TASK NAME	RESOURCES	STATUS	OCT 93 5	13	19	26
Make foundation						
Buy cement & sand	George	C				
Mix & place concrete	George	C				
Cure concrete		C				
Construct doghouse						
Buy lumber & nails	George	C				
Build walls	George	C				
Put roof on	George	C				
Paint doghouse						
Buy paint	Carol	C				
Paint first coat	Carol	C				
Paint second coat	George	C				

▌ Detail task	===== Summary task	○ ○ ○ ○ ○ Baseline	
▌ (Progress)	---- (Progress)	▶ ▶ ▶ Conflict	
▌ (Slack)	=== (Slack)	▪ ▪ Resource delay	
Progress shows percent achieved on actual		▲ Milestone	

-------- Scale: 8 hours per character ----------

Chart using the word-processing program on my computer. The letter *x* equals a quarter hour (fifteen minutes) of time.

This sample Gantt Chart shows a day's events laid out very neatly. The time duration of each event and the sequence are clear. It is easy to see that this person has little free time. There is a scheduling conflict, because the meetings with Clients A and B overlap, so a change will have to be made. Lunch could be taken early and the meeting with Client A moved up a half hour, or the meeting with Client B could be delayed a half hour. This display also shows clearly that any other meetings would have to be held in the mid-afternoon.

The figure on page 95 is a more complicated Gantt Chart. It was done with a project-scheduling computer program, so it is fancier than the earlier example, but the essentials are the same.*

This Gantt Chart shows a schedule for building a big doghouse. There are three summary (major) tasks, each of which entails three detail (primitive) tasks. The "resources" involved in this schedule are George and Carol, who have decided to build the doghouse together. The column of "Cs" shows the tasks on the critical path for the project. Except for purchasing supplies, the work is to be done in a single path. There are some dependencies in this plan that relate a predecessor task to a successor task. The foundation has to be finished before the doghouse can be constructed, and it is necessary to wait three days for the concrete to cure before the walls can be built. George has to buy the lumber and nails before the walls can be built, but he can do this any time before the foundation concrete is cured. For simplicity, the schedule shows the lumber and nails being bought the day before they are needed. During the painting task, the second coat cannot start until two days after the first coat has been applied to allow the paint to dry thoroughly. The overall project takes twelve days.

These two examples demonstrate the power of the Gantt Chart to illuminate your project schedule. Chapter 12 provides another example of how it all fits together.

Gantt Charts were invented a long time before computers were available, but it was hard to use them for large, complicated projects.

---

* This Gantt Chart was produced using *Time Line,* a project-management software product of the Symantec Corporation.

Making changes manually was very tedious, and it was difficult to change things around to look for better sequences. Computers have made Gantt Charts and the other project-scheduling systems much more convenient than even their inventors had ever visualized. The work of changing tasks and revising sequences is diminished, and alternative schedules can be created quickly. If you are computer literate, my advice is to buy one of the many program-management or project-scheduling software programs and use it for your planning.

For simple projects, however, you don't need a complicated software program, and if this is the case or if you prefer to use hard copy, buy some large sheets of paper with horizontal lines and draw your own Gantt Charts. As demonstrated above, you can create a simple Gantt Chart using any spread-sheet program or even a word-processing program. You can also prepare a Gantt Chart on a piece of paper using an old-fashioned pen and straightedge. If changes are expected to occur frequently, put the basic chart on the wall, cover it with acetate, and use a grease pencil to update the chart.

The critical path method is an offshoot of project schedules that allows you to determine the sequence of task accomplishment (the path) that governs the time it takes to accomplish the entire project. The longest path from start to finish is the critical path because it determines the minimum time required for the overall project. If the critical path can be shortened, the overall project time will also be shortened, and another path may become the longest—the critical one. This kind of analysis allows planners to identify the key events in their project schedules and perhaps to revise the plan to shorten the time or resources needed overall.

Gantt Charts are very useful for preparing and monitoring progress on projects that have many tasks moving along multiple paths—ones in which it is necessary to do things in the right sequence. These charts are fundamental to the program evaluation and review technique (PERT) covered in Rule 62. Gantt Charts were once considered advanced but are now basic tools that can help all planners.

Rule 38: List the Actors

Another way to make your planning easier is to make a list of all of the actors: the people, offices, groups, companies, or institutions that will affect your plan and either help or hinder you. Making things happen is not a solo affair—except for very small activities. Think about it! In just about everything you do or want to do, you will have to be involved with some others. These various entities are all actors in the drama you are about to produce.

When you are starting your plan, it helps to draw up a list of all of the various outside agencies that will be involved. This list will allow you to determine what you will have to do with each actor to get his, her, or its cooperation or—even more important—to minimize interference.

There are several different kinds of actors, and each kind will affect you in several ways. These actors may include friends, supporters, funders, workers, suppliers, clients, customers, approvers, critics, or enemies.

Friends provide love and support without asking anything in return. They are nice to have, and although they seldom add anything substantive to your efforts, they are often a key ingredient in success.

Supporters will engage themselves actively and help you do the work. Most supporters do this without hope of monetary reward and act out of sympathy with your goals. Some supporters may not. The kind of help you will get from supporters may range all the way from moral support to hard labor.

Funders will loan or invest or (once in a blue moon) give you money to help make your thing happen. Since almost all of the things you want to make happen will cost something, funders are important actors indeed. Rules 55 and 56 deal with this group of actors in some detail. Funders are often friends and supporters as well, but that is not a prerequisite.

Workers will accomplish the tasks you set forth in the plan for wages, salary, or some other form of monetary compensation. Workers are different from supporters because they are motivated by reward rather than sympathy for the cause, but they can be very helpful if treated right.

Suppliers will provide the resources you need, and for special kinds of resources, you will have to consider carefully just who these people are. This is so important that it is discussed in depth in Rule 44.

Clients buy what you have to offer in a close, personal relationship. They have great influence individually on what you do and how you do it.

Customers buy the products and services that you offer if you are running a business. While customers are real people, they usually are not as close to you as clients and do not have as much personal influence on your plans. In the abstract, of course, your customers have tremendous impact on what you are trying to do.

Approvers have the power to stop you by withholding their approval of what you want to do. These are the people who seem to be able to say no by themselves but have to send the paperwork to a higher level to get a yes. You have to learn early in the process just who the approvers for your plan are going to be.

Critics do not approve of what you are trying to do and will point out flaws in your plan. They may influence others to oppose your plans as well. Critics, however, are also a source of valuable information that you need to take seriously, because friends and supporters may not always be willing or able to point out the weaknesses of your plan. By making small but judicious changes in your plans, you may be able to convert critics to supporters or even friends.

Enemies are against what you are trying to do and will take an active role in trying to stop you. One of the valuable results of making your list of actors is to identify known enemies and take steps in advance to counter or nullify their opposition.

Some of the actors may fall into more than one category. It is not uncommon for a friend also to be a supporter and even a funder. An approver can often be a critic and may turn out to be an enemy. Relatives are another kind of actor that may be friends and supporters but sometimes are critics or even enemies, particularly if they are not workers or suppliers. It all depends on what you are trying to make happen.

When drawing up your list of actors, name each human being with whom you will interact on the left side of the paper, then write the organization, title, or position of that person and his or her potential effect on your project next to each name. You may find it useful to group the actors under some headings, such as those given above.

Remember that actors may be organizations as well as individuals, so list both, but try to identify a specific person in each organization as soon as possible so you will have a human being with whom to interact instead of just an impersonal office.

I like to look up the people and groups that are going to be involved in my plans and learn as much about them as possible. If you are dealing with an organization, get the brochure or annual report and study it. Reading the biographical summaries of individuals will give you an idea of their backgrounds and preferences and perhaps some inkling of how they will play their assigned roles in the plan. You will already know many of the people in your plan personally, but if there are some you don't know, it is a good idea to go out of your way to make their acquaintance. It is good if your first meeting with an important actor can be devoted to getting acquainted instead of dealing with crucial negotiations.

A list of actors for a project to start up a small retail service business polishing widgets might be as shown in the accompanying figure. Note that the actors are the organizations you will have to deal with, not just the individuals.

Actors for Widget-Polishing Store

Individual	Organization	Role
Customers	———	Pay for polishing widgets
Anne Carr	City Bank	Source of credit
James Haven	Landlord	Rent space for store
Joe Smith	Supplier A	Widget polishes
Edgar Bruff	Supplier B	Polishing equipment
Sally Smith	Repair Shop	Keep equipment running
Bill Jones	Custodial Service	Clean the store
Jennie Lind	Ad Agency	Attract customers
Simon Legree	A-1 Polish Co	Compete with you

One important by-product of your list of actors is an estimate of the complexity of doing what you want to do. Generally speaking, complexity goes up exponentially as the number of actors increases. It doesn't matter whether the actors are well disposed or not, for it is just the sheer number of actors that bears on complexity. The more actors involved, the more time you have to spend in communicating with them, checking with them, and checking on them.

Obviously it is better to have supporters and friends than critics or enemies, but real life has some of both kinds of actors. By making a list of potential actors in your project early in the planning process, you may be able to avoid or get around some of them, benefit from others, and convert a few to your cause.

Rule 39: Draw an Organizational Chart

An organizational chart is a useful planning tool that helps you match the tasks that need to be done with people to do them. At some stage in the planning process, you will have to figure out an organization to implement the plan, and if the project is a big one, you will also have to figure out the organization you will use to do the planning itself. An organizational chart will help you to do so.

Every project requires an organization. Even a one-man project requires organization of the time and efforts of that individual to assure that all tasks are done, that the most important or urgent tasks are done first, and that they are done in the proper sequence. If more than one person is needed to do the work, then there has to be an organization that divides the work among the workers. Organizing the people is based on organizing the work—or ought to be, although many existing organizations have allowed their work to be organized along current lines out of sheer inertia. In your planning, you are likely to have the opportunity to tailor your organization to fit the work to be done, so make the most of it.

Each organizational chart starts at the top with one person in charge—the boss. In theory and in the computer programs for making organizational charts, this is a strict rule. In real life, however, it is all too common to find that there are indeed several bosses. But since it's your plan, you can mandate one boss and preserve for the moment the important principle of unity of command.

The basic organizational element is a work center—a group of

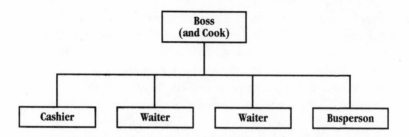

people (and associated equipment) to perform one primitive task or a few closely related primitive tasks. When you start making your organizational chart, you first list the tasks and then the people.

In small organizations where the boss is the direct supervisor of every worker, the differentiation is by the tasks each person performs or the time (shift) during which each person performs the same tasks. The diagram above is an organizational chart for a restaurant. The boss doubles as supervisor and worker because he is also the cook. Each of the others has specific primary duties, but in this small organization, it is likely that the workers will be expected to fill in for one another during breaks and absences.

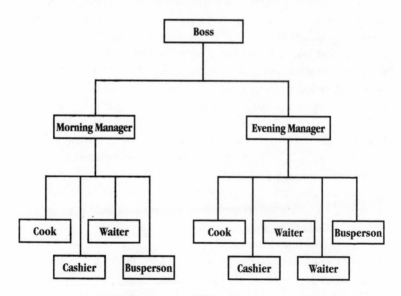

Suppose the restaurant is so popular that it is busy from breakfast to late supper and needs two shifts of workers. The preceding figure shows how the organization could be expanded to cover two shifts: morning and evening.

In this expanded organization, the boss may not be able to run everything himself or herself. He or she can become either a pure supervisor or perhaps the manager-cook for one of the shifts, leaving the supervision of the other shift manager somewhat loose. Note that each suborganization needs a single boss, so we are now introducing another layer of supervision. Since the breakfast crowd is smaller than the dinner crowd, only one waitress is needed in the morning.

Business booms again, and it is necessary to add some overhead in the form of workers who do not deal directly with either the customers or the food but support those who do. The boss—now a

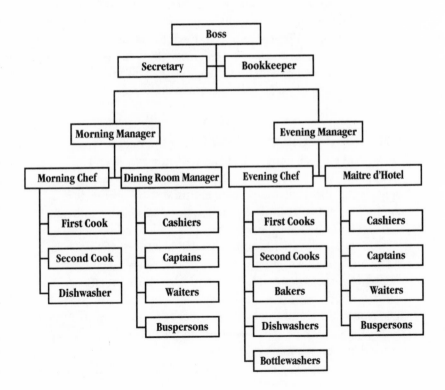

full-time manager—needs a bookkeeper and a secretary, and each shift has grown so big that it is necessary to create separate groups for preparing the food and serving it. This is illustrated in the final organizational chart.

In this larger organization, it is necessary not only to differentiate among the duties but also to define seniority or relative skill within a particular set of duties. This is done by assigning titles to particular jobs. Thus, we now have first cooks and second cooks, and we have captains who supervise the waiters for a particular set of tables in the dining room. We can also add receptionists, hat-check persons, bartenders, head bartender, beverage manager, orchestra leader, and master of ceremonies in the organization as the little diner expands to become a full-fledged nightclub.

Remember that the work to be done should dictate the organization rather than the other way around. You should establish a firm and clear line of authority from the top (boss) to the bottom, so that guidance and direction can proceed down the chain and feedback and problems can proceed up the chain. Finally, you need to modify the organization as the work load changes so that the tasks to be done and the organization to do them remain in close accord.

Rule 40: Prepare a Flow Chart

A flow chart is a planning tool that illustrates how you intend for things to happen when your plan is implemented. It is a schematic diagram representing the paths taken between nodes by information and action for a particular process. Each node represents an individual, work center, team, division, department, or entire corporation.

A flow chart simplifies complex relationships by reducing large and internally complex groups to single actors within the process flow. Thus, each node is represented by a single symbol that stands for the entirety of the activity represented. Different kinds of geometric figures, such as squares and rectangles, may be used to depict different kinds of nodes within the flow chart, and the nodes are labeled to show what they represent.

Paths of information or action flowing between nodes are represented by lines. Information may be of several types: direction, guidance, approval request, approval, reporting, comments, and just plain information. Different kinds of lines—solid, dotted, dashed, double—may be used to represent different kinds of information, and the lines may be labeled to indicate the nature of the action.

Decision points may be shown in the flow diagram, usually by diamonds. Information flows into the decision points, and several paths representing the possible decisions flow out. The most common decision point allows a simple yes or no response. Not only is this kind of decision common in real life, but it assumes particular importance for programming computers, which prefer to deal with bivalent decisions.

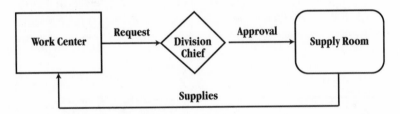

The diagram above is a simple flow chart illustrating the process for a work center to obtain some necessary office supplies. In this flow chart, the work center requests supplies, and the request is approved by the division chief and sent to the supply room, from which the supplies are shipped to the work center.

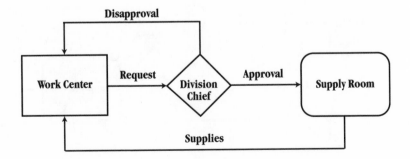

This process works well if the supplies are on hand and the division chief is in a generous mood. But we have to allow for some decisions in the process. The preceding diagram includes the possibility of the division chief disapproving the request for supplies and relaying that disapproval back to the work center for resubmission or, perhaps, belt tightening.

The process would be complicated even more if the supply room were out of the supplies wanted by the work center. The following chart includes this possibility. In this case, the supply room informs the work center that the supplies are not available and also orders the supplies from the warehouse.

A carefully prepared flow chart can be of great assistance when you are planning a complex operation involving interaction among many actors. This technique has been used for a long time in science and engineering, and it has proven invaluable for programming

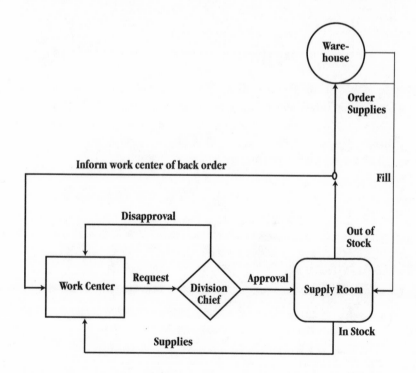

computers. Systems analysts spend hours drawing flow charts of complicated networks and systems so that the programmers can write the code to tell the computers exactly how to replicate the flow chart. These techniques can also be valuable to you. If you have a computer, there are several software programs that will allow you to prepare flow charts with standard symbols and internal rules of logic. But you can also prepare flow charts by hand, using pen and plastic templates to help you draw the various symbols. Just make certain you have plenty of paper and plenty of patience.

8   Resources

In order to accomplish anything at all, you need tangible goods and services—resources. Building a house requires lumber, nails, cement, paint, pipe, wires, wallboard, and a host of other items of hardware and building materials. Taking a trip requires a ticket, suitcase, passport, and the ability to obtain food, drink, and lodging. Throwing a party requires food, drink, invitations, a hall, and perhaps some people to help. These are all resources.

This chapter will not talk about costs; that topic will be covered in chapter 9. Costs are the money it takes to obtain the resources, but money is not itself a resource.* This chapter deals with the resources themselves.

The most important thing for you to understand about resources is that they will always be scarce. You will never have enough, and they will always be hard to get. In fact, a resource could be defined quite adequately as something in short supply. This being the case, you will find that your plans will always be constrained by an inadequate

---

* There is a lot of controversy over whether money is a resource. I have been in a room filled with economists (a terrifying predicament in itself), half of whom said vociferously that money was a resource, and the other half of whom said equally vociferously that it was not. I really don't care whether money is a resource; what is important is that money is required to obtain resources, serving as a medium of exchange (although it would be possible, of course, for you to obtain your resources by bartering).

supply of one or more resources. In fact, it is the scarcity of resources that requires you to have a plan in the first place. If resources were unlimited, you would not have to have a plan, or at least not a good plan; you could just throw resources at the project and muddle through by trial and error without regard for waste. You may have seen this approach to progress attempted by some wealthy individuals or by governments, and you may have noticed that the results usually are lacking. So you need to pay considerable attention to resources, and the following rules are designed to help you do that.

Rule 41: Have a Bill of Materials

The basic things you have to know about resources are exactly how much and what kind you need and when you need them.

The list of resources you need is called a bill of materials. That term comes from construction practice, but it applies generally as well. There is no time dimension to a bill of materials. Simply list every item you will need and the amount of each item that you estimate will be necessary.

My advice is to prepare a bill of materials for every job you are planning, from construction projects to trips to less tangible projects than those.

One of the most basic bills of materials is a list of items you would need if you were to construct a big doghouse, as in the accompanying figure.

Bill of Materials

4 sheets of 1/2" plywood (4' x 8')

5 pieces of lumber, 2" x 4" x 6'

1 pound #10 common nails

1 quart green enamel paint

1 pint putty

Completeness is a highly desirable feature of a bill of materials. Indeed, one of the primary purposes of making such a bill is to assure that you don't overlook some of the little items that are easy to forget. One is unlikely to forget the major items, but it is quite possible to overlook a small, inexpensive, but vital piece of hardware.

One of the virtues of a bill of materials is that it gives some assurance that you won't be held up on your project because you have insufficient resources. That is why it is important to take the trouble to list *every* item. There are few things worse than to be held up in the middle of a job because you don't have the two franizes you need to connect the oldgewarries. You will have to stop what you are doing, get in the car, and start the search for the missing stuff. The odds are that these missing items will be hard to find, or else you probably would not have overlooked them in the first place.

The bill of materials will also serve nicely as a shopping list. It would be great if you could obtain everything you need from a single, convenient source, but that seldom will be the case. If you don't have a shopping list on which you can check off items as you procure them, you are complicating the process and increasing the chances that you will miss something.

Preparing a bill of materials also provides a basis for estimating the cost of the project. Numerous times, compiling and costing a preliminary bill of materials has caused me to modify and in a few cases abandon a project because the cost was too high.

Make a bill of materials scrupulously early in the planning process, either for the entire project if it is a small one or for each task you have defined. *Write it down!* Trying to do it in your head will prove to be unmanageable and lead to mistakes.

Knowing what you need is important—just as important as what you want to achieve.

Rule 42: Add Up the Resources You Need

One important aspect of the Elephant Rule often overlooked in the frenzy to cut the critter up into bite-size chunks is that it started as an entire elephant.

After you do all of the cutting up and have figured out how to eat and digest each piece, you need to look at the whole thing again. The bill of materials for each piece provides you the cost of just that piece, but you are going to have to pay for all of the pieces.

Once you have made the various bills of materials, add them up into a single list of all of the resources you will need from start to finish to accomplish the whole plan. This advice may seem unnecessary, but many people get so tied up in the individual pieces that they fail to look at the whole elephant after that first, intimidating glance. This could lead to going back to the hardware store every day to get a few things instead of buying all you need for the entire three-month project on one visit.

A major advantage of combining the bills of materials is that you will have opportunities for economies of scale. The theory of economies of scale is that you can buy more cheaply in large quantities than in small quantities. That is, the unit cost of some commodity, such as peanut butter, paint, or perfume, is usually less when you buy a larger container of the stuff. We know from our grocery-shopping experience that this is generally true. We can buy a big box of corn flakes and get a lot more corn flakes for our money than if we bought the small box.* This is partially because buying in bulk reduces the proportionate cost for the packaging, but also because the sellers like to sell in large bunches.

Adding up the resources is a fairly easy process. Simply list each item by task number so that you can add up the total quantities of like items while simultaneously maintaining the capability to break down the large amounts into the correct allocations for each task. A barrel of nails is a wonderful thing to have, but its utility is decreased if you don't know how many nails to issue to each carpenter.

Chapter 9 will discuss estimating the cost of your plan. The first step in doing that is to have an aggregate bill of materials so that you know all of the tangible resources that will be required from start to finish.

---

* As we all know, even this basic truth is not certain, for the size of the box and the amount of stuff inside are sort of independent, and we may be buying some air space instead of corn flakes. Most stores now tell us the unit price of each item so that we can compare the cost for equal amounts, and that is helpful, but ultimately the only answer to modern consumption is an alert consumer, whatever that means.

Rule 43: Use Standard Items

Well, now you know what you need, and all you have to do is get it. Simple? Not at all. Obtaining the resources you need can be very tricky and discouraging, and you have to pay lots of attention to it in your planning.

A big reason why you have to plan to procure is because what you want may not be available. That is my experience, at least. I bought a tract house from a builder who apparently used nonstandard hardware every chance he could. That may have saved money for him, but it has caused me a lot of aggravation over the years as it came time to replace some broken items. Planning to use standard items is a lot smarter. I have spent hours looking for really strange hardware—drawer glides, door locks, and rubber ends for flexible door stops—that no hardware store in America has apparently ever even heard of. I look around me in the hardware store and envy those customers who can find what they need. I always ask and usually receive a pitying look from the experienced hardware salesman as he mutters something like, "Oh yes, that is a nonstandard item you are looking for, and I don't believe they are being made anymore." You can avoid this problem in your projects by some clever supply-side planning.

One thing that permits our big and complex world to function even as well as it does—which is not really all that well—is that many items are standardized. Take light bulbs, for example: The light bulb contacts are the same size as the light fixture sockets, so you can screw in a light bulb and expect it to fit properly. That is no accident. The makers of light bulbs and the makers of light fixtures got together and established a standard so that any light bulb can fit any light fixture of the same size. This makes it a lot easier to replace bulbs than it otherwise would be.

The necessity for standardization applies to all kinds of things: airline tickets, nails, pipe sizes, lumber sizes, and VCRs. How would it be if there were two different kinds of VCRs and two different kinds of videotapes, and tapes of one kind could not be played on a VCR of the other kind? Don't laugh, for that is exactly what we had when both the Beta and the VHS formats were going strong. Fortunately— except for those who bought Beta VCRs—VHS triumphed, and standardization prevailed. (You know I bought Beta.) Standardization permits interchangeability, and that is necessary for large, complex projects.

Standardization is promoted both by government and private industry—mostly by the private sector, as associations that manufacture items get together and establish industry standards.

Standardization has nothing to do with quality and price. There are cheap standard items and expensive standard items, so you do not give up high quality by going for standard stuff. Of course, you may—and many do—want to go extra special by getting unique items that are hard to obtain, and that is your prerogative. Just make certain that you understand and allow in your planning process for the extra time, extra effort, and extra bucks it will take to be unique.

Unless you are an expert in the kinds of resources you will need, my advice is to consult the suppliers before you plan to use certain materials. You need to know about the quality, selection, substitutability, and availability of the resources you plan to use. There is no use planning on an item that will not be available when you need it or that costs more than you can afford. The people with this information are the suppliers. They have an interest in selling things to you, and they will tell you about the items in their particular inventory. Most of the time the suppliers will give you good advice and the honest truth, because it is in their best interest to keep you as a steady customer. Sometimes you might run across a supplier who will trick you into buying something that is shoddy, unfairly priced, or cannot be replaced. You will just have to be alert to that possibility in your dealings with suppliers.

My advice is to make sure when you prepare your bill of materials that either the things you plan on using are standard and can be procured easily, or you take into account the delays and extra costs involved in using nonstandard resources.

Rule 44: Line Up Your Suppliers

Once you start implementing your plan, you are absolutely dependent on receiving the resources you need at the times and places you need them. It is really bad to have progress stopped or delayed because the load of bricks, the special copy paper, or the overhead projector did not arrive at the right time. It is also a planning failure when this happens. Part of the planning process is to look ahead, anticipate problems, and plan cleverly so that those problems do not happen. One of the corollaries to Murphy's Law is that the stuff you need is never available.

There are three reasons why resources might not be available in accordance with your plan: they are nonstandard; they are not in stock; or they are not carried by a particular store or vendor. Rule 43 pointed out the benefits of using standard items. This rule has to do with lining up your suppliers ahead of time.

Your resources either will be in the inventory of a particular supplier—a retail merchant, a wholesaler, or a manufacturer—or will have to be made, which takes time. If you simply go out to buy what you need, you are taking a chance that it is not in stock in someone's inventory and will have to be made. If the item has to be made, you will have to wait until it is manufactured and shipped to your supplier. If you have been a clever planner, you have allowed for this lead time in your plan, and you have placed the order sufficiently in advance to ensure that the item arrives at your location when you need it. Unless you have checked with the suppliers ahead of time, however, you may find that something you thought you could pick up on Wednesday afternoon will take six weeks to get, and that causes problems with the work schedule.

Some vendors have very large inventories. Anyone who has spent time in a mall, hardware store, or discount outlet knows that many items are for sale readily with no delays. If you are finishing the basement, you can be reasonably certain that you can obtain standard plywood, nails, Spackle, paint, and parts that you need to do that job. If your job is more complicated or you want some special items, you had better check on availability ahead of time to make certain you won't be disappointed.

The other factor in making certain you can obtain the necessary resources is to understand the nature of the distribution system for the items you want. Each nation or region has a different method of assigning various items to various kinds of stores. We are familiar with the U.S. system, but in Europe or Asia, we might have difficulty finding the right items, because they are sold in different stores than in our own system. When I lived in Germany, I had to learn where to obtain cosmetics, bread, and meat, each of which tended to have a special store. This was quite different from the supermarkets and drugstores of the United States, but it was easy once I got the hang of it. There was no difficulty with common sundries, but imagine how difficult this could be for really hard-to-get items.

This pertains not just to foreign lands, but also to our own American distribution system. If you are going to want some particularly special items, take the time to learn how and where those items are distributed and sold. Things are not always as simple as they seem. You can obtain some stationery items in a grocery store or drugstore, but if you really want office supplies, go to a store that specializes in them. Not only are the prices generally lower, but also the selection is wider, and items that sell infrequently are stocked as a service to office-supply customers. The same thing goes for many other items: There are probably some common outlets that provide a small selection of widely used items at higher-than-average prices, and these are offered as a convenience to customers who don't need or want to go to a specialized outlet. Then there is a full range of special stores that offer the really good, the really scarce, and sometimes the really expensive stuff.

Not all specialty stores carry the full line of merchandise that potentially is available. As a matter of fact, the specialty stores tend to offer products from only one or a few manufacturers, because they enjoy a franchise for a particular region or some other one-on-one relationship with a particular manufacturer. That means that you should really check a wide range of suppliers before you decide on the items you want. You can find out ahead of time the prices, models, options, and financial terms available. A little effort on this procurement planning can pay off handsomely when you actually go to buy the stuff.

Even though you have made your plans carefully and have selected the items to list in your bills of materials very carefully, you still face the problem of availability. You do not want to run up to the store someday and find that the items you plan to use that afternoon are not available. The way to prevent this from happening is to line up your suppliers ahead of time. Visit them. Tell them what you want to do and what you would like to have. Place your orders and give the dates you would like the materials to be available. Make sure that the suppliers have confidence in your ability to pay, for they work on a narrow cash-flow margin and really don't want to sell to people who might be slow payers. If the suppliers are going to have the materials in stock for you, they will have to order the stuff, receive it, pay for it, and store it while waiting for you to come and get it. That means that the suppliers will have to lay out money and effort, and if you are unreliable about either actually buying the stuff you said you wanted or paying for it promptly, suppliers are going to avoid doing business with you in the future. This is true for any commodity—hardware, building supplies, travel, catering, or computers.

The way to ensure that you will be able to get what you need at the right times is to work ahead of time and establish a good track record so that your key suppliers will have confidence in you. Remember that the success of your plan is completely dependent on your suppliers. Just because you are the customer does not make it good planning or good business to act like an arrogant fool. My advice is to establish a good, continuing relationship with a supplier or a group of suppliers. This will not only assure that you can get the resources when you need them, but it also can come in handy when you run a little short of cash or credit and want to buy the resources on favorable financial terms.

If you have a large project and a continuing need for certain kinds of resources, it is particularly important to do this kind of planning ahead of time. But it goes for small projects and everyday life as well.

Rule 45: Set Priorities for Resource Allocation

Since you are unlikely to have more resources than you need, it will be necessary for you to plan on allocating the available resources among competing demands. This means that you will have to establish and stick to priorities. Just setting priorities, however, is a difficult task because there are three different systems or ways to set priorities: absolute, proportional, and relative.

An absolute priority system is one in which all of the demands of a higher-priority claimant are met before any of the demands of a lower-priority claimant.

A proportional priority system is one in which more demands of a higher-priority claimant are met than those of a lower-priority claimant in some predesignated proportion.

A relative priority system is one in which the demands of higher-priority claimants are given general preference over demands of lower-priority claimants, but there is no prescribed proportion.

The difference between proportional and relative priority systems is the degree of specificity. Proportional priority systems specify exactly how priorities will meet demands, while relative priority systems operate more generally, without exact proportions or quantities of demand to be met. Proportional priority systems are feasible when a specific amount of supply is available to meet a specific (larger) amount of demand. Much of the time, however, the amount of supply that will be available later on is not known, so relative priority systems tend to be applied in practice to provide guidance on resource allocations to the persons in charge.

In order to understand the differences among these three systems, let's look at an example in which there are 100 units of supply to meet a total of 150 units of demand from four claimants. The table below shows the division of the demand among the claimants.

Division of Demand among Claimants

Priority	Demand	Supply
Claimant 1:	60	
Claimant 2:	40	
Claimant 3:	30	
Claimant 4:	20	
Total:	150	100

In an absolute priority system, the 100 units of supply would be allocated among the claimants as shown in the following table. All of the demands for Claimants 1 and 2 would be met but none of the demands for Claimants 3 and 4.

Allocation of Supply Absolutely

Priority	Demand	Supply
Claimant 1:	60	60
Claimant 2:	40	40
Claimant 3:	30	0
Claimant 4:	20	0
Total:	150	100

The disadvantage of an absolute priority system is that it does not necessarily provide something for every claimant. In some cases, however, that may be an advantage.

The proportional system may be used to ensure that each claimant receives something. Many different proportional priority systems are possible, depending on the scheme used to allocate the supply. In the next table, the proportional priority system used is that each claimant would get an amount of supply equal to the overall ratio of supply to demand. In this case, the supply of 100 to a demand of 150 means that the ratio is two-thirds, so each claimant would receive two-thirds of the amount demanded.

Allocation of Supply Proportionally I

Priority	Demand	Supply
Claimant 1:	60	40
Claimant 2:	40	27
Claimant 3:	30	20
Claimant 4:	20	13
Total:	150	100

This simple proportional system may not be exactly suited to the circumstances, however, and a more complicated arrangement may be needed. The next table illustrates a proportional system in which each claimant would receive half of the amount demanded, with the amount left over being allocated absolutely to the claimants in order of priority. The initial step in making this allocation would be to assign to each claimant half of the amount demanded; this would use up seventy-five units of supply. The remaining twenty-five units of supply would then be allocated to Claimant 1, whose total demand would still not be met, so Claimants 2, 3, and 4 would get none of the excess over half. As can be seen, there are many different possible ways to set up a proportional priority system.

Allocation of Supply Proportionally II

Priority	Demand	Supply
Claimant 1:	60	55
Claimant 2:	40	20
Claimant 3:	30	15
Claimant 4:	20	10
Total:	150	100

Still another way to approach priorities is the relative priority system, illustrated in the next table. In this example, supplies would be allocated in order of priority with no set proportions but generally. In this case, the amount of supply to be allocated was not known ahead of time, and the priorities were exercised piecemeal. The results shown have applied no particular specific formula but do follow the general guidance of the priorities. Although this approach to prioritization is the least satisfying from a rational viewpoint, it is the one most often applied in practice.

The illustration on the next page merely hints at the complexity that usually occurs in real situations involving prioritization and allocation of resources. One major problem is that complexity is increased by the nature of the resources—each resource will have some characteristics that affect the allocation process.

The number of claimants also complicates the situation. It was easy to develop illustrative solutions for a problem involving only four claimants, but in real life there are usually more claimants and the needs are distributed over time. When there are large numbers of claimants, the priorities can be simplified by grouping the claimants into classes and assigning a priority to each class.

Allocation of Supply Relatively

Priority	Demand	Supply
Claimant 1:	60	50
Claimant 2:	40	20
Claimant 3:	30	20
Claimant 4:	20	10
Total:	150	100

The key to setting up a prioritization scheme is to establish the constraints, primarily the amount and location of supply, and the objective function—what you want to accomplish or how you will know you have succeeded. For prioritization and allocation, the objective function determines the system selected to divide the supply among claimants. This is the essence of setting resource-allocation priorities. My advice is to keep your method simple and clear cut, for no matter how you set priorities, someone is going to complain that he or she is not getting enough.

Rule 46: Consider the People You Need

Thus far, resources have been considered in terms of hard goods and hard services—equipment, lumber, computers, and similar items. This rule addresses the most important resource of all: people.

You cannot make things happen without people. People alone have the will to do things. All of the other resources have to be shaped by people, carried by people, assembled by people, or operated by people before they can add value to your project. Even the most highly computerized robotic factory still depends on people to run it, change it around when needed, and repair it when it breaks.

So it is time to consider the numbers and kinds of people you need to implement your plan.

Rule 38 advised you to list the actors that would influence your plan; these included organizations as well as individuals, however, and most of the actors are going to be outside your own organization. Now you need to consider the workers you will hire to help you carry out the tasks you have identified.

People come in only two basic types (male and female), but there is an infinite variety of makes and models. The human attributes most important to you as a planner trying to achieve a goal are aptitude, skill, experience, and character.

Aptitude is an ability to learn. It is not the same as intelligence, although I admit to being confused by the distinction. You may understand aptitude as being "quick on the uptake" or "bright." In my opinion, it includes more than just mental ability, for mental attitude is involved as well. Willingness to learn, having an open mind, and enthusiasm are all important components of aptitude.

Skill is the ability to use one's knowledge to perform a particular task or set of tasks. It involves knowing the basics of a job—the procedures to be followed, the measures of quality, the tasks to be performed, and the context of these tasks in the larger enterprise. Skill is the fundamental cornerstone of building a work center, and the key is to assemble people with various skills who will form a team able to produce a high-quality product with little waste.

Experience is an indication of time spent in performing a particular task or group of tasks. It ought to be and usually is a measure of a person's skill. There are three general levels of performance: apprentice, journeyman, and master. Although these terms have been applied primarily to the crafts trades, they are useful for indicating experience levels for all kinds of work. Apprentices perform at what is called the entry level, and they produce less, work more slowly, and require more supervision than workers at the higher levels. Journeymen produce at a standard or desired rate, work quickly, and require little supervision. Masters have high productivity, work quickly, set the standards for their skill in quality and craftsmanship, and are the supervisors. You most likely will need some of each. Grade and pay generally increase with experience. An apprentice is paid the minimum, while a master earns top dollar and is often a work-center leader or team manager.

Character is perhaps the most important attribute for a worker. Character is an amalgam of honesty, integrity, loyalty, and all of the other good things you know about. It also includes such mundane things as showing up on time, giving a day's work for a day's pay, and trying hard. This attribute is long in demand but somewhat short in supply. Look for it, and treasure it when you find it in a worker, for it is probably more important than the other three attributes combined.

The organizational chart you set up according to Rule 39 has provided you with a list of the jobs you need to have done to implement your plan. This is your staffing table to be used as the basis for advertising, recruiting, interviewing, hiring, and training people to fill the jobs.

9 Costs

The cost of your project is one of the most—perhaps even *the* most—important consideration in the planning process. Costs are expressed in money terms—dollars, yen, or marks. Money is not important *per se*, however; it is only important as an expression of the costs of the goods and services you plan to use, plus other charges, such as interest and taxes. Costs are the basis for your budget and your spending, or cash-flow, plan.

Easy consumer credit leads some people to think that costs are not a major concern. There are so many ways today to defer facing up to costs that some people persist in living as if costs were not a constraint. Charging a trip or a purchase to a credit card makes it too easy to defer consideration of the cost you incur—until the bill comes in later. This allows you to go ahead and plan and implement small projects without even considering costs, much less living with the constraints imposed by costs.

I know an inveterate consumer who never considers costs and even brags about it. This consumer's spending plan consists of charging to the maximum credit limit immediately and then paying the minimum monthly amount from that point on *ad infinitum*.

This strategy, of course, is guaranteed to impose the maximum in interest charges while denying any future ability to purchase on credit—at least with that card. Consideration of costs and the ability to pay needs to be done before the plastic is used and not afterward. The same thing goes with any plan for funding your projects, be it consumer credit, bank loans, or using your own cash.

My advice is to consider costs up front, just as soon as you have an idea of the resources you will need for your project. Price out the resources and add up the costs. You will find that considering costs it is not as easy or straightforward as it may appear. Costs are not easy to count, and there are many subtle difficulties in determining the true costs likely to be involved. The next six rules are designed to help you deal with costs more effectively.

Rule 47: Estimate Your Costs

Cost estimation is a real art. Many mistakes are made by naive planners who fail to take into account every item for their project that will cost money.

There are two basic kinds of costs: one-time and continuing. One-time costs are investments that need to be made just once in your plan. These generally are substantial investments in equipment or facilities, such as buying a truck to deliver your products or buying or building a factory or showroom. These are considered one-time costs even though you may spread the payments out over many months or years. One-time costs are incurred when you make an investment in a tangible item.

Continuing costs are those that occur over and over again in regular, repetitive cycles. Once you have purchased a truck, you will incur the continuing costs of gasoline, oil changes, new tires, insurance, registration fees, repairs and maintenance, and in some states, property taxes. Continuing costs also include such things as rent, office expenses, and salaries. Continuing costs are incurred from the operation of the items you acquired by investing.

There are two kinds of continuing costs: fixed costs and variable costs. Fixed costs are those that exist whether or not there is any useful output. Variable costs are those that exist to defray the direct costs of producing an output and that are directly proportional to the quantity and quality of the output. Variable costs are incurred only in conjunction with an activity, such as producing a unit or units of output.

If you operate a small company that manufactures widgets, the difference between fixed and variable costs will be very clear, because you will incur the fixed costs whether or not you produce a single widget. They are independent of production. Fixed costs include rent on the factory, your office expenses, and anything else that has to be paid even if your production line is idle, including possibly your salary. Fixed costs are also called indirect costs or overhead.

Once you start producing, you incur variable costs, such as wages for the people making the parts, electricity to power the machinery, and the raw materials, parts, and components you buy and shape or assemble into widgets. Variable costs are proportional to production— the more you make, the higher your variable costs. The cost diagram below shows the fixed and direct costs for a company that manufactures widgets.

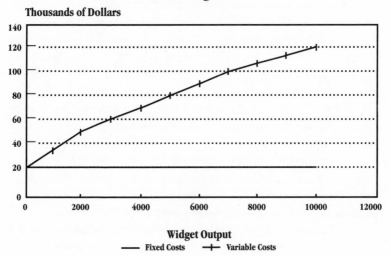

Cost Diagram

This company has a fixed cost of $20,000 per month and a variable cost that increases as the monthly production of widgets increases. Producing two thousand widgets per month would incur a variable cost of $30,000 and therefore a total cost of $50,000; producing ten thousand widgets a month would incur a variable cost of $100,000 and a total cost of $120,000. The unit cost of a widget at a monthly production rate of two thousand is $25, but at a monthly production rate of ten thousand it is only $12. This is because the fixed costs are a smaller part of the total cost at the higher production rate and also because the variable unit costs go down with high production rates. This is the "learning curve," or "economies of scale," effect.

When you sell the widgets, you have to set a price high enough to cover both the variable and the fixed costs plus pay off your taxes and a portion of your initial investment costs in order to make a profit.

These cost-estimating principles apply to all forms of human activity, but they have to be set up differently for each specific plan. The same breakdown of costs used for estimating them during the planning process should be used in cost accounting when you collect and record them during implementation. Costs appear to be very mysterious because the practitioners of cost analysis have complicated the matter enough so that you must hire their services to help you in planning a very expensive and complex project. Most of us, however, can deal with costs if we apply to them the basic planning rules, particularly the Elephant Rule (Rule 6): Costs have to be broken down systematically into smaller and smaller pieces until they make sense individually and can be estimated accurately. Then it is just a matter of aggregating them to obtain an overall estimate.

My advice is to pay serious attention to costs, for inability to keep them in line is a major factor in planning failures. When I worked for a "Beltway Bandit"—one of the consulting firms located just off the Capital Beltway, which encircles the nation's Capital and its government agencies—I saw a manager in another division go down the tubes because he could not hold his costs down enough to make money on his large consulting contracts. The man was a technical genius with an international reputation as an analyst, but he was no manager, and he eventually had to be replaced with a less brilliant person who knew how to hold the line on costs. I admit to feeling a bit superior to the ousted manager, because I thought then that controlling costs was easy and that anyone could do it. Later, when I became a manager, I found that controlling costs was not so easy, and I became less critical of others who had problems in this aspect of management.

There are three requirements to controlling costs. The first is to have a cost estimate that is reasonably accurate, the second is to know what costs are being incurred (not at all easy), and the third is to have the guts to cut costs when required. Controlling costs does not lead to popularity, but it could lead to the survival, profitability, and success of the plan.

Rule 48: Seek the Total System Cost

It is important when estimating the costs of your plan to include all of them. A big mistake made in this area is to forget costs, either because it is not immediately apparent that they are costs, or because they occur sometime in the future. One way to ensure that you include all of the costs—or at least more of them—is to think consciously about the total system cost.

Take, for example, the guy who got a great deal on a pair of skis on sale. He was really happy about his inexpensive introduction to the great sport of skiing—until he found out about total system cost. It turned out that his modest investment in some equipment was just a start. In order to use the skis, he had to buy ski boots, ski wax, and poles. He had to be dressed correctly, so he bought a skiing outfit with special (expensive) clothing, from thermal underwear to a light-weight outer parka. He also had to have ski glasses and probably lots of other things just to look like a skier. So he incurred a lot of initial costs even before he actually went skiing.

When it came time to use the skis, he started incurring the operating costs. He had to pay for travel to a ski slope, lodging at a ski resort, and meals between skiing sessions on the slope. In order to ski, he had to pay for a lift ticket. After his initial session, he probably shelled out for some instruction. Then he had to pay for the *après ski* part—entertainment, beverages, and *gemütlichkeit.* He soon found that the initial cost of a pair of skis was just the tip of the iceberg for what it really cost to ski. Assuming our newcomer liked to ski, he would then have to pay the operating costs again and again, several times a year, for many, many years into the future. The total sum spent on skiing mounted until it reached astronomical proportions. An initial small investment on a pair of skis had turned into a lifetime of costs amounting to thousands and thousands of dollars. When all of the other initial costs and the annual operating costs thereafter were summed, that was the total system cost for skiing.

The concept of total system cost is that all of the additional costs that can be ascribed directly or indirectly to a particular piece of hardware, a structure, or a program should be included in the cost of having or operating that hardware item, structure, or program. This includes not only costs incurred initially, but also all of those that will occur from the start of the system into the future for a defined period. Thus, the ten-year system cost would include the initial costs plus the annual costs for the first ten years of the system's operation.

The total system cost allows the planner to differentiate between two systems on a true cost basis. For example, System A might have a low initial cost but very high annual operating or maintenance costs. System B might have a high initial cost but very low annual operating or maintenance costs. If the total system cost for System A were greater than that for System B, the wise choice would be to purchase System B, even though its initial cost is higher. This kind of decision is controversial, however, because it is easy to confuse initial costs with downstream costs.

Many people make this kind of total system choice intuitively, as when buying good clothes that will last longer than cheaper clothes: The total system cost of having cheaper clothes is greater if we factor in how soon the clothes will have to be replaced. We also show some idea of total system cost when we seek to purchase an automobile with good gas mileage. The total system cost of an automobile is seldom the major factor, however, because buying a car is such an emotional thing to most Americans: We often buy a car with an initial cost several times what would be necessary for just having a means of transportation, and if you have to consider the cost of gasoline when buying a really big car, you can't afford it. Nonetheless, we do consider the total system cost—gasoline, maintenance, and even repairability—in buying cars, and that is one reason why gas mileage even for big cars has been improving in recent years.

My advice is to apply the concept of total system cost in your planning where it makes sense. Many of your plans will be for one-time events; it is important in these cases to include all of the costs. In doing this, experience will be a great help, and if you do not have the requisite experience, seek counsel from someone who does. You do not want to be forced to face up to a cost that you didn't consider. While there are ways around this, such as allowing for contingencies and including safety factors, it is better to determine all of the costs in the first place.

If your plan involves buying or building something tangible that will last for several weeks, months, or years, give some thought to the periodic operating costs. This may be valuable in making a decision—or tradeoffs—between two different kinds of machines. For example, you should take into account the relative cost of electrical versus gas air conditioning for your new house, and the cost comparison should be made on the twenty-year system cost for air conditioning—not just the initial cost of the two systems. The probable length of service of the units should be estimated, and the total system cost should include the cost of buying a new unit sometime in the next twenty years. Include in the operating costs not only what it will take to run the unit (electrical power or gas), but also the likely cost of periodic maintenance and repair. Make your choice only after you have taken into account all of the various ways in which the items could cost you.

As noted above, the use of total system cost will sometimes lead to a decision in which you buy an item with a greater initial cost in order to achieve savings on operating costs in the future. This is probably the greatest virtue of using total system cost—it leads to planning decisions that are not readily apparent at first glance.

Rule 49: Don't Count Sunk Costs

One of the most difficult cost concepts is that of sunk cost. A sunk cost is one that has already been incurred and into which you have already sunk some money.

The rule is that you don't even consider sunk costs when you are making a decision on how to spend money in the future. This rule is based on the concept that what is past is past and you need to focus on the future—on what is the best way to proceed from this point.

This is a very difficult thing for us to do. It requires that we ignore what we have already spent in figuring out our future spending. This is completely opposite from the way most of us approach financial decision making.

Suppose we have a project into which we have sunk a half million dollars. We have assessed the situation, and we have to decide how to spend another $50,000. Suppose further that the situation is grave and our project has not done well. Our normal instinct would be to add the new money to the old project, hoping in that way to make it prosper. We make the fact that we have spent that enormous sum already the central focus of our planning process, but that is the wrong way to proceed. This leads to throwing good money after bad, which happens every day of every week.

Adherence to the rule on sunk costs is counterintuitive. We feel that everything we have done has some worth and ought to be a consideration when we plan the next move. But the rule tells us instead that the future starts now and what we have done up to this point makes no difference to what we should do now.

It is easy to understand just how clever it is to ignore the sunk costs when making a decision. For one thing, it gets us out of a sentimental feeling toward what we have already done, which clouds objective appraisal. Time and time again people have continued with projects with complete track records of continuous failure. This kind of unfortunate project is known as a folly. We also know, however, that there have been projects that were called follies— Fulton's Folly, the Wright Brothers' Folly, Edison's Folly (the light bulb)—that paid off through stubborn and illogical perseverance. This gives us pause at cavalierly laughing off the past so fast that it means nothing at all.

I am unable to give you advice that will help you to distinguish among follies that really are doomed to failure and those that ultimately will succeed. I can point out to you, however, that the former exceed the latter by a great deal, and those in the latter class usually were accomplished by men of great conviction and drive, for whom rational cost estimation was not a concern.

I understand full well the attractiveness of putting more money into losing projects in the hope that the additional funding will bring about a miraculous recovery and achieve the success so long sought and so long denied. When I left the government, my initial venture in the private sector was with a small consulting company, and I became part owner and professional optimist. We did not do well. I was not a good manager at that time, and we tended to insult our customers— not a good way to get repeat business. The head man was an intellectual genius but a perennial flop as an entrepreneur. I was having so much fun at the work that I lost my head about the business. Cool calculation would have revealed that we should fold our hand early, take what little we had left, and try something else. Instead, I stayed on for more years working and striving because I just knew that a bit more money or one lucky break would make it right for us. I put in a lot of my own money and lost it all because I failed to recognize that my decisions should be made on what the future holds and not what the past involved. My loyalty overcame my good sense, and I was saved only when the tensions of constant failure frayed our good humor, the head man and I argued, and I was in effect fired. That was the best thing that could have happened, for freed from the sunk cost of years of effort, I was finally able to make sound decisions for the future.

Ironically, the business at which I failed was the historical analysis business, which appeared to preach the exact opposite of sunk cost. Our motto was that one had to understand the past in order to profit from it. That is not inconsistent with ignoring sunk costs, however. The fact that one has already invested $500,000 should not be ignored, but it also should not lead one automatically to the conclusion that adding to the sunk cost is the best or even a reasonable way to proceed into the future. Sometimes it is best to sink the sunk costs and start all over, and understanding what is meant by sunk costs will help you discern when that is appropriate.

Rule 50: Remember to Count Costs You Avoid

Another important concept in estimating costs is that of cost avoidance. This occurs when a course of action allows you to avoid incurring a cost that you otherwise would have. If you avoid a cost, that is a plus to be included into the total cost estimate.

Cost avoidance can be very important. If you decide to take up tennis instead of skiing, you avoid the money it would have taken to travel to ski resorts and pay for ski lifts. Although this is offset by the costs of tennis, it is still worthy of consideration.

Planning decisions often involve choices among several alternatives. The general approach to these choices is to line up their costs and their benefits and then pick the alternative that appears to meet your measure of merit. You can pick the alternative that gives you satisfactory benefits for the least cost, you can pick the one that gives you the best benefits for a reasonable cost, or you might pick the one that gives a reasonable amount of benefits for a reasonable cost. There is no one correct way to pick the best result from a cost-benefit analysis, but if you omit the cost avoidances, you can really distort the costs.

Suppose you are moving to a new house and have to make a decision about selling your old house or renting it out. The figures show that you could benefit slightly from keeping the old house and renting it, because the mortgage is low enough that the rent would almost cover the average monthly expenses of the house. That is, you would have a small negative cash flow on the rental property. If you keep the old house, you would not add to your tax burden, because you can deduct your expenses, and you might achieve a capital gain in a few years when you finally do sell the house. You draw up a list of costs and benefits, and the numbers show that it is better to rent the old place because the anticipated capital gain will far exceed the out-of-pocket costs over the next five years. You have already decided to rent, when you mention all of this to your wife, who points out that the water heater in the old house is about to go and the roof leaks and will have to be replaced. The possible costs of these repairs will be several thousand dollars—enough to make the rental deal look bad. By selling the place you will avoid these costs, although you probably will have to take a lower sale price because the purchaser—having read this book—will take the need to replace the water heater and roof into account when making an offer.

The cost avoidance idea can be applied improperly, and you have to be wary of people who claim they are saving you money by buying items on sale. My wife has been good at this: Over the years she has saved thousands of dollars for me, but somehow I don't seem to have that money in the bank. The key factor, of course, is whether you would otherwise have bought the item or not. If you have to buy a pair of shoes, it obviously is better to buy them for $80 rather than $100. In this case, you have saved $20 in cost avoidance. On the other hand, if you buy a pair of shoes that you don't need for $80 (or any price), you have wasted your money. The middle ground of this situation is when you are induced to buy at $80 a pair of shoes you would not have bought for $100 because of price considerations. That might be a bargain, but it does not involve a cost avoidance.

The concept of cost avoidance relates to the basic idea that a decision to do nothing is still a legitimate decision. A decision not to spend money is a cost avoided, and these are some of the best savings. My advice is to consider not only the total system cost for what you are going to do, but also the benefits of avoiding costs that would have been incurred by what you have decided not to do.

Rule 51: Count Opportunity Costs

Another form of cost you should consider in your planning process is the opportunity cost. This is a benefit that you forgo by selecting a particular course of action in your plan. You have lost the opportunity to obtain that benefit, and this is counted as a loss.

Suppose you have two ways to go on a plan. If you take Alternative A, you will gain a benefit worth $500 from the sale of some property. If you select Alternative B, you will not be able to sell the property, which will remain in your hands but will be unusable. In this situation, selection of Alternative B would cost you the $500 you otherwise would have gained from the sale of the land. In lining up the pros and cons of the two alternatives, you should list for Alternative B an opportunity cost of $500.

Opportunity costs are seldom considered by planners, unless they have had considerable training in economics, for ascribing costs because of something you have decided not to do is a fairly subtle idea. It is, however, a very powerful idea that can have great impact even on day-to-day living and planning.

Each time we make a choice, we eliminate from our plan the opportunity to make other choices at that decision point. If we come to an intersection, we can go left, right, or straight ahead. When we go left, we cannot at the same time go right or straight ahead. We have foreclosed the alternatives forever. Even if we go left and then decide a mile down the road that we have made a mistake, turn around, return to the intersection, and then go off in a different direction entirely, we cannot re-create the conditions that pertained at the time of the original decision to go left. Life is full of these decision points.

Just because we cannot simultaneously go left, right, and straight ahead, however, does not mean that we cannot consider beforehand what would happen if we went one way or the other. Indeed, one of the purposes of the planning process is to force us to consider the consequences before making a choice. In this case, we would be wise to think about what would happen if we went left, what would happen if we went right, and what would happen if we went straight ahead. We do this kind of thinking all of the time, much of it instinctively, and we even consider the opportunity costs in a general sense.

My advice is to consider the costs of lost opportunities in a formal sense, and include them in the evaluation of alternatives and the planning for each choice you make. Though opportunity costs may not result in a need to pay for something, they do represent benefits that might be used in the future to offset some of the other costs of your plan. Just ask yourself what you are going to lose out on by choosing a particular alternative.

Rule 52: Take Inflation into Account

You should take inflation into account in the planning process. Money is not worth what it used to be. The sad fact is that for most of human history, money has lost its value as time progresses. This is called inflation. Prices tend to rise so that the real value of a unit of money—a dollar, say—is less today than it was last year and will be less next year than it is this year.

There have been some periods of deflation in history, during which prices decreased and the purchasing power of money increased, but such an event is unlikely unless there is a global depression. Inflation may be bad, but deflation is worse, so let's just deal with the present economic circumstances.

We are all aware of the existence of inflation and acknowledge its existence with charming folk tales. Who among us has not told of the wonderful days when a movie cost a quarter and a candy bar cost a nickel? We look at advertisements in old magazines and long for the good old days when things were so inexpensive compared with today's prices. And even the younger folks among us have tales of only a few years ago when things were "much cheaper" than they are now.

It is easy to long for the good old days of low prices, but it is also necessary to consider that wages and salaries also were low in those days. When I was first commissioned in the Army as a second lieutenant in 1950, my monthly salary was $200. Today the monthly salary of a brand new second lieutenant is $1,400. So pay also has increased, and some economists claim that income has increased more than prices so that we are better off than we were. This may even be true overall, but I am sure there are many cases of people who have not done so well or who have done worse due to inflation. And while prices in general may have gone up, some prices, such as the cost of a TV set, have gone down a great deal in absolute terms. Inflation may be good or bad, but it is a fact of our present economic life, and you need to know how to cope with it. The effect of inflation on the planning process is that it costs more to do things later.

If you plan to build a house, assuming you own the land free and clear, this year the cost may be $150,000, but a year from now it may cost you $159,000 to get exactly the same house. This represents a 6 percent increase in the cost of labor and materials in the course of a year. The same kind of thing is true of all multi-year spending. You need to apply an inflation factor to future spending.

When estimating labor costs, for example, it is advisable to add a percentage increase to both the direct labor costs and the costs of benefits. The cost of employing a word-processor specialist full-time this year might be $32,000 in salary plus an additional $5,000 in payroll taxes and benefits, for a total cost of $37,000. Next year, it is likely that taxes and health care and insurance will increase and that the employee will expect and receive a pay hike, so the overall cost will go up from $37,000 to $39,220 if inflation is 6 percent that year. If you are doing a five-year total system cost, this person's services will cost you the amounts shown in the accompanying table, assuming a 6 percent annual increase.*

Year One	Year Two	Year Three	Year Four	Year Five
$37,000	$39,220	$41,573	$44,067	$46,711

You need to add an increase for inflation to the costs of other resources as well, including and particularly hard goods. The rates of price inflation may be greater or smaller for particular resources, and you will have to learn the territory to make fine estimates.

The optimum timing of your spending is also affected by inflation. It might make sense to buy some items early to avoid later price increases. This would depend on whether you have funds available, the cost of borrowing money, the rate of inflation, and other factors affecting the future price of the items under consideration. Generally, this kind of analysis can be approached by bringing all of the estimates down to the present value of the money involved (Rule 67), and it affects decisions to buy long-lead-time items (Rules 87 and 88).

Inflation is the major reason why cost overruns occur when projects are delayed beyond their original implementation dates. With rare exceptions, delay means additional cost, and unless the planner has taken inflation into account, he or she will be caught unaware by price increases.

---

* The average rate of inflation from 1978 through 1990, as measured by the Consumer Price Index, was 6.3 percent, according to data on page 151 of the World Almanac for 1992.

10   Money

Finally, we get down to money, the nub of it all or—as people are wont to say—the root of all evil.

Money is not a resource in the sense the term was defined and used in chapter 8, but it is a resource in the sense that you need it to get anything done. Money is a medium of exchange that is the ultimate in fungibility, meaning you can transform it into many different forms: food, clothing, airline tickets, lumber, trucks, labor. Money is used to obtain resources and defray expected costs and expenses and to reward your success with profits and benefits. In short, money is the prerequisite for doing something. You need it to implement your plan, and you need it even to do the planning, for it costs money to pay for your time and the time of your helpers, as well as the paper, pens, computers, and whatever else you use in the planning process. So money is necessary.

Someone is going to say at this point that I am wrong about money being necessary—that it is possible to plan and even to achieve without money, using a barter system or subsistence agriculture or some other nonmoney means. That is true in the extreme, but I don't advise you to try to get along without money. Like it or not, money is the medium by which our activities are facilitated.

Both money and time are essential to proper planning—or even to improper planning—but there is a difference: Time is immutable. It flows at a constant rate in one direction, and we have to fit our plans into it since we cannot change time. Money, on the other hand, is variable both in amount and availability. We can have lots of it or little of it, and we can have it now or tomorrow. We can even have different kinds of money—dollars, francs, yen, or rubles. Since money is variable, we can plan initially for different amounts, because our needs for money will to a certain extent determine how much money we will get.

Money is a measure of the resources you will have to accomplish your plan and achieve your goals. It is a measure of the costs you plan to incur. So it is necessary to keep track of your money and plan for its use. The following four rules are designed to help you manage money, plan for its use, and get it when you need it. This is not, however, a book on personal finance, and I am not going to advise you on how to keep money or make it grow. My emphasis is on how to plan to use it and how to incorporate considerations of money into your planning process. Remember, money in itself is not the goal of your planning—money is just something you need to use to achieve your goal. If you want money for itself, my advice is to read another book.

Rule 53: Prepare a Budget

A budget is a plan for spending money. You should have a budget as part of your plan, and you should have a budget for everything else you do or plan to do that involves money. A budget works in a general way to give you an idea of how to plan your spending.

There are many different ways to budget, but the basic idea is to set up in advance the various expense items for which you will spend your anticipated income.

You may have heard about some household budgeting schemes in which couples change all of their money into cash each month and put the appropriate amounts into envelopes: so much for rent, so much for food, so much for the movies, and so on down to so much for the baby's shoes. This system, while superficially sensible, never works. Having cash in hand makes it hard to resist the temptation to take a few dollars from one envelope to pay for some unbudgeted item.

Credit cards have wreaked havoc on household budgeting, particularly when one of the spenders fails to inform the other about large charges. This has had the unfortunate effect in many households of stopping even the pretense of budgeting.

Budgetless living is possible. Army couples used to brag about eating beef in the first part of the month right after payday but eating beans during the last part of the month just before the next payday. The approach that encourages spending all the money until it is gone, however, is really good only for those with a regular income that comes in month after month after month, so that bridging the gap from one monthly paycheck to the next is irritating but not life threatening. Living without a budget is possible but not recommended, at least not by me.

Budget of the Association for FY1999

Income		Expenses	
Dues:	$36,000	Postage:	$ 600
Interest:	2,000	Lawn care:	24,000
Cake bake:	500	Insurance:	2,200
Misc.:	100	Legal fees:	1,000
Total income:	$38,600	Total expenses:	$27,800

Budgets are the main activity of civic, neighborhood, and alumni associations and similar groups. These organizations have to accomplish some activities, all of which cost money, and they have to allocate the money to various items. The budget is always a major source of contention at the annual meeting, where the treasurer presents his or her report and is greeted with sharp questions from a few members no matter how good the finances look. Generally a budget runs for a year in this context, and it looks something like the table above.

This imaginary but typical budget shows that the association plans to generate an excess of $10,800 in income over planned expenditures. This is certain to create a commotion among the membership, most of whom will want their dues lowered immediately. This commonsense proposition normally is countered by the board of directors, which proposes some kind of contingency fund or emergency fund. And so the budget controversy continues *ad infinitum* to some and *ad nauseam* to others.

The biggest and most prominent budget around, of course, is the budget of the U.S. Government. The high jinks and tomfoolery that surround this particular spending plan are enough to give the whole subject of budgeting a bad name. The president, with the assistance of the entire Executive Branch, prepares a budget proposal that fits the administration's policies and spending priorities. The president submits the budget to Congress, which immediately throws it away and creates its own budget from whole cloth. This situation got so bad a few years ago that a new law was passed requiring the president and the Congress to agree at least on the total amount to be spent. The latest evidence suggests that the new law does not appear to have had any useful effect on the process. It is heartening, however, that the federal government still recognizes the necessity for a spending plan, because even a controversial and hodgepodge plan is better than no plan at all.

My advice is to have a budget as an integral part of your plan. As you cost the resources and the nonresource items, you simply accumulate them into categories useful for your spending plan. You can assign dollar amounts to each of these categories, then compare the total amount you plan to spend to the total amount you plan to earn or obtain as financing.

If you plan to spend more money than you plan to get, you need to adjust the budget—unless you are the federal government.

Ordinary households, associations, and businesses cannot last long if they continue to spend more than they make, although this basic truth has been well camouflaged in recent years. A deficit is when you spend more than you make, and a deficit has to be financed in some way. Young people can finance a deficit by hitting up their folks for a grant. Everyone can finance a deficit by selling assets, and the pawnshop business owes its existence to this proposition. Most people finance deficits by borrowing money, thereby creating a debt. The problem with running up a debt is that it costs money to owe money, for the lender charges you interest for the privilege of using his money. So running up a debt costs you more money, which leads to more borrowing, which leads to more debt and more interest, and so on into a downward spiral of financial disaster, which could lead ultimately to bankruptcy. This accumulation of massive debt whose interest payments were too large to handle is the reason why many old and respected U.S. corporations bit the dust in the early 1990s. Like some individuals, these business entities lived high on the hog in the '80s and paid for it in the '90s.

The way to avoid this kind of problem is to work out a budget, making sure that you have captured the anticipated costs of your plan plus some allowance for Murphy's Law.

Rule 54: Check the Cash Flow

Checking the cash flow is the most important rule in money planning. While profit and loss are important, and control of costs is important too, managing the cash flow is absolutely essential.

Cash flow may be considered part of cost control, but in my view it is more than that. You can estimate and control costs and still go down the tubes because of poor cash-flow management.

Cash flow is the balance over time between available money and anticipated expenses. Available money consists of cash on hand, anticipated revenues, and credit. Anticipated expenses include outlays of money for goods, services, taxes, debt payments, and other things. The rule is always to have sufficient money available to cover anticipated expenses. That is more easily said than done, however.

All of us have probably had the sad experience of receiving a large bill that we did not anticipate and for which we did not plan. Perhaps this was a tax notice, an insurance premium notice, or a major purchase that we had forgotten about until the day of reckoning. This situation requires us to scramble to make the payment by shorting some other obligation, borrowing, delaying payment, taking money out of savings, or some other unsatisfactory method. Some people live their entire lives in this kind of financial chaos, and though this is their prerogative, it is not necessary and can be mitigated by a little cash-flow planning.

Cash-flow planning, of course, cannot mitigate or erase poverty or low income; it can only assure that you have a reasonable balance between your income and your outgo. I have been telling my wife for years, "It ain't the income that counts, it's the outgo." Her usual response has been to urge me to increase my capacity for income to match her capacity for outgo.

It seems to me, however, that cash-flow planning is equally important for those with modest incomes as for those with large incomes—perhaps more important. If you are receiving only a few pennies, it makes sense to count each one of them and make it do the best it can for you. Cash-flow planning will help you do that.

One of the best features of cash-flow planning is that it will help you avoid inadvertent debt. We Americans are exposed to great temptations to borrow money. This is because the credit card industry makes its profit from the interest we pay when we borrow from them.

In the old days, I am told, people actually saved up money to make large purchases. Today, however, we buy now and pay later. This causes problems when people buy too much now and cannot afford to pay later when the bills come due. The sharp increase in personal bankruptcies is evidence of this. Even the largest U.S. corporations did the same thing in the 1980s, when they assumed large debt burdens that they later could not afford. Cash-flow planning will help you avoid getting into such problems inadvertently. It will not guarantee that you will become prudent, but it will inform you when you might tend to go off the deep end.

The difference between budgeting and cash-flow management is the distinction between obligating money and spending it. You obligate the money when you contract to make a purchase or pay for a service. You spend the money when you actually write the check or hand over the cash. Obligations for large capital investments or continuing services are made up front, but the outlays of the money are made over a period of time depending on the terms of the contract in each case. Failure to appreciate that you will still have to pay out cash for purchases made earlier often results in cash-flow spending plans that are too big. You have to face up to your previous obligations of money in your cash-flow planning.

I manage my own consulting business by cash flow. Each month I list all of the expenses I anticipate for the next three months. This includes firm numbers for items I have ordered with a credit card or purchase order, as well as rough estimates for expenses I know I will incur but for which I do not have firm numbers. For example, I know from experience just about how much money I will spend each month for petty cash expenses, and I will forecast that amount for each of the next three months. I include in the anticipated expenses extraordinary payments for quarterly income tax, property tax, or other items that I know from experience will be coming up. I keep a three-month list of anticipated expenses because this warns me that I have to accumulate enough cash to pay them, and I can start that process.

My next step is to make a list of possible revenues. There are three categories: cash, accounts receivable, and future income. Cash is the amount in my checking account. When I send an invoice for services already provided, I list the amount of that invoice in the accounts receivable section, and I count this as almost as good as cash, for I am assured that this money will be forthcoming. Then I list the future work of which I am reasonably certain, and list the future revenues from that work as future income. There is a degree of risk in this forecasting, particularly with respect to the time element. I have had to wait as long as six months to receive payment for an invoice, and this really upsets the cash-flow plan. And sometimes the work I have forecasted does not occur, and I have to delete an item from the list of future income. It is easier to project expenses than income, and I have to keep fiddling with the income list.

I compare the possible revenues with the forecasted expenses over three months, with the objective of making the two sums balance. If I am certain of a major expense that will occur in the fourth or fifth month, I bring it into the equation too, just to make certain that I will have enough money to cover it.

When revenues exceed expenses, I make a payment to a savings account or pay more on a debt item. When, as is normally the case, the expenses exceed revenues, I go over the expense items again and eliminate optional items or delay them until the two sums balance. Sometimes it has been simply impossible to cut expenses to match income; then I have had to dip into savings or borrow money to pay the bills. This is a bad policy, but everyone has to do it at some time or another. When I do use some savings or borrow money, I list as an expense item the repayment of the loan or replenishing of the savings to my safety level. I try to keep enough money in a quick-access savings account to handle a major cash-flow emergency, such as an unexpected trip or medical expense. By scheduling the repayment of a loan or a savings withdrawal, you can prevent a downward spiral into financial disaster.

Cash-flow planning provides you with the information required to make hard choices about expenses, but it cannot guarantee that you have the good sense to make those hard choices. Nevertheless, even if you don't want or need to be fiscally prudent, it is better to approach insolvency knowingly than simply in complete ignorance of your cash-flow situation.

One result of cash-flow planning is that you have little discretionary spending power. If you do a complete job of projecting expenses, your revenues will be almost completely allocated to future expenses even before you get the money. My wife complains about this a bit. When I tell her I just received a nice check in the mail, she usually suggests some imaginative way to spend the money, but I can generally tell her truthfully that the money is already spent—or at least already earmarked for one or more of the items on my future expense list.

Cash-flow planning can minimize financial discomfort by letting you know in advance where you stand and how you can spend your money in the best way to meet your needs and possibly satisfy your desires. My advice is to do some kind of cash-flow planning for yourself, your household, your business, or the project you are planning. It does not have to be elaborate, but it does have to be honest. There is no point in fooling yourself about your own money prospects.

Rule 55: Have Credit Available

No matter how good a job you do at budgeting and managing your cash flow, there will be times that you will need to borrow money. Perhaps you will need some funds to pay bills, or buy a new piece of equipment, or take advantage of a good deal. The ability to borrow money depends on your credit. So you need to keep up your credit and have the ability to borrow money quickly and without a lot of fuss.

The problem with credit is that the general approach of the banking industry is to loan money only to those who don't need it. If you are running a business and need money to keep going until things improve, you will have a rough time, but if your business is generating lots of cash, you can borrow all you want. If you are rich, credit is easy; if you are poor, forget it. There are exceptions, of course—during the 1970s any South American nation could get massive loans, and during the 1980s any crackpot land developer with a golden tongue could borrow large sums of money. Both of these practices rebounded on the lenders in numerous bad loans, so they have responded by restricting loans to individuals and small businesses.

You can arrange to have credit available to you in several ways so that you can borrow money when you need it. The trick is to get the credit when you don't need it but not to use it until you really do need it.

Credit can be obtained from your local bank or savings and loan, a credit union, or a second mortgagor. You can establish open lines of credit that will allow you to borrow when you need to by writing what looks like a check. You can probably get lines of credit up to several thousand dollars without much trouble if you have an income and a reasonable credit history.

One way to get credit is to become acquainted with the manager or loan officer at your local bank. This works better with smaller banks than with the huge chains that are now forming in the U.S. banking industry. When our bank was small and friendly, I used to be able to go down and borrow several thousand dollars on a signature loan from my friend, the bank manager. He knew me and was well aware that I kept several accounts in his bank and had a net worth sufficient to cover the amounts borrowed; it was quick and easy. Unfortunately, the small bank merged with another small bank, was bought by a larger chain, and after several more unions emerged as the fifth- or sixth-largest bank in the United States. The bank became unfriendly, and my ability to obtain loans was gone—each time I applied (once in a desperate hurry), I was put off, asked to file the same old papers again, and finally refused. I had seen this coming and had taken the precaution of setting up other lines of credit, but it has always bothered me that my bank is no longer a source of convenient loans.

A credit card, of course, is a source of a loan. You can charge what you need on your card, and you can even take cash advances up to your credit limit. Since it is still relatively easy to get a credit card, this is a convenient source of a loan for almost everyone. The catch is that borrowing with a credit card is very expensive—the highest interest rates, in general, of any loan. So I don't recommend using a credit card to borrow money.

A good way to get a line of credit for emergencies is to set up an open loan with the savings and loan or credit union where you keep some savings. If you have funds on deposit with an institution, they are more favorably disposed to loan you money than if you are a complete stranger. For my business, I use an open line of credit with my credit union to adjust my cash flow for important items that have to be paid right away.

You have to be careful about credit. The world is full of companies and people who will be glad to loan you money but charge you exorbitant interest for the privilege.

The most important thing to remember about credit is that it is not a solution or a panacea, for in the end you have to pay the money back plus interest. So my advice is to have credit available to bail you out of cash-flow problems, but do not rely on it. Just as soon as you borrow money, start paying it back and continue to do so until it is all paid up. Then it will be ready for you the next time you need money fast.

Rule 56: Get the Financing First

You will need money to implement your plan. For small projects, you will use money from your earnings or your savings or, perhaps, borrow the money and then pay it back.

For large projects, however, unless you are rich, you will have to get the money from someone else—that is, you will have to obtain financing. My advice is to get the financing first—before you start implementing.

Not everyone agrees with my advice. Some very serious people advocate starting the project on a shoestring so that you can have something to show people to attract the financing. Frankly, that kind of approach is all right for young people with more vigor than sense, but I tried that and have lost all heart for it.

I spent three years developing a concept and a prototype for a computerized war game based on some authentic combat simulation work for government customers. The concept was great, but we had insufficient money to develop the game, so we worked on it in spare time and tried to come up with something good enough to attract an investor. It was a real Catch-22. We had enough money to work on it, but not enough money to do a job good enough to attract the money to do it right in the first place. Because of this sad experience (the games are still in limbo), I decided that my approach henceforth would be to get the money first and do the job properly.

There are thousands of good ideas out there that just might be successful if they were funded. There are also thousands of bad ideas that were funded and failed. As I presided over several good ideas that never got off the ground for lack of funds, I watched with envy as others with poorer ideas attracted large amounts of financing and were able to live well—if briefly—before plunging into financial chaos. I was really jealous of one company that attracted $25,000,000 in capital from investors and went out of business three years later without ever having developed the service for which they were funded. In the meantime, the managers lived well with big salaries, company cars, opulent offices, and first-class airline tickets. This was really hard to take while I was sitting around with my great idea and a hard-headed approach to cost control and could not get anyone to give me the time of day.

There are two ways to get funding for your plan: You can form a business, then either borrow the money or sell shares in the business. For the purposes of this discussion, a business can be a sole proprietorship (just you), a partnership, or a corporation. The corporation form has the distinct advantage that, in the event things go down the tubes, your liability is limited to your investment in the corporation.

Borrowing the money allows you to retain ownership and control the destiny of your business, but it adds interest payments to your costs. In Rule 55 I advised you to have a line of credit available, but there I was talking about just a few thousand to get you over a cash-flow crunch. Now I am talking about big-time borrowing, from tens of thousands up to millions, to finance your plan, business, or project. Strangely enough, it is probably just as easy to borrow big-time as it is to borrow small amounts. Borrowing the money is possible but arduous, and you have to be able to provide collateral in some form.

Venture capital is available from individuals and companies who have money and like to invest it into promising ventures. My experience with venture capitalists has not been promising, however, for they were interested primarily in putting expansion money into proven companies with good track records, and they appeared to want an arm and a leg to do it. I could find no venture capitalists interested in helping me start up any of several promising ventures, so I gave up on these investors. My experience should not deter you from sounding these people out, however, for my ideas might just have been bum ones.

Equity funding, obtained by selling shares in the business, allows you to avoid interest costs but means that your ownership and possibly your ability to direct the affairs of the business are weakened. Obtaining money by selling shares is subject to federal and state laws and regulations, so before you do this you should consult an attorney who specializes in this area. I once hired an attorney for $20,000 to prepare a prospectus to sell shares in a brilliant new company I was part of, and we sold just enough stock to pay the attorney off. Lots of people raise lots of capital through private and public offerings of stock, so you might want to investigate this. Be prepared for a visit to Wonderland if you decide to go this route.

You can make your deal more attractive to investors by putting some of your own money into it. This demonstrates to investors that you are really committed to making things happen. They know that if your own money is at risk, you will try harder than if you are simply playing around with someone else's money. I was really shocked on one of my first attempts to obtain investment money when my prospect listened to the deal and then asked if I had taken a second mortgage on my house to put money into the deal. Apparently, this was his measure of just how serious I was about it all. On the other hand, I know another entrepreneur—a successful one—who has made millions and boasted that he never put a nickel of his own into his projects.

It is not easy to obtain funding even for good ideas, but it is done every day, so you should definitely consider it, keeping in mind the few bits of information provided in this rule. My advice is to avoid trying to do things on a shoestring. I have tried that method and have seen others do it, but never with great success. Even if you have to wait a bit, get the financing you need to implement your plan properly the first time.

11   Advanced Concepts

This chapter presents some advanced planning concepts that are considerably more than basic. The eleven rules herein show that difficult matters often boil down to simple principles. Some of these rules are steeped in jargon and have mysterious words or phrases in them, such as "zero-sum game," "parallel paths," and "satisficing." Well, all words are mysterious until they become familiar through understanding and usage. So the more you use these advanced concepts, the less mysterious they will be. Just focus on the concepts, then learn the words and make them your own. All of these words represent fairly simple ideas. Just add them first to your recognition vocabulary and then, as you practice your planning, to your working vocabulary.

Some of you may be daunted by the prospect of dealing with really difficult stuff, but let me assure you that the basic ideas of these tools are really simple. It is true that the actual use of the tools is complicated, but then so is planning for complicated things. The purpose of this chapter is merely to expose you to these concepts; if you believe they will be useful, follow up with additional research in other books.*

What I am trying to do is enable you to make use of some pretty powerful stuff in your own planning. So bear with me as we advance boldly into the land of the advanced concepts. It will get even more scary later on as we lose some grasp of the definitive, but it will all help you to be a better planner.

Rule 57: Play a Zero-Sum Game

Game theory establishes some general rules for playing and winning at games, and several different aspects of game theory are important for planning into an unknown future. Rule 65 will cover game theory in more depth, but I want to introduce the subject now in order to consider the concept of the zero-sum game.

Game theory can be applied to any case in which two or more human beings vie to achieve certain goals. Gin rummy is a card game in which two people vie to reduce the point total in their hands to zero and "go out" or "gin," scoring the point total the other player is caught holding. Hands are played until one person achieves 100 points in score to win a game. Gin rummy, like all games, is played with rules. In most recreational games, both sides know the rules. In some recreational games and in life, there are times when one or both sides either do not understand the rules or play by different rules. So it can get complicated rapidly, which is why some theory has been helpful in simplifying the use of games and increasing their usefulness in planning.

An important aspect of game theory is the definition of "winning." The object of all games is to win, but there has been some confusion about what, exactly, that means. Winning often is linked to the rules: If you get 100 points at gin rummy, you win that game and count

---

* I am indebted to Richard A. Levin and Charles A. Kirkpatrick and their excellent book, *Quantitative Approaches to Management* (New York: McGraw-Hill, 1971), for their simple yet elegant explanations of PERT, inventory models, and game theory.

the points for yourself. In Monopoly you win if you stay in the game until all of the other players have gone bankrupt. In chess you win if you can place the opponent's king in a position of not being able to move without being captured. Winning may also be established by counting up the number of points, dollars, or honorary degrees one can accumulate. Points count mostly in recreational games, while money appears to count heavily in the grand game of life.

One of the important classes of games is the "zero-sum game." This means that the total number of good points in the game is fixed. The essence of a zero-sum game is that the only way you can get more points is by taking them away from the other player or players. Zero-sum games exist in real life when the amount of resources is constrained. If you are dealing with a fixed amount of lumber that has to be allocated among various building projects, the only way you can increase the lumber for Project A is to decrease it for Projects B and C. The fixed amount of the critical resource involves you in a zero-sum game.

Most people are involved in zero-sum games when they deal with their personal finances. The amount of money available to a family tends, in the short term, to be fixed. So the funds available to spend or save are constrained, and if you buy a new car you cannot buy a new coat, or you cannot spend as much on travel, or you cannot save as much as you wanted. So personal spending tends very much to be a zero-sum game, although credit cards have blurred this fact and have brought many people to address personal finance otherwise until ultimately the bills come rolling in.

Anytime there is a fixed amount of some resource for your plan, you will have to figure out how to allocate that resource among the various projects that could use it. This means you will play a zero-sum game. This is a useful idea; many planning problems occur because people overallocate resources among their various projects and cannot cope when one or more of the projects fail due to a lack of that resource.

The essence of a zero-sum game is that when I get something more, you get something less. I can "win" only by taking from you. Being involved in a zero-sum game can be ferocious, particularly if both sides understand that it is a zero-sum game. These games tend to be taken very seriously by all competitors who may not mind if they don't win, but who don't want to lose what they have. Zero-sum games are often ended by the capitulation of one of the sides. It is almost impossible to conclude a zero-sum game by negotiation because there is seldom anything to negotiate. The winner wants to keep winning more, and the loser cannot obtain an acceptable outcome except by continuing to play and hoping for a reversal of fortune. The winner, of course, can end the game by being magnanimous, but the nature of the game tends to work against magnanimity. Because it is so hard to end zero-sum games on any basis acceptable to both sides, they are played seriously and hard and sometimes even lead to cheating or violence by the loser.

Because of the nature of zero-sum games, much thought has been given to creating situations that are non-zero-sum games, in which many or all players can benefit from an outcome, although to varying degrees. Thus, you hear a lot about "win-win" situations, in which everyone benefits. Essentially, the goal of a negotiator is to establish an outcome in which all sides can win something (or claim to win something). In real life, however, there are many situations in which resources are constrained, and you have to deal with a zero-sum game. Learn how to recognize these, or your plan will have great problems when you meet a shortfall.

Rule 58: Move along Parallel Paths

You can schedule your projects so that the tasks are performed consecutively in series, or you can try to schedule them so that some of the tasks are performed concurrently along parallel paths. Generally, it saves time and resources to do as many tasks concurrently as you can handle.

The reason for this is Ohm's Law, which implies that the usual friction or resistance encountered along any path behaves differently for series and parallel circuits.*

---

* Ohm's Law really says that the electromotive force (E) is equal to the product of the current (I) and the resistance (R). So the law is $E = IR$.

A series circuit is one in which the task proceeds from Point A to Point B, then from Point B to Point C, then from Point C to Point D, as shown in the diagram below.

Series Circuit

In a series circuit, each event has to be completed before the next event can start. That is, the electrical current flows from one end to the other through the wires and gizmos (capacitors, chips, resistors—this is not an electricity book) successively. For the series circuit shown here, the resistance, cost, or friction of the three segments is additive, so that if the resistance of each segment is R, the total resistance to get from Point A to Point D is 3R. Since the series circuit offers only a single path, there is little ability to shift resources or emphasis to improve performance, and the circuit is vulnerable to disruption because a single failure along the way stops all progress in going from Point A to Point D. So series circuits, either in electricity or in planning, have some inherent disadvantages.

In a parallel circuit, several paths are used to move from Point A to Point D, as shown in the following diagram.

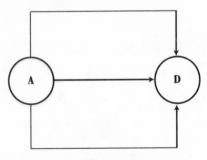

Parallel Circuit

For the parallel circuit shown here, the electricity flows directly from Point A to Point D (without going through any intermediate points) along each of the available parallel paths, generally dividing up in inverse proportion to the resistance offered by each path, so that overall resistance is much less than for a series circuit. The overall resistance of a parallel circuit is considerably less than the sum of the resistances along all of the paths. In the case where the resistance of each segment is R, the total resistance to get from Point A to Point D is in fact only one-third of R (R/3).

If you want more electrical current, you have to either increase the electromotive force (voltage) or decrease the resistance, often by setting up parallel circuits. That also holds true for endeavors other than pushing electrons through wires. To get something done, you have to apply force in the form of energy, effort, will, resources, or dollars to overcome resistance in the form of ignorance, antipathy, indifference, and physical barriers. So old Uncle Ohm gave us not just a way to solve circuit problems but also a general guide for living—and planning.

The point here is that moving along parallel paths has several advantages when you are preparing your plan. By planning multiple paths, you allow the work (current) to proceed along each path in accordance with the difficulty (resistance) of each path. You can increase the progress by applying more effort (electromotive force) to a particular path without having to do it for every element as you would in a single-series path. You have flexibility in shifting resources from one path to another depending on circumstances. If there is a disruption, progress will be halted in only one path, and the entire project need not be stopped. So there are definite advantages to planning parallel paths.

There are also some cautions, however. You may have figured out by now that each of your separate parallel paths is in actuality a series circuit, with all of the characteristics of that kind of path. So you will have to deal with series kinds of events at some level of detail. That is not entirely bad, for one of the beneficial characteristics of series circuits is that a single disruption halts progress for the whole circuit and thereby acts as a safety switch if damage or harm would result from a continuation of progress. This operates somewhat like the fuses or circuit breakers in your home, which are designed to disrupt an overloaded series circuit before it heats up the wires and causes a fire.

Another problem with parallel planning is that the difficulty of scheduling, monitoring, and managing increases geometrically as the number of paths increases. Managing one path is simple; managing two paths requires more than double the attention; and managing ten paths may be one hundred times more difficult. So there are some limits on the number of parallel paths you should use.

My advice is to recognize the advantages of using several different parallel paths when making your plan, but do not go overboard with them until you are confident of your ability to control them.

Rule 59: Do Some Sensitivity Analysis

In order to do sensitivity analysis you need to appreciate the meaning of the phrase *ceteris paribus:* "Other things being equal." The whole idea starts with the scientific method and the great difficulty in figuring out cause-and-effect relationships.

Science is hard. It is possible to generate scientific data by observing phenomena or conducting experiments, and it is possible to apply mathematical statistics to determine if there are relationships among various kinds of data, pointing out how one set of data behaves with respect to other kinds of data. It is very difficult, however, to be able to conclude definitely that one kind of data *causes* another kind of data.

When analyzing data obtained from observations of natural phenomena, it is possible to draw inferences that are plausible but counterintuitive (not what we expect). Most of these are also wrong. There has to be a definite causality link established in science. Demonstrating that the height of children correlates positively with their age does suggest that growing older causes children to get taller, and this is so—at least up to a point. Demonstrating that the height of children correlates with their grade in school, however, should not be the basis for concluding that getting promoted from the first grade to the second grade will cause a child to get taller. Lots of books have been written about this kind of thing, and if you really want to get involved, I suggest you read them. The scientific method is really neat, and it is also misunderstood by a lot of people—including a lot of scientists.

The great difficulty in detecting and proving cause-and-effect relationships leads scientists to create experiments and make observations in which all but one of the possible variables is held constant. If particular results ensue from changes in only one variable, it is reasonable to conclude that the results are caused by the changes in that one variable. That works fairly well for physical scientists, who can set up experiments that do hold all but one variable constant, but it does not work well at all for social scientists or observational scientists, who cannot control the many variables that affect their areas of study. Still, all scientists would like to be able to describe the behavior of only one variable at a time, and they do this by saying, "Other things being equal."

Simply saying it, of course, does not always make it so, but it does mean that the importance of a single variable working alone is recognized, and that if everything else really were equal (meaning constant), the variable of interest could be a cause of a particular result. Since all real-world problems tend to be multivariate (a word meaning "hideously complicated"), it is important sometimes to try to establish the influence of a single variable—*ceteris paribus*. The process for doing this is called sensitivity analysis.

Sensitivity analysis seeks to establish how sensitive the results are to changes in the value of a single variable. This is done by holding constant the values of all of the variables except the one whose influence is being checked.

Sensitivity analysis is very useful to see just how far out on a limb you have crawled by making a certain assumption or taking at face value a certain "fact." You can determine just how important that assumption or fact is to your plan by conducting a sensitivity analysis for it. If the results are insensitive to changes in the assumed value, then it is not very important and you need not necessarily go back and revise or improve the assumption. If, on the other hand, slight changes in the assumed value cause great changes in the results, you had better go back and improve the validity of the assumption.

The way you do a sensitivity analysis is by setting out the model of the plan, which may be an equation or a drawing or a word description, and then figuring out how the results would change if you were to redo the calculations for a range of values.

Let's say you are going on a trip with a fixed budget of $1,200, and you have made an assumption that you can get a round-trip ticket for $500. The amount of money you will have to spend on hotels and meals and fun is going to be quite sensitive to the amount you actually have to spend on the airline tickets. If your assumption is really bad and you end up spending $1,000 for the ticket, you will not even have enough money to take the vacation. So you can figure out that the first thing you have to do is find out the actual cost of the airline ticket to replace your initial assumption.

That was a fairly simple example of the process, but many planning problems are much more complicated. Suppose you are building a house, again with an idea of how much you want to spend. One of the options you have to consider is the cost of the land. You could run a sensitivity analysis that varies the cost of the land and gives you an idea of the kind and size of house you could build for a range of potential properties. That would allow you to make a better choice of land plus house than if you simply ignored the influence of the price of land on the total package.

If you get to a point where you have reached a result but you don't really understand what it means, you might want to conduct some sensitivity analyses to help you figure out what is causing that result. You can do this by changing the values of several variables one at a time to see how each affects the results. You cannot regard these kinds of analyses as definitive or proof of cause and effect, but you can use them to gain insight into the workings of the mechanism.

My advice is to utilize sensitivity analysis informally much of the time to get a better idea of which horse is pulling the plow. If you are really uneasy about some of your assumptions or facts, use sensitivity analysis more formally to investigate the influence of that assumption or fact on your plan.

Rule 60: Examine the Worst Case

It is very useful in some planning cases to see what would happen if everything went wrong. This is like when you are set for a relaxed weekend, and your wife goes to bed with the flu, the dog gets fleas, the children get into a fight with the neighbor kids, and your brother-in-law shows up for an impromptu barbecue—expecting you to provide the beer and steak. Suddenly, everything has gone down the tubes!

Sometimes you cannot even plan for the worst, but most of the time it is useful to think about what would happen in that event. This is called worst-case planning.

Worst-case planning is justified in some circumstances and not in others.

During the Cold War, the Joint Chiefs of Staff (JCS) habitually engaged in worst-case planning. They did this because they needed to have some assurance that the United States could prevail even if everything went to hell in a handbasket. When estimates of Soviet strength came in with both a high value and a low value, the JCS took the high value. The JCS assumed that there would be no warning of a Soviet attack on NATO. They assumed that U.S. and NATO losses and problems would be high. They deliberately built a worst-case scenario that posed the most difficult set of challenges to the U.S. armed forces, and then compared our capability against that. Although this process has been criticized because it created the greatest demands for U.S. and NATO resources and responses, it was probably a prudent process, because the consequences of under-estimating Soviet capability could have been great. On the other hand, it is now clear (with the luxury of hindsight) that the Soviets were not up to the JCS assumed worst case. They needed time to prepare for an attack, and their strength was not as great as we had thought. So in retrospect, we might have been better off adopting a planning scenario that did not assume that everything went wrong.

Adopting the worst-case scenario simply because it is the worst, therefore, has little to recommend it. My advice for you planners is to plan for a case that appears to be reasonable, but still do some thinking about what would occur if the worst case happened.

This goes back to your assumptions: You made assumptions (Rule 10) and challenged them (Rule 11). Now you need to get some idea of what would happen if all of your assumptions turned sour.

Suppose you are planning a party and you assume that you will have 20 percent no-shows. You invite one hundred people but expect eighty. The worst case would be if all one hundred actually did come to the party. You have food and drink for eighty. It might be worth giving some thought to what you would do if all the guests come. Have you more beer and soft drinks in the basement? Are the stores open for more ice? Can you dig up more chow from the freezer? Without making a big deal out of it, you can prevent panic and have some idea of what to do if your worst case happens.

Worst-case planning can also be applied to your daily schedule. You failed to heed Rule 26 and made a tight schedule for yourself on the basis that your meeting with Mr. X will take only thirty minutes, but when you get there, the worst happens. Mr. X is in an expansive mood, and you leave his office ninety minutes later, already an hour behind schedule. Granted, it is always possible to take corrective action at that time, such as calling your secretary and having the next meeting canceled or simply giving up and going home to bed. But knowing that Mr. X has a tendency to be long-winded, you might have benefitted from some worst-case planning in advance, allowing for some optional time in your daily schedule right after that meeting.

If you are building a house, it is always good to at least address a possible worst case, particularly if you are selling your current residence to move into the new place. Timing is everything—and no more so than when making moves of the household. We have all read stories of people who had to leave their former residences and camp out in motels waiting for their new houses to be finished. I am not saying that you should plan for a delay, but you should at least examine a worst case that assumes there will be a maximum delay. That worst-case analysis might lead you to extend your time in the old house, warn your parents of a possible extended visit by the kids, or make another such prudent plan that would be implemented in the event the new house was not ready at the promised time.

Some people are really pessimists who believe that everything is already the worst case, but that is not true: No matter how bad things are, they can get worse. Good planning involves some consideration of what you would do if they did get worse.

Rule 61: Try Satisficing

Game theory was built originally around three concepts: maximizing, minimizing, and optimizing. These three concepts have great utility for game theorists, but for regular people, a new concept of "satisficing" may be best.

The three original concepts deal with ways to express the goals of a player.

Maximizing is the goal of getting the most of a particular benefit, or setting up a situation in which the probability of a good event is highest. That is, you seek to maximize the good outcomes.

Minimizing is the goal of getting the least of a particular disadvantage, or setting up a situation in which the probability of a bad event is lowest. You seek to minimize the bad outcomes.

Optimizing is the goal of getting the outcome that meets most closely the success criteria you have set for the game. Optimizing is a difficult concept that has significance in mathematical analyses but is hard to apply in daily life because it requires definition of the most favorable outcome.

In most simple games, the goal is to maximize or minimize. You try to maximize the amount of money you make or minimize the probability of a heart attack. You increase your salary by working hard, sacrificing free time, and being attentive to the boss. You can maximize your salary (*ceteris paribus*) by working as hard as you can, giving up all your free time, and becoming a slave or sycophant to the boss. Similarly, you decrease your chances of having a heart attack by stopping smoking, giving up sweets, and exercising regularly, and you minimize the possibility of a heart attack by creating a regimen devoted exclusively to that end. Either of these objectives causes you to behave in a way designed to achieve one particular goal to the utmost.

Most people do not want to achieve a single goal to the exclusion of all others, however. They do not want to maximize or minimize, or even optimize, but just want to achieve an acceptable balance. Most people do want to make more money, but few are willing to do what it takes to maximize their salary. Most people do want to avoid a heart attack, but few are willing to devote their whole existence to a healthy heart regimen. In real life there are many goals: We all try to achieve some of them more than others, but we approach few with the idea of maximizing or minimizing them.

Because of the nature of human beings, the concepts of maximization, minimization, and optimization, so useful in mathematical models of games, tend to be inaccurate guides to real outcomes. In recognition of this, a new criterion for success in a game has been developed.

The concept of satisficing says that there is a reasonable outcome that is not the optimum and is less than the maximum or more than the minimum, and that people want satisfaction rather than the best, most, or least. With respect to money, for example, a satisfactory goal may be to attain a certain level of salary and be willing to put out the work, make the sacrifices, and cultivate the boss enough to do that, but not be willing to make the extra effort needed to maximize salary. With respect to heart attacks, a satisfactory goal may be to reduce the probability of a heart attack to a degree by taking some steps to change diet and exercise, but not going to the extreme lifestyle changes required to minimize the probability of a heart attack. This is satisficing.

Many outcomes meet the criterion for satisficing, and this makes it easier to plan the outcomes. By definition, there is only one solution that provides either the maximum or the minimum, and it takes a lot of extra effort to define and achieve the single, best solution. If, on the other hand, you establish a satisfactory level of outcome, it is likely that there will be several solutions available to you. Not only will it be easier to find a solution, but also you will avoid the extra effort required to achieve a maximum, minimum, or optimum. To achieve one of these extremes, each extra increment of results requires a large increment of effort, so you will be in the area of diminishing returns and will have to really use up energy and resources to get to a maximum or minimum. So by settling for less than the best, you will make it a lot easier on yourself.

Satisficing is a very useful concept. It relieves you from the burden of planning to do things you really don't want to do, and it allows you to set reasonable expectations that can be met. My advice is to think about what is satisfactory to you in terms of the outcome of your plan and try to do that.

I realize that this advice is completely contrary to many of the mottoes and slogans offered in the literature of human fulfillment. "Be all you can be" and "Never settle for less than the best" are familiar slogans that may have good value for advertising but are really misleading when it comes to rational planning. Writers who tell you to maximize or minimize (without putting it in those terms, of course) are giving you bad advice. Life is too complicated for simple solutions, and trying for the best possible outcome in one or even a few areas is a prescription for fanaticism and ultimately failure.

Rule 62: Try PERT

Program evaluation and review technique (PERT) is a method of scheduling and budgeting resources that permits a project to be accomplished on time by minimizing delays due to conflicts and interruptions. PERT is concerned with events (specific actions that occur at particular points in time) and activities (work required to complete a task). PERT establishes a network to define the time and resource relationships between events. Arrows are used to show the connection between events, signified by circles. A simple PERT network is shown in the diagram below.

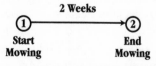

Event 1 is the start of a task, and Event 2 is the end of that task. The arrow represents the time or resources required for the task, or both, and its length is proportional to the amount of time and/or resources. In PERT it is customary to use weeks as the measure of time, using the five-day workweek as the standard. So if the total required time is ten days, that equals 2.0 weeks of working time, an elapsed time of twenty-two days is $22 \div 5 = 4.4$ weeks. Suppose Activity 1–2 is mowing the grass, as the diagram illustrates. Event 1 is the time you start to mow, and Event 2 is when you finish the job. At a scale of ½" = 1 week, the arrow between indicates the mowing took 2.0 weeks (a big lawn!).

Using PERT notation, a network can be established showing the relationships among many tasks. The next diagram shows a more complicated PERT network in which two task paths have to be followed to get to Event 4. One path goes from Event 1 to Event 2 (2.0 weeks) and then to Event 4 (3.0 weeks); thus the total path 1–2–4 takes 2.0 weeks plus 3.0 weeks, or 5.0 weeks. Path 1–3–4 takes a total of 6.0 weeks, so the earliest time that Event 4 can be completed is 6.0 weeks.

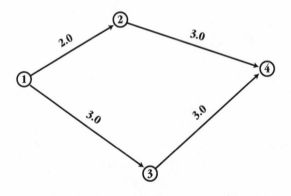

A still more complicated, but essentially simple, PERT network is shown in the next diagram. Because of dependencies, three paths have to be followed from Event 1 to Event 6: 1–2–4–6 (10.0 weeks), 1–3–5–6 (12.0 weeks), and 1–3–4–6 (11.0 weeks). Path 1–3–5–6, which takes 12.0 weeks, is the critical path.

In this case, we can calculate the earliest possible dates for each event. Event 4 is attained by paths 1–2–4 (5.0 weeks) and 1–3–4 (6.0

weeks), so the earliest possible date it can be accomplished is 6.0 weeks. The earliest possible date to accomplish Event 6 is 12.0 weeks, over the critical path of 1–3–5–6. If you want to shorten the time it takes to achieve Event 6, you should focus your attention on the critical path, initially on decreasing the time it takes to get from Event 3 to Event 5. Reducing the 3–5 task by a week will cut a week from the overall project time, but reducing the 3–5 task by still another week will not cut overall project time by that amount; this would instead make 1–2–4–6 the critical path, and you should then turn your attention to the 4–6 task.

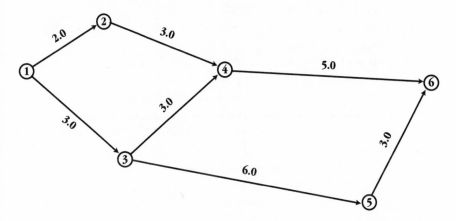

Addressing the PERT network in a repetitive manner and replanning after each iteration allows the planner to approach a complicated system in a systematic manner, applying corrections to the activities that will provide the greatest payoff in time or resources.

PERT can be simple or complicated, ranging from the hand-drawn networks above to very sophisticated computer programs. If what you are trying to get done involves more than just a few tasks, my advice is to use a computer program to plot your tasks and identify the critical path.

It is possible to apply some simple statistical methods in PERT that will enable planners to allow for uncertainty over how long it will actually take to complete certain activities. In reality, things often go wrong: The lumber is delivered late, you miss a connection at the airport, or there is an accident on the job site. So you cannot really count on its taking exactly 4.5 weeks to accomplish a certain task, for in real life it might take as long as 6.0 weeks or as little as 4.0 weeks.

This introduction to PERT is very basic and merely hints at its possibilities. Even so, however, this should make it clear to you that PERT is a powerful planning tool that can be used to simplify and modify very complicated schedules to provide a satisfactory solution within time and budget constraints.

Rule 63: Use the Inventory Model

If your plan involves buying and stocking resources, you may be able to make good use of the inventory model. The inventory model relates demand and production so that you can determine how much inventory of a particular item you should hold. This is important because holding inventory is costly in terms of rent on a supply room or warehouse and pay for people to tend the inventory stocks. You would like to maintain as little inventory as possible, but you always

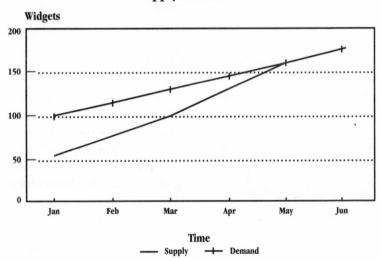

Supply & Demand

want enough so that you do not lose sales because you are out of an item wanted by a customer. The chart on the preceding page shows sample demand and supply curves for an item.

Demand is the number of items you want to have at a given time. For commercial applications this is your sales forecast. For military applications it is the number needed to equip the forces and replace losses incurred in combat. Your object is to meet the stated demand.

Supply is the sum of the number of items you already have in inventory and the number you will produce or will receive from the manufacturer in the future.

This supply and demand figure could represent the six-month sales and supply projections for a widget-manufacturing company. The recently rejuvenated sales force has projected sales of widgets as shown by the demand line. The plant manager says that production of widgets can be increased as shown on the supply line.

Demand exceeds supply, and the company will not have sufficient widgets to fill orders for the first four months until supply can be increased to meet demand. You may lose sales to some of your competitors because you cannot fill the orders promptly. A solution to this problem is to maintain an inventory of widgets in your warehouse and use these to fill orders until production can be increased. The amount of inventory needed is equal to the area between the supply and demand curves—115 widgets in the figure.

The purpose of keeping items in inventory (stock) is to ensure that you will not lose sales, delay projects, or degrade performance because you have insufficient items to meet the demand. The difference between demand and supply (the shortfall) is the number of additional items you need to have to eliminate the shortfall. You may reconcile a shortfall by increasing your inventory, increasing your orders from production, reducing demand, or implementing some combination of these actions.

If supply exceeds demand, this indicates you either have too many items already in inventory or have ordered more items from production than you need. You may sell some items to reduce your inventory, cut back on your orders, or implement some combination of these actions.

The best solution to a shortfall depends on the relative costs of buying items ahead of time and holding them in inventory versus buying them only when needed. The latter option is complicated by the lead time of the item—the time that elapses from the placement of the order until the item is delivered and in your hands ready to sell. Another factor is a reduction in unit price of the item because you purchase it in large quantities. These three factors—inventory carrying costs, lead time, and unit price of the item from the manufacturer—are related in the inventory model.

The inventory model is used to compute several important planning numbers: the economic order quantity, the reorder point, and the safety stock level.

The economic order quantity (EOQ) is the number of items that offer the least total annual cost for ordering and holding inventory. Ordering costs refer to the work necessary to place an order, not the cost of the items ordered. They include the salaries of the people who formulate, process, and pay for the order. Carrying costs include rent and utilities for storage space, salaries for people to take care of the inventory, losses from stocks that become too old to sell, and interest foregone on the money spent for the items in inventory. Generally, the economic order quantity occurs for the number of annual reorders at which the annual carrying cost equals the annual ordering cost.

The reorder point is the inventory level (number of items on hand) that triggers an order for another EOQ of the item. The reorder point is the product of the number of sales (uses) of the item per day and the lead time in days. If you forecast sales of fifty items a day, and it takes ten days to receive an order after you place it, you need to place a new order when your inventory hits five hundred (50 x 10) items.

The safety stock level is the number of additional items to be held in inventory to cover uncertainties in lead time and fluctuations in demand so that there will never be a situation in which there are no items to sell. Stock outages occur because sales are greater than expected after you have reached the reorder point or because the lead time is greater than expected. These possibilities may occur for a variety of reasons, and you hedge against them by buying extra inventory. Safety stocks increase storage costs but decrease the costs of lost sales. The ideal safety stock level minimizes the carrying costs of the inventory and also the costs of lost sales, but these objectives are somewhat at odds. The methods for deriving a safety stock level use probabilities based on historical trends in supplier reliability and the manner in which sales have fluctuated. These are beyond the scope of this book but can be learned from most business management texts.

Proper application of the inventory model requires that you know at all times both the number and the sales history of each item you have in your inventory. If you have calculated reorder points for each item, a resupply order will be placed whenever a reorder point is reached, and you will have some assurance of a reasonable balance between carrying too much inventory and not enough. This is why so much attention is paid in grocery stores and other retail outlets to inventory, and why electronic cash registers that both ring up the price and enter an inventory change report are so useful to these stores.

My advice is that if you are involved in planning for a business that keeps an inventory of items for sale or as components of products you manufacture, you need to learn a lot more about inventory and production models.

Rule 64: Calculate the Expected Value of Future Events

Another powerful planning tool is the concept of calculating the expected value of future events. This concept is somewhat counter-intuitive but can help you decide how to treat in the planning process events that you believe are possible but not likely. Expected value is the product of the probability of an event and its value (or cost).

Probability is an expression of your belief about the extent to which a future event is likely to happen. The idea is both simple and complicated. We all understand that some future events are more likely to happen than others, and we have words to describe various degrees of likelihood. Some of these common terms and a possible (!) numerical probability-rating scheme for them are shown in the following figure.

Common Terms for Probability

Expression	The Event	Probability
Certain	Will happen	100%
Probable	Is likely to happen	60%
Possible	May happen	40%
Impossible	Will not happen	0%

The only two points on this scale that are really valid are for certainty and impossibility. All of the words and numbers in between are highly subjective and difficult to define. Nevertheless, we use these words frequently in our daily lives and in our planning. We are all familiar with the predictions of the weatherpeople: A 50 percent chance (probability) of rain means that it is just as likely to rain as it is not to rain, and a 90 percent chance of rain is enough to warrant taking our umbrellas to work, while a 10 percent chance is insufficient to cancel plans for the picnic. We even apply probability in our planning to the extent that we project the likelihood that a supplier will be late in a delivery and allow for that in the schedule, or we add 15 percent to the estimated cost because we know there is a chance that the items we need will require paying a premium price. It is also possible to think of probability in mathematical terms, and this is taught as part of statistics courses. So we are fairly comfortable with the idea of probability and its application to our lives and plans.

If we combine the probability of an event with its consequences, we go beyond what most of us are comfortable with, because this leads us to conclusions that are sometimes different from our original conclusions.

The expected value is the product of the probability of an event and its value. The next figure illustrates what this means with an example of pari-mutuel betting on a horse race. The table shows your estimated probability of winning and the payoff for a $2 ticket for three horses in the eighth race.

The Eighth Race at Upsan Downs

Horse	Probability of Winning	$2 Ticket Payoff
Goldenrod	60%	$ 4
Dahlia	30%	$ 20
Azalea	10%	$120

Which horse do you bet on to win? Is it Goldenrod, the favorite? Or Azalea, the long shot? If we calculate the expected value of your winnings, you will have a better idea of how to bet. The next figure includes the calculated expected value for each horse.

The Eighth Race at Upsan Downs

Horse	Probability of Winning	$2 Ticket Payoff	Expected Value
Goldenrod	60%	$ 4	$ 2.40
Dahlia	30%	$ 20	$ 6.00
Azalea	10%	$120	$12.00

The correct answer according to the expected values is to bet on the long shot, Azalea. If your probabilities are correct, your best long-term strategy is to bet on horses whose combinations of probabilities and payoffs are highest. Of course, most of us don't do that at all and persist in betting on the favorite and losing at the track because we don't win enough when we do win to cover our losses in the other races. Thus, expected values often lead to results contrary to our normal impulses.

The expected value approach can provide a way to allocate resources to hedge against unlikely but possible events. The table on the next page shows the probability that bad weather will hamper construction on a housing development and the number of extra days it would take to complete the work under different weather conditions.

	No Rain	Light Rain	Heavy Rain	Downpour
Probability	10%	40%	40%	10%
Extra Days	0	10	50	200
Expected Value	0	4	20	20

In this case, the expected values reveal that the consequences (costs) of rainy weather are great enough to warrant putting forty-four "extra" days—the sum of the expected value for each weather category—into the original schedule as a hedge. Although this increases the cost of the project, it would be better to do this in the plan than to have unplanned delays if the heavy rains do occur. If we had not used expected value, we might still have allowed for rain days, but fewer than the forty-four indicated by this approach.

Expected value has also been applied to the problem of allocating funds to prepare for emergencies. The everyday emergencies that occur frequently have a tendency to attract attention and funds because they are imminent and urgent. But the adverse consequences of less likely but larger emergencies, such as catastrophic earthquakes, are so great that their expected value costs are high enough to warrant allocating some of the available funds to prepare for such emergencies. The same thing applies to preparations for war, another unlikely event whose consequences are so great as to warrant some investment for preparedness.

My advice is to appreciate at least the ideas behind expected value judgments. The extent to which you can use this concept depends on your confidence in your ability to estimate the probabilities of future events and your willingness to take a long-term viewpoint.

Rule 65: Add Some Game Theory

Some aspects of game theory have already been covered in Rules 57 and 61. This rule is intended to provide only a general introduction to this fascinating—but complicated—area.

A game is a conflict over time between two or more people or groups. Sometimes there are established rules, more or less understood and followed by the players, but sometimes there are no rules or the rules are unknown to the players. In planning for a project involving several groups with different goals and viewpoints, it may be helpful to treat the situation as a game. Game theory is an explanation of human behavior in games, and attempts to formulate some general approaches that can be useful in the planning process.

Almost all people play games or have played games. Childhood games provide lessons in following rules and competing. Parlor games and card games are ways that we can compete with others in an organized but nonthreatening way. Game players recognize that it does not take long to learn how to play the game to maximize the chances of winning. You learn how to operate within the rules and in light of human nature to give yourself an advantage.

Some people are better at playing games than others. Champion bridge players, chess masters, and professional Monopoly players win more than their fair share of games that ought to be matters of mere chance. This is because they understand and apply the rules of the games to their advantage. They are witting users of game theory.

Game theory is well developed for two-player, zero-sum games, and elegant mathematical solutions have been derived for these and for larger games. The treatment is based on logic, assuming that each player wants to win and will use a strategy believed to lead to victory. In the mathematical treatments, it is assumed that the players are equal in intelligence and ability and that each knows the outcome of each possible strategy. Based on these assumed conditions, the theory states some rules of behavior a player can use to improve his or her chances of winning.

The results of game theory have not been very useful directly for planning because they seldom fit real life. Most games in life have more than two players—you, the competition, the public, the government, and other interested or influential players. Many real situations are not really zero-sum games, because both sides may gain something—although less than desired. Game theory is based on the assumption that players have full information, and this is seldom the case in real life. Finally, the assumption that a player frequently changes strategy is seldom true in real life, where the tendency is to stick to a chosen strategy for a fairly long time.

So it is unlikely that game theory will have a big payoff for you in terms of predictions of specific payoffs for one strategy over others—there are too many uncertainties for that. Some reference to game theory, however, can provide insights that, when added to other facts, may lead you to select one strategy instead of another. Thus, despite some disadvantages, game theory can be a good basis for planning when the actions of another person or group are important to your own progress. Even if you do nothing more than consider the likely reactions of others to your plans, you will have improved your planning process. Game theory offers you an opportunity to consider the reactions of others in a systematic manner.

My advice is to incorporate into your planning process the recognition that there are ways to play the game that will improve your chances of winning. If you want to learn more about how to do so, you should learn more by reading books about game theory.

Rule 66: Use a Venn Diagram

Sometimes things get so complicated that it is useful to try to figure out how the different pieces of your planning puzzle fit—or don't fit—together.

A helpful tool with a funny name is a Venn diagram, named after the inventor, John Venn (1834–1923), a British logician who sought to simplify logic and set theory. Venn and his colleagues used these diagrams to work in Boolean algebra, but they can also be used to get a better idea of how things relate in the planning process.

A Venn diagram is basically a way to visualize how different sets relate to one another. A set, or class, is a group of members (events, people, things) distinguished by a particular condition or conditions for membership. Set theory is a valuable branch of mathematics and logic, and I have been told that young children now are introduced to it in elementary school.

The concept of a set is useful in planning, for it allows you to concentrate on a single aggregation or group of members with the same attributes, instead of looking at each individual member.

There are many different sets. There is a set of left-handed plumbers comprising all plumbers who are left-handed. There is a set of tools in your toolbox comprising all tools in the toolbox. There is a set of airlines with flights from Miami to Los Angeles. There is a set of hardware stores that carry a particular brand of paint. The number of sets that can be defined is limited only by your imagination and patience, plus the needs of the planning process. In fact, there is an infinite variety of sets, because you get to define them the way that makes the most sense to you.

In the vernacular, a set goes beyond merely aggregating members with identical characteristics to imply that the members fit together in some useful or logical way. The tool set mentioned above, for example, does not consist of several copies of identical tools but of one copy each of several different kinds of tools that complement one another to do a certain kind of work. This is consistent with the definition, because each different tool is admitted to membership in the group by contributing its unique capability to the set.

More frequently than you like, you will have problems relating different groups of things that influence your planning process.

The following illustration of how a Venn diagram works uses the example of a businessperson who has been offering three different product lines—A, B, and C—but wants to eliminate one because of storage space limitations. Since this is a savvy businessperson who understands the importance of feedback, a survey of customer prefer-. erence has been conducted for the three product lines. The survey nets the following responses from 500 customers:

Product A	**Product B**	**Product C**
350	250	150

The initial impulse from the survey is to eliminate Product Line C, because the fewest customers indicated their preference for that product line. But wait a minute! The tabulated responses add up to 750 answers—250 more than the number of customers who responded. It appears that a large number of those rascally customers indicated a preference for more than one product line. This situation is shown in the Venn diagram below.

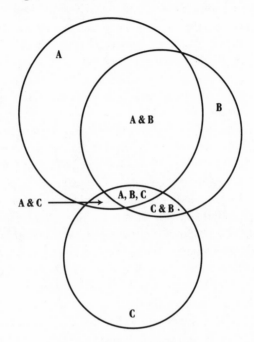

Three sets are involved: customers who prefer A, customers who prefer B, and customers who prefer C. These three sets overlap, however, because some of the members of the A set are also members of the B set, the C set, or both. There are seven possible areas: three groups of people who indicated a preference for only one product, three possible combinations of people who indicated a preference for two products, and one group of people who indicated a preference for all three products. This is shown clearly on the Venn diagram.

Going back to the responses, it is possible to tabulate the multiple answers into those seven areas as follows:

A	A & B	B	B & C	C	C & A	A,B,C
160	150	40	30	80	10	30

When these responses are indicated on the Venn diagram, the result is as shown in the accompanying figure.

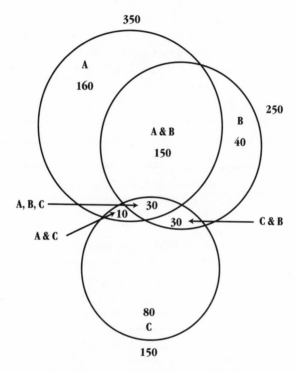

Some of you may be able to grasp the significance of this more refined set of responses right away, but for the rest of us the diagram helps. Even though this particular diagram is not to scale, the virtue of the Venn diagram is that it shows clearly the relationship of these three customer preference sets and allows us to make informed use of the data to achieve a correct solution, which is to drop Product B rather than Product C because the number of customers in the B set showing a preference for some other product as well is 210, while the number of customers in the C set who would be satisfied with another project is only 70. Thus, 140 more members of the B set would tend to switch to either A or C products if Product B were dropped. Looking at it another way, the number of customers who indicated a preference for only Product B is 40, while the number who indicated a preference for only Product C is 80, so dropping Product B will lose fewer customers.

Another common use of a Venn diagram is simply to show how different sets relate when some entities belong to one or more sets but not all. The Venn diagram below was used to show how the nations of Europe fit into three major organizations: the North Atlantic Treaty Organization, the European Community, and the Western European Union.* It would be possible to show the same relationships with words or lists, but the Venn diagram makes it very clear who belongs to what.

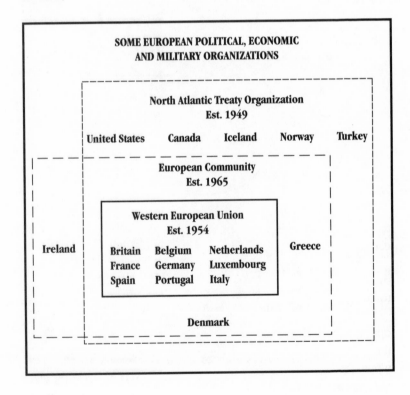

SOME EUROPEAN POLITICAL, ECONOMIC
AND MILITARY ORGANIZATIONS

North Atlantic Treaty Organization
Est. 1949

United States   Canada   Iceland   Norway   Turkey

European Community
Est. 1965

Western European Union
Est. 1954

Britain	Belgium	Netherlands
France	Germany	Luxembourg
Spain	Portugal	Italy

Ireland   Greece

Denmark

---

* From *The American Sentinel,* September 20, 1992, p. 5.

A Venn diagram is just a special kind of picture that can help you visualize your planning problems and clarify how things and sets of things relate.

Rule 67: Consider the Present Value of Money

One of the ways you can discriminate among various alternatives for investing your money is to calculate the present value of money. This is the final rule in the advanced concepts chapter because—to me at least—it is very advanced.

Present value is the converse of inflation, which was considered in Rule 52. The effect of inflation is that money loses its value over time because prices increase. The effect of present value, however, is that money will be more valuable in the future, provided you invest it so that it earns interest or some other form of a return on the investment. The definition of expected values is as follows:

> The present value of an amount that is expected to be received at a specified time in the future is the amount which, if invested today at a designated rate of return, would cumulate to the specified amount.*

The present value of $1,000 invested for a year at 6 percent interest is $943.40. This is the amount that at 6 percent interest would earn $56.60 to reach a value of $1,000 in a year.

Most investments pay off over several years, and the projected stream of earnings from each alternative investment can be discounted to give an expected value for each alternative investment.

The critical factor in calculating the present value of an investment opportunity is the selection of an interest rate. Since rates change from time to time, it is possible that calculations made at the start of a project would be invalid later on.

---

* Robert N. Anthony and James S. Reece, *Management Accounting* (Homewood, Ill.: Richard D. Irwin, Inc., 1975), p. 614.

For those who are interested, the formula for the present value of N dollars to be received in n years with interest rate i is:

$$\frac{N}{(1 + i)^n}$$

Rather than calculate present values, however, you can use published tables for various interest rates and years over which the payoff is expected. These tables can be found in economics or accounting texts.

One way to appreciate (if not understand completely) the impact of present value is to consider how it affects those sweepstakes that are used to solicit your purchase of magazines, books, videos, audio cassettes and compact discs, and other miscellaneous products. The sweepstakes letter always says you are going to be a millionaire, and that you have won $5,000,000 provided your number matches the number selected in a random drawing. You know the drill.

The fine print is that if you win, you will receive the grand prize of $5,000,000 in thirty equal payments of $166,667 each. What is the catch?

Well, the catch is that the present value of thirty payments of $166,667 is much less than $5,000,000. While the sum of the payments will total to $5,000,000, the present value will be only $2,294,171 if you use a discount rate of 6 percent, or $1,571,320 if the discount rate is 10 percent. Thus, the company has only to invest the lesser present value amount to be able to pay you the grand prize, and you will not get a full present value of $5,000,000. Though this might be disappointing, my advice is to accept the grand prize if you win it. Even $1,571,320 is better than nothing.

Using the present value approach can be helpful when you consider investing money on capital goods, equipment, or other resources that will pay a return to you over a period of several years. While many business planners do not use present value estimates because they are so heavily dependent on forecasting a future interest rate, others say that it is better to do the calculations and then make a choice than to simply ignore the present value of money.

12   Project Planning

Project planning is one of the great inventions of the twentieth century, just as double-entry bookkeeping was one of the great inventions of the fourteenth century. These kinds of intellectual achievements appear so simple (once they have been discovered) that they seldom attain the fame accorded to mere mechanical inventions, such as the light bulb, telephone, radio, television, computer, and pogo stick. They are, however, just as important.

Project planning is a systematic method for scheduling work to be performed. It was applied initially for construction and engineering jobs, such as building bridges, roads, houses, and large structures, but it has been applied also to the manufacturing and service industries. Project planning makes possible the astounding feat of preparing and providing several thousand high-quality fast-food meals a day, the construction of a huge jet airliner, and the operation of a vast transportation industry that moves millions of people each day with little disruption or danger.

Corollary One to the Elephant Rule (Rule 6) says that when eating an elephant, it is inefficient and even undignified simply to start gnawing away; it is necessary to identify the order in which one goes

181

about taking bites. Which bite do you take first? The trunk? The tail? An ear? The order in which you plan to eat your elephant is important, because it determines the bites you will take and chew first, second, third, and so on until the entire elephant is eaten. If you have several teams of elephant eaters assigned to the project, consuming the elephant will require coordinating their respective biting areas on various parts of the elephant: a trunk team, a left side team, a right rear leg team, and so on. This will allow the elephant to be eaten faster but requires you to coordinate the biting and chewing processes so that all of the teams finish at the same time.

This chapter will use as an illustration the job of painting a room. This is a commonplace chore that many of you will attempt at some time, and it can benefit from some common sense. The rules follow the planning steps for a couple named Carol and George to paint their bedroom: breaking down the job into tasks, assigning times and costs to the tasks, assigning responsibility, defining the relationships among the tasks, establishing the schedule, and refining the plan. By the end of this chapter, you will be able to paint a bedroom, and you might even be able to apply these principles to something larger.

Rule 68: Break the Work into Tasks

The first step in project planning is to break down the work into tasks. This is done a step at a time. There are two general approaches: top-down and bottom-up. Either approach will work, but don't try to do both simultaneously or you might end up somewhat confused.

For the room-painting project, the top-down approach appears to be easier and more natural than the bottom-up approach. This means you look at the whole thing and then break it down into logical major tasks. Many times the initial breakdown into major tasks will be readily apparent, particularly if you have experience in the kind of project you are planning. Sometimes, however, you may find that this first step is a difficult one, and you may feel like the first-time golfer hitting the ball off the first tee in front of all the old hands: afraid that you will make a fool of yourself. In this case, you just have to do it, knowing that you may have to go back later and revise your first cut.

If you are at a loss to identify the major tasks, start with the parts of a story: beginning, middle, and end. That translates as preparing, doing, and finishing up. There will always be a preparation phase or task, and there will usually be a finishing-up phase. The doing phase may be split up into several major tasks.

Most of you have had some experience in painting and will recognize that there are three basic parts to the job: preparation, painting, and cleanup. It is often said that preparation is the most important part of painting, and all of us who have ever hired a painter (or plumber, electrician, or other kind of home handyman) understand well the importance of cleaning up. Let us accept the three major tasks for painting a bedroom to be as follows:

1. Preparation
2. Painting
3. Cleanup

The next step is to take each of the major tasks in turn and break it down into tasks and then subtasks. What needs to be done in preparation for painting? Well, one obvious thing is to obtain the paint and other supplies needed for the job. Another more or less obvious task is to protect the contents of the room—furniture, rugs, clothes, and bric-a-brac—from paint. Less obvious, unless you are an experienced painter, is the necessity of taking down pictures, fixtures, curtains, and curtain rods; taking off doorknobs, locks, and electrical and telephone outlet plates; and removing all nails and hanging hardware from the walls. Once you have taken the nails out, it is a good idea to fill up the nail holes with putty or Spackle before painting. Depending on the condition of the room, it might also be necessary to putty up large holes or cracks before painting.

What else? Reviewing this unorganized list of things to be done indicates that two tasks have been omitted—one important and the other critical. It would be a good idea to clean the room: vacuum the rug and wash the walls and woodwork (trim). And most important—and most difficult—you need to select the color to paint the room.

The following is a list of those tasks considered for Major Task 1.

Major Task 1. Preparation
- Buy paint
- Buy other supplies
- Protect contents of room
- Remove hardware from walls
- Remove hardware from windows
- Remove hardware from doors
- Remove nails and hanger fixtures
- Fill up and putty or Spackle holes and cracks
- Buy putty or Spackle
- Wash walls and woodwork
- Select paint color

This is a mixed bag of tasks listed in the order they have been thought up, not in the order they should be done when implementing the plan. Some of the tasks need further breakdown, and others can be combined. Also, consideration has not yet been given to making the task list conform to the people (resources) available to do the work. This list of tasks can be revised to take into account timing, resources, and similarity. The revised task breakdown for Major Task 1, preparation, is as follows:

Major Task 1. Preparation
  Task 1.   Obtain supplies
     Subtask 1. Decide on paint color
              2. Make up bill of materials
              3. Buy paint
              4. Buy putty or Spackle
              5. Buy other supplies
  Task 2.   Protect contents of room
     Subtask 1. Remove pictures from wall
              2. Take curtains down and put in hall
              3. Move bric-a-brac to hall

4. Move furniture to center of room
5. Cover furniture with a cloth
6. Place drop cloths on floor

Task 3. Clean room
  Subtask 1. Wash walls
            2. Wash door
            3. Wash window frames
            4. Wash woodwork

Task 4. Prepare room for painting
  Subtask 1. Remove hardware
    Sub-subtask 1. Doorknobs and locks
                 2. Outlet plates
                    1. Electrical
                    2. Cable TV
                    3. Telephone
                 3. Door stops
                 4. Window locks
                 5. Other hardware
  Subtask 2. Remove nails and picture hangers
            3. Putty or Spackle holes

Now the second-order tasks and the third-order subtasks are listed in a general time sequence, and each is identified by a number, as shown by the very first subtask: Subtask 1.1.1. Decide on paint color.

Each task can be broken down into as much detail as seems appropriate to you. Sub-subtask 1.4.1.2. (Remove) Outlet plates, has been broken down to a fifth level to show the kind of detail that is possible. If you are a real stickler for detail, you can line everything up to the fifth level or beyond, but for most of us two or three levels of detail are enough, and for the rest of this example, only two levels of detail will be used to illustrate the process of planning a room-painting project.

Once the entire project has been broken down into tasks, the ordered list of major tasks and second-order tasks is as follows:

Major Task 1. Preparation

1. Obtain supplies
2. Protect contents of room
3. Clean room
4. Prepare room for painting

Major Task 2. Painting

1. Sand walls
2. Sand woodwork
3. Wash walls and woodwork
4. First coat walls
5. First coat woodwork
6. Resand walls
7. Resand woodwork
8. Wash walls and woodwork
9. Second coat walls
10. Second coat woodwork
11. Touchup

Major Task 3. Cleanup

1. Remove excess paint
2. Clean brushes
3. Clean room
4. Shampoo rug
5. Replace furniture and contents

These second-order tasks are what it takes to paint the room, and we will follow these through the project-planning process.

Rule 69: Estimate Times and Costs

Project planning involves the assignment of times and costs or resources to each primitive task. These may be aggregated carefully to achieve estimates of overall times and costs for second-order tasks, major tasks, and the entire project. This has to be done carefully because of the relationships between the tasks and the effects of having more than one person doing things in parallel.

In this example, the two painters—Carol and George—are the resources. This is standard project-planning procedure, and it indicates that the person named will either do the work or supervise a team doing the work. In either case, the resource person is responsible for getting that task done.

The next step is to go through the task list and list the number of hours you believe will be required to perform each task. This can be done based on experience with similar tasks, by careful analysis of each primitive task, or some combination of these approaches. At this point, you should tentatively assign a resource to each task. The

	Hours	Resource
Major Task 1. Preparation		
1. Obtain supplies	2	George
2. Protect contents of room	3	Carol
3. Clean room	2	Carol
4. Prepare room for painting	4	George
Major Task 2. Painting		
1. Sand walls	2	George
2. Sand woodwork	1	George
3. Wash walls and woodwork	1	Carol
4. First coat walls	3	George
5. First coat woodwork	4	Carol
6. Resand walls	2	George
7. Resand woodwork	1	George
8. Wash walls and woodwork	1	Carol
9. Second coat walls	3	George
10. Second coat woodwork	4	Carol
11. Touchup	1	Geo&Carol
Major Task 3. Cleanup		
1. Remove excess paint	2	Carol
2. Clean brushes	1	George
3. Clean room	2	Carol
4. Shampoo rug	1	George
5. Replace contents of room	2	Geo&Carol

resource will be responsible for the task. This assignment is tentative because conflicts due to dependencies may require shifting resources around to reduce overall project time and cost.

This is our initial list of tasks, times, and resources. The hours total forty-two, but even if we were to simply go through the subtasks in sequence, the job would take more than forty-two hours because of delays and dependencies.

Rule 70: Schedule Each Major Task

Scheduling the tasks and subtasks in each major task involves considering the time dependencies between them. Some tasks and subtasks have to be finished before other tasks can be started. This time dependency is established by the logic of the tasks. For example, it is impossible to buy the paint until the color has been decided upon. Thus, it is necessary to finish Subtask 1.1.1. before starting Subtask 1.1.3. The room has to be ready before you can start painting, so you have to finish Task 1 before starting Task 2. Sometimes the next task can be started immediately, but sometimes a time delay is required. These kinds of prerequisite dependencies are usually readily apparent.

Some tasks can be done concurrently. For example, buying the supplies and cleaning the room can be done simultaneously provided you have enough people to do both at the same time, for there is no physical or logical reason why these two tasks cannot be performed concurrently.

The accompanying Gantt Chart, as explained in Rule 37, illustrates how this works for painting a room. In this chart, an x equals one hour, and # is used to denote a major or parent task. This is how the timing for Major Task 1 might look before some planning logic is applied:

Major Task 1. Preparation

1.1. Obtain supplies	George	xx
1.2. Protect contents of room	Carol	xxx
1.3. Clean room	Carol	xx
1.4. Prepare room for painting	George	xxxx

This chart lists the second-order tasks, the resources tentatively assigned to each task, and the estimated time to accomplish each task. The next step is to establish some simple relationships, resulting in the following Gantt Chart, which shows it would take eleven hours overall to accomplish Major Task 1 if every task were done consecutively.

Major Task 1. Preparation   ###########
1.1. Obtain supplies   George   xx
1.2. Protect contents of room   Carol   xxx
1.3. Clean room   Carol   xx
1.4. Prepare room for painting   George   xxxx

Some obvious improvements can be made. Tasks 1.1. and 1.2. can be done at the same time, for George can go to the hardware or paint store while Carol removes items from the room. The room should be cleared before we clean it, but that means that George is sitting around for an hour with nothing to do, so we might want to reassign George to do Task 1.3. instead of Carol and have him start Task 1.3. before Carol finishes Task 1.2. A revised plan that reduces the time for Major Task 1 to eight hours overall is shown below:

Major Task 1. Preparation   ########
1.1. Obtain supplies   George   xx
1.2. Protect contents of room   Carol   xxx
1.3. Clean room   George   xx
1.4. Prepare room for painting   George   xxxx

This schedule, however, means that Carol has nothing to do for five hours—one hour waiting for George to finish Task 1.3. and four hours while George does Task 1.4. Applying two resources to Task 1.4. could shorten the time even further. Looking at Task 1.4. in detail shows that George could remove hardware and nails, while Carol (who has an artistic temperament) follows him to putty the holes and cracks. Doing this allows Task 1.4. to be completed in three hours instead of the original estimate of four hours, and the revised schedule shown below takes only seven hours overall.

Major Task 1. Preparation   #######
1.1. Obtain supplies   George   xx
1.2. Protect contents of room   Carol   xxx
1.3. Clean room   George   xx
1.4. Prepare room for painting   Geo&Carol   xxx

This is a pretty good result. Carol still has an hour of slack time in which she is waiting for George to finish Task 1.3., but overall resource utilization is good, the work is to be done in a logical order, and the overall time for Task 1 has been reduced from eleven to seven hours.

Rule 71: Allow for Delays and Lead Times

Sometimes the time dependencies are more complicated than simply starting one task after another is finished: There has to be a delay between the end of one task and the start of another, or one task has to start a certain time before the end of another task so that the two tasks are completed at the same time. When Major Task 2, painting, is addressed, it is necessary to allow for delays while waiting for the paint to dry between coats.* A first try for a Major Task 2 schedule is as follows:

Major Task 2. Painting   #####################
2.1. Sand walls   George   xx
2.2. Sand woodwork   George   x
2.3. Wash walls and woodwork   Carol   x
2.4. First coat walls   George   xxx
2.5. First coat woodwork   Carol   xxxx
2.6. Resand walls   George   xx
2.7. Resand woodwork   George   x
2.8. Wash walls and woodwork   Carol   x
2.9. Second coat walls   George   xxx
2.10. Second coat woodwork   Carol   xxxx
2.11. Touchup   Geo&Carol   x

---

* Some painters declare that new, quick-drying paints make it unnecessary to wait for paint to dry between coats. I prefer to play it safe and wait.

Following this schedule, it would take twenty-three hours to complete all of these eleven tasks, because they would be done consecutively, starting each task immediately after the preceding one. Some tasks have to be delayed, however, to schedule the time it takes for the paint to dry. Even if both George and Carol worked together on sanding and one painted walls while the other painted woodwork, there is a problem. A revised schedule taking this into account follows.

Major Task 2. Painting   ##############################

2.1.	Sand walls	George	xx		
2.2.	Sand woodwork	Carol	x		
2.3.	Wash walls and woodwork	Carol	x		
2.4.	First coat walls	George	xxx		
2.5.	First coat woodwork	Carol	xxxx		
2.6.	Resand walls	George		xx	
2.7.	Resand woodwork	Carol		x	
2.8.	Wash walls and woodwork	Carol		x	
2.9.	Second coat walls	George		xxx	
2.10.	Second coat woodwork	Carol		xxxx	
2.11.	Touchup	Geo&Carol			x

The schedule above has reduced working time by assigning to Carol all of the woodwork tasks and using George on the walls. This permits some concurrent performance, so that the first coat can be done in seven hours. It is necessary, however, to wait eight hours for the first coat to dry before sanding to prepare for the second coat, so it will take thirty-one hours to complete the painting: twenty-two hours for two coats and another nine hours to complete the final touchup, allowing eight hours for the second coat to dry.

This process suggests that the task breakdown would benefit from some reorganization and simplification. All of the wall tasks are aggregated and assigned to George and all the woodwork tasks are given to Carol, while an explicit distinction is maintained between the first coat and the second coat. The task of washing after sanding has been broken down so that George washes the walls and Carol washes the woodwork. The revised breakdown of Major Task 2 is as follows:

Major Task 2. Painting
2.1. First coat
  2.1.1. Walls   George
     2.1.1.1. Sanding
     2.1.1.2. Painting
     2.1.1.3. Washing
  2.1.2. Woodwork   Carol
     2.1.2.1. Sanding
     2.1.2.2. Painting
     2.1.2.3. Washing
2.2. Second coat
  2.2.1. Walls   George
     2.2.1.1. Sanding
     2.2.1.2. Painting
     2.2.1.3. Washing
  2.2.2. Woodwork   Carol
     2.2.2.1. Sanding
     2.2.2.2. Painting
     2.2.2.3. Washing
2.3. Touchup   Geo&Carol

Revising the task breakdown makes it possible to use a simplified schedule for Major Task 2 as follows:

Major Task 2. Painting ##############################
2.1. First Coat Geo&Carol xxxxxxx
2.2. Second Coat Geo&Carol   xxxxxxx
2.3. Touchup   Geo&Carol   x

This schedule allows eight hours of drying time between the first coat and the second coat and another eight hours after the second coat until the final, touchup task. Painting requires thirty-one hours all together.

A reasonable Gantt Chart for the final task, cleanup, is shown below. Once again, the time to do the work has been shortened by reassigning resources and scheduling some tasks concurrently. In this case, Task 3.2. is scheduled ahead of 3.1. because George is a fanatic about clean brushes, and he can move on to removing paint from the windows without delaying Carol's cleaning. This schedule also allows eight hours for the rugs to dry after George shampoos them. The overall time for this major task is now fourteen hours.

Major Task 3. Cleanup   ##############

3.1. Remove excess paint	George	xx
3.2. Clean brushes	George	x
3.3. Clean room	Carol	xxx
3.4. Shampoo rug	George	x
3.5. Replace contents	Geo&Carol	xx

A Gantt Chart showing the entire project after it has been revised and scheduled is shown on page 194. The total time to do the work for all three tasks is fifty-two hours, or six and one-half days.

Rule 72: Make the Project Plan Relevant

The final step is to make the project plan relevant to your needs. In the bedroom-painting example, the project is complicated further because both George and Carol have full-time jobs, and they are able to paint the bedroom only on weekends. This is all right, however, because project planning shows them how to approach the job efficiently. The Gantt Chart on page 195 shows how the work for each task can be assigned to a specific day by specifying the number of hours for each task on each day. In this case, it works out very well for the painting project.

PROJECT: PAINT BEDROOM

Task 1.	**Preparation**		#######		
1.1.	Obtain supplies	George	xx		
1.2.	Protect contents	George	xxx		
1.3.	Clean room	Carol	xx		
1.4.	Prepare room	Geo&Carol	xxx		
Task 2.	**Painting**			#############################	
2.1.	First coat	Geo&Carol		xxxxxxx	
2.2.	Second coat	Geo&Carol		xxxxxxx	
2.3.	Touchup	Geo&Carol			x
Task 3.	**Cleanup**				###############
3.1.	Remove paint	George			xx
3.2.	Clean brushes	George			x
3.3.	Clean room	Carol			xxx
3.4.	Shampoo rug	George			x
3.5.	Replace contents	Geo&Carol			xx

	First Weekend		Second Weekend		
	Sat	**Sun**	**Sat**	**Sun**	**Mon**
Major Task 1. Preparation	7				
Major Task 2. Painting					
Task 2.1. First Coat		7			
Task 2.2. Second Coat			7		
Task 2.3. Touchup				1	
Major Task 3. Cleanup				4	2

The final plan is for George and Carol to spend the first Saturday preparing the room and obtaining supplies and that Sunday putting the first coat on the walls and woodwork. They will wait until the following Saturday to put on the second coat, and the room can then be cleaned up and the rug shampooed on Sunday. Then George and Carol can put the furniture and contents back after work on Monday when the rug is dry, and the job is done. True, they will have to sleep in the spare bedroom for a week, but that is a mild inconvenience for having a brand new paint job in their bedroom.

There are a multitude of other considerations that are unique to each particular project, and one useful benefit of project planning is that each of these special considerations can be worked into your schedule if you follow the logic of the planning system faithfully. Another satisfactory schedule could have been made if George and Carol had decided to take a week off from work to paint the bedroom. Can you work that schedule out for yourself?

Don't let the mechanics of the process get you down. You can do your project planning freehand with pencil and paper, or you can use one of the many software programs that help you do the planning. I did this one using a word-processing program on my computer to show you that it can be done. For larger projects, however, I use special project-planning software that does a lot of the formatting, displays, dependencies, and aggregations more or less automatically. Learning these computer programs is hard, but once you master them, they make project planning really easy.

The purpose of this chapter has been to expose you to the possibilities of project planning. While you may be able to paint your bedroom without going through all of the steps shown above, you might have done a better job more efficiently if you had done so. Certainly, you need this kind of tool for larger projects. If you do not approach a project in a systematic, logical manner, the time to do the job and the cost of the job are likely to be greater than necessary. Project planning offers a way to make things happen without wasting time or money.

13 Business Planning

One of the American dreams is to own one's own business. Whether this is a good idea or not seldom occurs to those hardy and hopeful entrepreneurs who start a small business. They dream of self-reliance and freedom from bureaucratic bungling, when in reality all they have done is take on the toughest boss of all—themselves.

The owners of small businesses may not have to please bosses, bigger bosses, and biggedy bosses up the line, but ultimately they have to please their customers—or fail. So owning your own business is no panacea, and it can benefit from some advice.

From my own experience, I can tell you that nothing impels you to work so hard as the knowledge that your income depends on it. When you own your own business, in reality it owns you. You work longer hours and with more intensity than is even conceivable

197

for corporate or government employees. And for this, the rewards fortunately are also great. You do feel a sense of satisfaction and you do have fun, and sometimes you make some money too.

This chapter is dedicated to owners of small businesses, who have to plan how to conduct their businesses and often have to prepare plans in order to obtain the loans or equity financing enabling them to start up the businesses. Specifically, the subject is that thing called a "business plan."

All of the planning rules presented earlier in this book apply to business plans, and there are also some special rules included in this chapter. Business plans primarily are designed to attract funding, but the best business plans are those based on your real intentions of how to run the business and make a profit. If you prepare one business plan for the business and another business plan for investors, you are doing both a disservice. The best thing is to prepare an honest plan and then use it to attract money. If it doesn't attract money, your plan is likely to be faulty, although the converse is not necessarily true. Even a great plan cannot turn a defective business concept into a winner. A good plan does not guarantee success, but in my opinion it is the necessary basis for any success in business. This chapter is intended to help you prepare a business plan for your concept, without prejudice to the concept.

Rule 73: Explain What You Are Going to Do

The first essential ingredient of a business plan is a simple explanation of what you are going to do. Many business plans provide copious numbers and detailed projections in numerous tables and exhibits, but without ever saying what it is that the business will offer in the way of products or services.

The absence of a clear, concise statement of the business concept indicates that the entrepreneurs really do not know what they want to do. No business idea should be so complicated that it cannot be stated in a paragraph. If it takes twenty single-spaced pages of text to explain the business, it is probably too complicated to be workable. Granted, those are my prejudices, but I am confident that they are shared by most people who are being asked to invest in or loan money to a business.

Your explanation has to be written in plain American English with a notable absence of jargon or technical terms, because it has to be read by people whose sole qualification may be that they have money to make available to you. They may be technically qualified in your business area, but that would be a bonus. You have to convince these potential angels that what you are doing makes sense.

This is not always easy, and the process of boiling down your inchoate scheme to a paragraph or (at maximum) a page may force you to rethink the concept. What, exactly, are you going to make? What service, exactly, are you going to provide? How are you going to do this? To whom are you going to sell the product or service? How are you going to market the product or service? These are the essential elements of your concept.

You may also wish to insert some information that tells the reader just why you think you can make this product or offer this service in such a way as to be profitable. What special experience or qualifications do you have for this business? What is the special new idea or procedure that will give you an edge over the competition? Will your costs and prices be lower? Will your quality be higher? Or will your marketing scheme be so much better that you can make a profit?

In general, three factors influence sales of a product or service: price, quality, and marketing. Contrary to popular belief, marketing—or advertising—cannot over the long run promote sales of an inferior product; it can only stimulate sales of a satisfactory product. There are obvious trade-offs among these three elements. Low-quality products imply low prices, while high-quality products imply high prices, and both require appropriate marketing. The trick, of course, is to provide high quality at a low price—easy to say, hard to do. You have to decide on the mix of price, quality, and advertising that will enable your business to generate sufficient sales to cover expenses and taxes plus make a profit for you and your backers. That mix has to be stated in your business concept.

Astute readers will have noticed that this is the same advice covered in some detail for all planning in chapter 1: You are asked to think about what you want to do and how you want to do it, and then write a concept paper explaining it. For a business plan, this initial step requires more than ordinary care, for it will play a large role in determining whether you will obtain the funding you need to start or expand your business.

Once you have laid out the business plan, you need to consider both future costs and future income, and initially at least this should be done separately.

Rule 74: Check Out the Competition and the Market

Unless you have an absolute lock on a particular product or service by means of a patent or a territorial franchise, there will be other businesses in your area of operations offering the same or similar things. That is, you will be competing with some others.

Competition is good news and bad news. The bad news is that if a lot of other businesses are competing with you, you will have to fight hard to capture some share of the market. The good news is that having a large number of competitors indicates that there is a market for that product or service.

In order to beat the competition, you will have to do one or more of the following four things: charge less, provide higher quality, advertise better, or out-hustle. Charging less is difficult for a given level of quality, and as the airlines have demonstrated amply in the past decade, can lead to difficulties for all. Gasoline price wars are fine for consumers but bad for operators of service stations and do not change market share very much. Lowering the price can be effective for a while, but long-term success depends on other factors, such as quality of service and good treatment of customers. Providing higher quality is good but tends to limit your market. If this is a deliberate marketing ploy, OK, but don't just hike up the quality without realizing that you are also hiking up your costs. Advertising or marketing can improve sales but also increases costs, so you have to balance the two. The final item—hustle—is entirely at your discretion. If you have the energy to work long hours at a fast pace, your chances of success will be good—particularly if the competition has grown fat and lazy and complacent.

My advice is to learn all you can about the competition before you even start up the business. It is not wise to open an Italian restaurant only to then find that there are three other Italian restaurants in the same neighborhood. If you had known this in advance, you might have opened a Mexican restaurant or moved your Italian restaurant to a different location free of close competition. If you are going to sell a widget, you should know ahead of time who else is selling widgets, what their widgets are like, and how much they cost. If you are offering a computer service, you need to know what other businesses offer the same service, how much they charge, and how many customers they have. There is at any point in time a limited market for any service, and you have to know the degree to which your potential market is already occupied by your competition.

No team in the National Football League would take the field on any given Sunday without having scouted out the opposing team. Much effort is taken to learn the strengths and weaknesses of the players on the other team, the plays they favor, the defenses they use, and the way they play the game. Films are reviewed, scouting reports are received seriously, and scrimmages are held during which the third string plays the part of the adversaries. This is just good sense in football, and it is good sense in business, too.

If you find that there is no competition, you may rest for a short time until you consider why not. It is possible, but not likely, that your product or service is so new that there has not been time for competitors to get established. If this is so, and you truly are in on the ground floor, you should rejoice and count your blessings and profits. On the other hand, you might also want to consider that the reason no one is competing with you may be because there is no market for your product or service. There are few people selling wagon wheels because there are so few wagons on the road these days. So one thing you need to do is a market survey just to see if people will buy what you want to sell. This is so elementary and self-evident that I would not bring it up except that people start businesses every day without the faintest idea of the market or the competition. This, to say the least, is the epitome of poor planning and invariably leads to poor performance.

Rule 75: Project Your Income

The essence of a business plan is the projection of costs and income for several years into the future.* These figures will determine whether you will obtain financing, and that is strange, because they really are not very useful as far as predicting whether a business will succeed. These tables are called *pro formas* in the jargon of the funding world, and that means you are really doing it just to satisfy the formal requirement. It is barely possible to project costs with confidence, and it is very difficult to project income at all. Nevertheless, you will have to do this for your business planning, so you might as well do it the best possible way.

Your first decision is how far ahead you want to project your costs and income. Generally, you want to project far enough into the future for the income to exceed the costs and even show a cumulative profit. Investors like to see a business show a profit, even if it is only in some flaky tables in a business plan. New businesses generally lose money for the first few years, because the initial costs have to be amortized (paid off) before a profit is realized. The first encouraging step for a new business is to reach the crossover point at which current income exceeds current costs. After this point, assuming the business continues to prosper, the excess of income over costs can be used to pay off losses incurred before the crossover point. This continues until the cumulative income is sufficient to cover all the cumulative costs from start-up. After that, your business will really begin making money. For most small businesses, the crossover point can be reached in two years or less, and you can show a profit in three or four years. Generally, it is sufficient to project your costs and income for five years after the start-up.

---

* I had a hard time selecting the terms to signify money coming in and money going out. Some people use the terms "revenue" or "sales" for money coming in, and the term "expenses" is often used for money going out. There are probably subtle distinctions of which I am not aware, but I believe that "costs" and "income" are adequate for my purposes and will be understood by the reader.

All cost and income projections are based on assumptions about how many and what kind of resources are needed and how many and what kind of sales will occur. This is basically guesswork, but you can make it credible by stressing the tentative nature of the forecasts and exposing weak points (questionable assumptions) openly. As long as the logic is straightforward and you do not try to pull any fast ones, the projections will be accepted for what they are—educated guesses influenced by hope. Incidentally, it does not hurt to appear to be optimistic, but it does hurt to appear to be devious.

The really important part of a business plan is forecasting income. While you can price a piece of lumber or a word-processing person and have a reasonable basis for costs, there is no really solid basis for forecasting sales. This is true for a new business and particularly true for a new business introducing a new product or service. Business history is full of stories of products that did not sell (the Edsel, New Coke) for reasons that are still not clearly understood. Yet it is vitally important in preparing a business plan to provide reasonable, credible forecasts of income.

I have prepared several business plans and must confess that I have inserted income estimates that were essentially pulled out of thin air with little other than blind faith to support them; of course, I didn't get any funding for these plans either. I have also seen some business plans with income estimates that were reasonable enough to attract funding. The difference lies in making clear the nature of the basic assumptions upon which the income estimates are based. If you are offering a service at a certain price, show the number of customers you plan to serve each month and demonstrate that this number is a reasonable assumption based on circumstances for that particular service. The same thing goes if you are offering a product for sale: Simply demonstrate that the number of units you plan to sell each month can be achieved. Be conservative by understating what you believe you can accomplish, for it is better to overproduce than to fall short of your estimates.

A set of income projections based on fundamental, reasonable assumptions clearly laid out is a prerequisite for an effective business plan.

Rule 76: Project Your Costs

Costs may be projected in accordance with your plan of operations. The two key costs for businesses are labor and the initial investment in tools and machinery.

The initial investment should cover what you need to purchase in order to carry out the concept of your business. If you need to buy a computer, a truck, a building, or an airplane, list the costs of these items as initial capital outlays. Then add the labor required annually to operate the machinery and tools. Labor costs carry with them a lot of other expenses, such as insurance, payroll taxes, benefits, and in some cases overhead. So it is permissible to list the direct salaries you plan on paying and then augment them with a factor to take care of the other costs associated with labor. Don't forget to pay yourself a salary if it is your own business, and count your labor charges as a cost. Too many businesses have gone down the tubes early on because entrepreneurs are so eager to get into business that they fail to allow for their own pay.

Next, you need to list the costs for overhead: rent, telephones, attorneys, and the like. Finally, there is that cost category called "general and administrative costs" (G&A), which amounts to overhead on the overhead. Actually, overhead is supposed to be chargeable directly to a specific aspect or program of the business, while G&A is more general and covers whatever else is not. Investors hate overhead and G&A, so you should be as specific as you can about these costs, listing them under advertising, accountants, and executive salaries, or whatever they really are. Don't use overhead to try to hide items, such as entertainment, that you believe investors might not like. Simply list the items as clearly and as specifically as you can, and provide or have available backup rationale explaining in some detail how you arrived at the estimate for each cost item.

Projecting the costs before projecting the income is neither necessary nor desirable in the planning process. For one thing, you might be tempted to inflate your income projections once you see how large the costs are. For another thing, your costs will depend in great measure on your customers and sales. Therefore, I suggest you do income first and then estimate the costs needed to generate that income.

Rule 77: Explain How You Will Spend Your Capital

All businesses need capital to start up. The amount differs, and some business can get started with very little if the only input required is the blood, sweat, tears, and labor of the owner. But most businesses require some equipment, an office, a telephone, and other things to produce the goods or deliver the services offered for sale. Many businesses require large sums of money up front just to get started, and most of the up-front money has to be spent before a single widget is produced or a single service is delivered.

It is said that most small businesses fail because they are undercapitalized, and I believe that is true. Most entrepreneurs underestimate the capital they will need to get started and survive long enough to make a profit consistently. Few businesses do well enough to make money right away. As a result, there are many starters and few finishers, but those who fail one time often learn from their experience, try again, and ultimately succeed. One lesson most people learn from this experience is that they need substantial capital available to call on when sales do not come up to expectations or there are unanticipated problems in production.

So it is wise to ask your investors or creditors for more than you really need. This is ticklish because they are unlikely to be sympathetic to a funding request they consider to be wasteful, careless, or unduly luxurious. Nevertheless, most people with money have gone through the mill enough to understand at least that prudence calls for more capital instead of less.

The key to all of this is to tell your investors or creditors exactly what you intend to do with the money they are going to make available to you.

When you go to a bank for a loan, they want to know what you are going to do with the money. That request is more than just idle curiosity. If you intend to take the money and spend it on what they would consider to be foolishness—a wild party or a Hawaiian vacation—they probably would not approve the loan, figuring your ability to repay is not enhanced by your spending plan. (Credit card companies are indifferent to how you spend money, but they charge high interest and limit the amount you can use.) If, on the other hand, you intend to start a business, the loan officer will be more sympathetic because your purpose is to make more money, some of which will be used to repay the loan. So purpose is important.

I have already covered the basic elements of cost projections in Rule 76, but I want to reemphasize two points in the context of explaining how you will spend the initial capital.

First, you should be as specific as possible with prices, transportation charges, and all other costs connected with purchasing the initial equipment and supplies for the business. You should list the number, makes, and models of the equipment items you are going to buy. You should describe the office you intend to buy or lease, and also the terms of the lease. You should list the job titles and job content of the people you plan to hire, and you should be as specific as you possibly can be with overhead, furniture, and other necessary stuff. The people who are letting you use their money for your purposes deserve to be given complete information.

Second, you have to be open and aboveboard about soft items, such as your compensation, contingency reserves, and other special items. With respect to your own compensation, you have to judge whether you want to pay yourself what you are worth or something more. It is probably in good taste not to pay yourself great sums of money until after you have demonstrated a capacity to show a profit. In fact, you probably should pay yourself only the going rate or less for the first few years in the business. While you need to earn enough to live and support your family adequately, investors do not want to sustain you in a luxurious lifestyle. If you want to have a sum for contingencies, say so and set that amount aside openly. Do not try to hide it in overhead or some other catchall category. It would be a good idea to identify some downstream use for the contingency reserve in the case that the contingencies don't happen. Finally, you may want to spend some money on entertainment, lobbying, public relations, or other purposes that may be considered as nice to have but not essential. My advice, as always, is to be honest and identify these items for what they really are. Not only is this the right thing to do, but it precludes charges of false statements and fraud later on if things do not do well. Simply itemize all of these

items and be ready to explain them in greater detail if called upon
to do so.

You will find that in addition to helping you make a more credible
presentation to your sources of funds, the exercise will allow you to
understand better just how you should spend your capital to give
you the greatest chance for success.

Rule 78: Calculate Your Profits

Remember that your purpose is to make a profit for yourself and
your partners or shareholders. This is where gross and net come in.
Gross is great, but net is better.

There are many variations in terminology about profit and loss
and ways to calculate rates of return. To save time and controversy,
I am adopting the terminology used by the Internal Revenue Service
on Schedule C (Form 1040), Profit or Loss from Business.

Gross receipts or sales are aggregates of the money you receive
from sales of your goods or services. From this you have to subtract
any sums you paid out in returns or allowances and, most important,
the cost of the goods or services sold to generate the gross receipts.
The difference is your gross income.

Cost of sales includes the expenses of buying supplies, paying
workers, shipping goods, providing services, or any other part of your
business that can be attributed directly to the manufacture or purchase
of your products. This definition works well for businesses that make
something for sale or buy something wholesale to sell at retail, and
maintain an inventory of items. It does fairly well for a business that
offers a tangible service, such as a dry cleaner or a restaurant. It does
not do very well for a business that offers an intangible product, such
as consulting reports or books on how to plan. The key thought is
direct, and the test is whether the expense can be justified on the
basis that it goes *directly* to making the product or delivering the
service.

From gross income, it is necessary to pay for your expenses,
including advertising, general transportation, commissions and fees,
employee wages and salaries and benefits, legal and professional

services, office rent and costs, supplies, maintenance, general vehicles and equipment, travel and entertainment, insurance, state and local taxes, and interest on debt. These expenses cover overhead and general and administrative expenses not directly attributable to a product or service. With any luck, your gross income will be sufficient to cover all of these expenses, and therefore you will show a net profit.

Net profit in IRS terms is before payment of federal taxes, so those have to be computed and paid before you realize the real goody, which is the net profit after taxes.

Note that servicing the debt of the business by paying interest on loans is included in the expense before net profit is calculated. It is essential that you allow enough money to perform this debt servicing. In the 1980s many businesses borrowed a lot of money for expansion or takeovers on the assumption that sales would increase to cover the additional interest payments. In the 1990s many of these businesses were unable to pay the interest on their debts when revenues did not increase sufficiently, and either went into bankruptcy or simply went out of business. It is tempting to finance a start-up or expansion by borrowing money, but it is also risky.

Federal, state, and local taxes deserve considerable thought in your business planning. If you are a corporation, you will have to pay corporate taxes, and if you pay some profit to the shareholders in the form of dividends, they also will have to pay taxes on the dividends as income to them. If you have employees, you will have to pay FICA tax (Social Security and Medicare) for your employees (you pay half and the employee pays half), and you will have to pay federal and state unemployment tax and possibly some other taxes depending on where you are located. Localities and states make you pay for the privilege of doing business in their jurisdictions, and you had better check out their rates and practices before you settle in. If you are a sole proprietor, you will have to pay self-employment tax on your profits, and this consists essentially of both halves of the FICA tax.

You have to understand these tax burdens before you get into business, for they are really a problem. The rules and forms are so complicated that you will not be able to cope with them unaided and will have to hire a small-business accountant to help you. Of course, this costs more money, but it is a wise thing to do. Above all, you must pay your taxes on time. You might be able to slide a bit on some payments to suppliers, but you absolutely cannot fool around with the IRS. I once inherited a responsible management position in a small company where the departing office manager had failed to pay any bills for several months. I managed to straighten all of this out—except for the IRS. This person had simply not paid the payroll taxes for several months, and we were in default. Although I was honest, admitted fault, and promised to pay, I was treated like a criminal by an IRS agent. I normally have great sympathy for the IRS, which has the difficult job of collecting taxes from Americans, but this situation was really bad. I was humbled and humiliated, even as we were paying off the back taxes, penalties, and interest. I wasn't even the person who had made the mistake, but I certainly paid. The IRS even went after my personal money to pay the corporate taxes, and so I learned something about the true nature of limited liability.

I am not the only one who has learned this sort of lesson. One of the biggest mistakes made by small-business people is failing to make payroll tax payments. A great Mexican restaurant in our neighborhood failed despite good food and loyal clientele because the owner used the tax money for something else, and the IRS got him. My sincere advice is never to be late paying the taxes.

Once you have paid the federal taxes on your net profit, you finally have some real profits. You can do three things with net after-tax profits: reinvest in the business, pay a dividend to the shareholders, or reward yourself. Probably the best use of the profits is to finance expansion of your business. Buy the new computer you have been wanting, get six more delivery trucks, hire another salesman, build your own office building, or in some way add to your productive capacity. You will, however, be under some pressure from your investors to pay some of their investment back by declaring a dividend to the shareholders or partners. Generally speaking, companies that are widely and publicly owned pay something back to their shareholders as well as reinvesting. Companies that are closely held or privately owned tend to put most or all of the profits back into the business. If you have raised money from investors, it is likely that there is some prearranged repayment plan for them that constitutes an obligation for you to meet. Finally, you may wish to reward yourself for your faithful service by giving yourself a bonus to make up for the years of hard work at a subsistence-level salary. Divvying up the profits is a fun thing to do.

14   Helpful Hints

The rules and processes presented up to this point have been fairly pragmatic suggestions for practical planning. They are eminently useful but perhaps also a bit too pragmatic. After all, planning is inherently risky because it projects into an unknown future. Also, the plans themselves are not the product, although they can seem to be after you have worked on them for several weeks.

This chapter provides some helpful hints to supplement the good advice given elsewhere. These rules are a potpourri of various tidbits of sometimes impractical advice. They are designed to sharpen you up to produce a better plan than otherwise might be the case.

Rule 79: When in Doubt, Guess!

At times in your planning process you will run right smack up against a crunch point in what you know—or rather, what you don't know. No matter how thorough your search for the data has been or how comprehensive your coverage of the field has been, you will get to a point where you just don't know something you need to know in order to move along.

I find this happening to me when I am writing historical case studies. As I am writing a narrative, all of a sudden I come to a date or a name or a fact that I just don't know. What to do? One approach is to stop work and research the unknown fact right there and then, and commence work when the dubious point is satisfied. Another method is to mark the problem somehow and proceed with the work. I prefer the latter method, but unless you keep track of the inaccuracies, it is risky. My own marking method is to put an *X* in the text when I do not know something to be certain. My drafts have a lot of *X*s marking first names, dates, and numbers of various kinds of things. This is better than my previous practice, in which I would insert fake numbers when I was unsure of something and wanted my staff to react. I found that instead of checking the numbers out and giving me the right answers (which is what I wanted), they often took my fake numbers to be correct. I had to quit that after some of my fake numbers became "correct" through the process of bureaucratic blessing by usage.

So if you are stopped at some point in the planning process by something you just don't know, make a guess and write it in the spot, being careful to mark the spot for further attention when you have the time and inclination, and proceed on with the process.

There will also be times when you simply will not be able to find the correct answer no matter how hard you try, and my advice in these situations is to guess and get on with it.

Guessing implies inaccuracy, and that is true, but there are degrees of inaccuracy (see Rule 30), and you can probably do all right with a more or less scientific approach to guessing.

Given the tendency of people to generalize, you doubtless will not find it in the least strange that three classes of guesses have been established by common usage in the planning business, as was discussed in Rule 10. Although these were invented and are used more or less in jest, they also make good sense. In order of merit from bad to good, these are the wild-ass guess (WAG), the scientific wild-ass guess (SWAG), and the informed wild-ass guess (IWAG).

WAGs are genuine guesses—something you do when you really don't know anything about the issue. You can always improve your WAG, however, by some simple gaming techniques similar to those you used on multiple-choice questions during your academic years. Remember? The straight probability of getting the right answer from a guess on a multiple-choice question with four choices is 25 percent. That wasn't enough to pass, so you had to improve your chances by some artful test-taking skills. One way was to pick an obviously wrong answer and exclude it, thereby increasing your probability of guessing the right answer from the three remaining choices to 33 percent. Not much of a gain but worth the effort. Now the real gain occurred if you were able to eliminate two of the choices as being obviously wrong; then you could improve your chances of picking a right answer from the two remaining choices to 50 percent, and that was good enough, when combined with correct answers from the questions you actually knew, to get you over yet another hurdle on the rocky road to graduation. Thus with a little thought, you can avoid a wild stab in the dark on your WAGs and at least get them into the proper ballpark.

SWAGs are WAGs improved by a scientific approach to the situation, like the test gaming described above but with the application of positive knowledge instead of just removing losers from the choices. That is, you apply scientific method (or at least a pale imitation of it) to make your guess better than it otherwise would be. This can be done by various means: dimensional analysis to get the units of a quantity at least correct; order of magnitude scaling to get the figure roughly right; carryovers from previous situations not entirely dissimilar; and application of general rules for the areas of application. These methods improve the probability that your guess is good enough to pass muster until you can get better information. A scientific wild-ass guess is always better than a simple WAG, and it is used more often than we think.

IWAGs are the best kind of guesses, for they are based on some informed knowledge of the area of application. You know the nature of the beast and the likely range for a quantity, but you don't know exactly what is going to happen, so you guess. This is a perfectly legitimate method used habitually by meteorologists on television to predict tomorrow's weather. The basis for an IWAG is your knowledge or the knowledge of a colleague about a particular area, which allows you to guess with confidence. This method is really the application of experience, and it works very well, particularly in complex areas where precision is not really a virtue.

Remember that you seek to improve your guesses as time and resources permit during the planning process. If you have made a WAG, seek information to upgrade it into a SWAG or even an IWAG. Also, keep these guesses in mind when it comes time to make sensitivity checks or question your assumptions, for every guess is really an assumption. Don't be afraid to guess; just remember that it is a substitute for certainty, and treat the information in your guesses accordingly.

Rule 80: Iterate and Reiterate

It is comforting to assume that planning is a finite process and that there is an end to it all. This is particularly comforting after you have spent a lot of time and effort putting together a workable plan that will fulfill your goals at the budgeted cost, and you are sick and tired of the whole thing and just want to forget about it. Unfortunately, your comfort would be false, for planning is a continuous process, and it is never ended.

Life goes on, and time flows by, and things happen whether we like it or not, so there is no cessation to activity. Thus there can be no cessation of planning, unless we default and allow ourselves to exist entirely at the mercy of outside forces. We have to recognize that all actions have consequences down the stream of time, many of which we cannot even foresee, and that every action begets a reaction, so that what we do multiplies, diverges, converges, dims, brightens, and so on into the future.

All of this philosophy is designed merely to get you in the mood to accept some advice on iteration. In process terms, iteration means doing it over. Reiteration is just doing it over again. But iteration has a special sense that means more than merely doing it over for no good reason. Iteration carries with it the sense that each new edition or version of the plan has benefitted from what went before. That is, there has been improvement because of the iterative process.

This is important, for planning cannot produce certainty, and each version of the plan can correct the mistakes of earlier versions while at the same time promoting other mistakes. Iteration at least can help us avoid making the same mistakes over and over again.

Iteration serves many purposes, but three of the most important are improving accuracy of data, integrating new information, and simplifying internal relationships.

It is quite likely that the early versions of a plan will include many assumptions or guesses about quantities, and iteration allows the accuracy of these data to be improved systematically and progressively. Suppose you didn't know the actual value for the length of a table in your first plan, so you inserted a WAG of 6.75 feet. Then later on, you had an opportunity to measure the table and found that it was closer to 6.40 feet in length. During the next iteration, you would insert the more accurate statement of the length into the plan and modify other numbers appropriately. Or suppose you had no idea of how much a particular resource would cost, so you guessed, making certain to have a high estimate. When you phoned the supplier and got a good estimate of the price, you could change the cost estimate in the next iteration. Iteration also helps narrow ranges of values where you have a pretty good idea of the upper and lower boundaries but no clear idea of the value. Your initial estimate might be that a location is between 200 and 300 miles away, and a subsequent iteration could change that range to 250 to 285 miles away, giving a better idea of what you would encounter. Improvements in accuracy of other quantities in the plan are a natural part of iteration.

It is often the case that new information comes to light after the plan is finished, and it is necessary to modify the plan in light of the new information. This can occur if you discover that a major competitor is opening new stores in the area in which you propose to expand your own outlets. Or suppose the cruise for which you have reservations has a change in schedule, or the guest of honor will be out of town the night you have scheduled a roast. These kinds of major new items may not occur frequently, but there will always be new facts and new forces that will influence your plan enough to warrant consideration in a forthcoming iteration. Incidentally, resist the temptation to ignore new information; you can probably fool yourself, but ultimately you have to conclude that you cannot fool the planning process. If new information is relevant, it has to be considered.

Finally, iteration permits you to look again at the complicated web of internal relationships you have patched together in your first versions or first two or three versions. Simplification is so important that the entire next rule is devoted to it, so suffice it to say that ironing out the rough spots is facilitated by careful iteration.

Even if you had time to do it right the first time, take the time to do it over and over and over and over again until you get it the way you want it.

Rule 81: Simplify the Plan

One of the all-time great slogans is exemplified by the acronym KISS, which means "keep it simple, stupid." Originally coined by and for infantry soldiers, it has found wide application in various lines of work. It has particular application in planning, where the natural tendency is to complicate things more and more.

Planning involves forecasting and scheduling future events, and the future is an area where one seer's opinion generally is as good as another seer's opinion. This means, among other things, that the complexity of the future can exceed even the complexity of the present—which already is too complex by far. The complexity of the present is at least limited by reality, and there is only one sets of facts and one set of relationships. The complexity of the past is limited by our understanding of the past, and while our histories are simplified, they are so only because we cannot understand the complexities of that past. In planning we are concerned with the complexities of the future, which are almost limitless because we can imagine alternatives that will never happen. It is really important, therefore, that planners adhere to the KISS rule.

A common tendency of planners is to get down in the weeds fast—down into a level of detail and concreteness that cannot be disputed easily by outsiders. Getting into the weeds, however, also limits one's vision and can make the plan opaque or even impenetrable. While in the weeds, moreover, it is impossible to see even a tree, much less the forest. So planners have to fight the tendency to provide more and more detail and more and more exhibits and charts and tables and graphs until the entire plan is covered with a patina of encrusted microdata. The truth is that more detail cannot hide a bad concept, but it can obscure a good concept so much that it won't sell.

My advice is to simplify your plan during its iterations. It is normal and understandable if the first version simply throws it all out there for the reader to organize and grasp, but is it inexcusable if the next versions are equally impenetrable. Your own review of the plan should suggest where connections need to be made, and relationships should be explained in the plan. Do not just simplify the presentation of the plan; while that is a good idea, it is insufficient. What you should do is simplify the plan itself. A complicated plan is hard to explain in a simple manner, but a simple plan encourages simple explanations.

One of the biggest areas for simplification is relating ends and means. While it may be apparent to you, the planner, how each element contributes to achieving the goals, it may not be evident to outsiders. If not, you need to review your task organization to assure that you have broken down the work properly. Another way to simplify a plan is to show the relationships between various elements, and you can use a Venn diagram or flow diagram to illustrate them. The time sequences of the plan can be simplified by using a project-planning system to display the relationships of events along the time line. Another challenge for simplification is to show how each element of the plan fits into a central conceptual framework, and this involves aggregating from the bottom to the top in a reasonable manner—which is covered in the next rule.

By advocating KISS, I am not ruling out the complexity that may be required to achieve the goals of your plan, but I am advising that you simplify the internal arrangements of your plan so they make sense.

Rule 82: Build a Conceptual Framework

One of the best ways to simplify your plan is to find some overarching principles that apply to your problem and can be used to describe in some general terms what you are doing. This is not easy, but it has been done in the case of some very complicated matters.

The equation $F = Ma$ is an example of a very complex set of rules and behaviors that can be explained simply—once you comprehend the nature of the field of application. This equation is Newton's Second Law, in which F stands for force, M for mass of a body, and a for the acceleration of a body. This law says that a body of mass, M, acted upon by a force, F, will be accelerated at a rate equal to the ratio of the force to the mass, or a. Or, looking at it another way, the force generated by a body of mass, M, accelerated at a rate, a, is equal to the product of the mass and the acceleration. The equation itself is a simple model or expression of a very complex system of physics, and the beauty or even the validity of the equation makes sense only in the context of the sophisticated conceptual framework of classical physics.

A conceptual framework is a philosophical construct that provides a skeleton or structure upon which you can fasten the various parts of the plan. In science, the framework that holds together and explains the observations is called a theory. In one sense, therefore, a conceptual framework is like a theory in that it holds together the various elements of the plan, but a theory seeks to explain why, while a conceptual framework just tries to cope with how. Since planning is an art as well as (or perhaps instead of) a science, I prefer to think of a conceptual framework as a way to understand the plan rather than a way to explain why it is. That last bit of philosophy may unduly obscure this subject, but it serves to assure you that you are not responsible for explaining all of the phenomena when you create your conceptual framework.

Essentially, you should seek some general rules or general principles or just plain generalities that seem to fit the plan you are devising. These rules, principles, and generalities may actually provide a matrix of two or three or more dimensions, with boxes into which you can fit various pieces of your plan.

Your conceptual framework may consist of a logical way to aggregate the tasks and subtasks of your plan into a coherent scheme. When you set about planning, one of the first things you had to do was break your plan down into smaller and smaller pieces in accordance with the Elephant Rule. This top-down approach resulted in a larger and larger number of sub-sub-subtasks to be accomplished in finite periods of time using finite resources and labor. Then you set about fleshing out the sub-sub-subtasks with the inputs and the outputs while simultaneously spreading them out along the time line. This probably resulted in both complexity and confusion, which makes it difficult to understand easily what you have done and how to go about the implementation. In this all too common situation, an aggregation scheme for the tasks is a useful kind of conceptual framework.

One of the essential features of natural science is the grouping of like things into sets. Charles Darwin was able to generalize his observations over a lifetime by classifying what he saw into logical sets of similar things and then figuring out a scheme of aggregation that made sense. After he did this, he was able to generalize to derive his law of natural selection. Similarly, you may be able to generalize from your own aggregation scheme.

I have to warn you that grouping things logically may prove difficult. About 90 percent of the aggregations of things will be obvious, but the remaining 10 percent of your assignments of things into aggregation sets will be uncertain, arbitrary, and controversial. This characteristic varies, and sometimes you will be unable to aggregate more than 50 percent of the items easily, but in all cases that I have encountered, there has always been a hard core of 10 percent of the items that defies logical classification. My approach is simply to be open, honest, and arbitrary in assigning the final 10 percent of the items to their aggregation sets. Once this is done, you have created a conceptual framework that specifies the sets to which each item belongs and also contributes to understanding the relationships among sets, which, by the way, are actually the rules used to establish the sets.

One important characteristic of a good conceptual framework is that it is comprehensive. It explains everything—every aspect of the plan, every task, and every element. It is simply no good to devise a conceptual framework that explains only half or even 90 percent of what is going on. This is also a requirement for a scientific theory, which is obligated to explain all observations or test results, not just those that suit the theorist. If there is only one exception to the theory, it causes the entire theory to be defective, and it is necessary to devise a new theory to take into account all of the data—including the former exception. The same thing goes for conceptual frameworks, which must be revised and redone until they cover all aspects of the plan. It is the requirement for comprehensiveness that explains why many planners do not prepare conceptual frameworks and why so many other people don't get excited about them. It is more fun to deal with the easy 90 percent and simply fail to come to grips with the hard 10 percent of the problem.

The very act of preparing a conceptual framework may cause you to learn things you never imagined before, and this effect was clearly working for Darwin. Once I prepared a conceptual framework for a relatively unimportant aspect of national security merely because no one had ever done it before. The result of my intellectual curiosity was that I discovered self-evident truths completely unknown to me— or anyone else. (Unfortunately, however, no one else cared enough about it to share my delight in the discovery, which remains available but inactive.) Setting about deliberately to aggregate the tasks or other elements of your plan into a comprehensive conceptual framework is worthwhile for its own sake, in addition to making it easier for others to understand and appreciate your good planning.

Rule 83: Try Supply-Side Planning

Rule 16 pointed out the difference between objectives planning and capabilities planning, and Rule 18 advised you to distinguish between supply and demand and treat them separately. Both of these rules stressed the difference between what you want to do and what you can do. This rule will discuss in more depth a particular application of capabilities planning called supply-side planning.

Supply-side planning rests on the premise that your plan is limited by availabilities of supplies to the extent that you cannot plan to meet a given demand but must instead just do the best with what you have. Your whole plan depends on the supplies available.

For general planning purposes, I have advocated first setting goals and objectives, next figuring out the resources it takes to do the job, and then getting the resources and doing the job. In most planning situations this works well enough, because the gaps between demands and supplies are small enough to be closed during the planning process, either by reducing demand or increasing supply, or through other means previously discussed.

In some cases, however, demand so far exceeds supply that it cannot possibly be met—ever. In those cases, the problem is not meeting demand—even a reduced or modified demand—but simply allocating available supply in the best possible way. Demand exceeds supply substantially during emergencies, in which there is a sudden increase in demand in a locality, or perhaps over a short period of time, that simply cannot be met by available supply. For these situations, supply-side planning may be useful.

Supply-side planning stresses allocation of available resources in accordance with some useful set of priorities and urgencies. The trick to supply-side planning is in deciding what is urgent and what is not, and this is not always clear. One problem is in deciding how to establish the priorities. Rule 45 identifies three ways to set priorities. In a system of absolute priorities, all of the demands of the top-priority consumer have to be met before any of the demands of the lower-priority consumers are met. In a system of proportional priorities, each consumer would receive the same proportion of demand. In a system of relative priorities, all consumers might receive some supply but in different amounts. Perhaps the top-priority consumers would receive 90 percent of their demands, second-priority consumers 75 percent, and third-priority consumers only 50 percent of their demands. It is possible that a lower-priority group might receive nothing under this kind of system. Establishing a system of priorities that includes the number of priority classes, the satisfaction level for each class, and the criteria for placing consumers into each class is a difficult and controversial job. One thing for certain is that priority systems of allocating supplies seldom satisfy everyone and sometimes satisfy no one.

Energy is a product that requires supply-side planning in an emergency in which its price or availability fluctuates. Energy is ubiquitous in our society, and our lifestyles from driving cars to recreation depend on abundant supplies of electricity, natural gas, and petroleum products. When an energy emergency leads to a sudden increase in price, hoarding, or decrease in amounts available in a locality, it is sometimes possible to use supply-side planning to ensure at least that emergency facilities and essential institutions get enough energy to meet their minimum needs. Supply-side plans may be implemented using a market mechanism instead of some kind of governmental intervention and may rely on prices to shift energy supplies into more-desirable consumption patterns. This approach is based on the premise that people with the most urgent demands for energy will pay higher prices to meet their essential needs, and the insufficient amount of energy will be reallocated appropriately in this manner. Whether or not your own economic agenda favors the market solution or imposition of some priority scheme, you will find that supply-side planning will help.

Rule 84: Try Some Long-Range Planning

"Long-range planning is what people do when they cannot cope with day-to-day business." *

Long-range planning is the orphan of the planning community. It is often extolled but seldom done. Long-range planning has a time horizon measured in years. A common time frame is ten to twenty years, although some long-range planning efforts extend only five or up to fifty years. The many jokes about long-range planning, such as the one above, reveal that Americans have a real problem with the whole idea. Another opinion about the futility of long-range planning is expressed in the saying by the eminent economist John Maynard Keynes: "In the long run, we shall all be dead."

The relative unimportance of long-range planning is also

---

* Rear Adm. Joseph C. Strasser, president, Naval War College, July 13, 1992.

expressed in the following rueful saying, repeated in many variations in too many offices: "In this office, short-range planning is now, mid-range planning is tomorrow, and long-range planning is next week."

Still another common story relating to long-range planning is the one about the person who is up to his rear end in alligators so much that he forgets that his long-range plan is to drain the swamp.

These stories illustrate why long-range planning languishes in the backwaters of government and business organizations. Day-to-day business consumes most people and leaves little time for speculating about the future, and long-range planning is too remote to be relevant to today's concerns.

This is a well-known phenomenon in organizations, so managers who want some long-range planning done generally cluster a small group of people together into a single unit and order them to plan long-range. This does provide long-range estimates and plans, but the long-range planners and their far-out plans seldom relate to what the rest of the organization has been doing or intends to do. So the long-range planners often have little impact on what is going to happen. Finding a satisfactory solution to the problem of having good long-range plans that are relevant to the current needs of the organization is not easy, but for those organizations that do take long-range planning seriously, there are benefits. In this era, we have witnessed many large companies once at the top of their class simply disappear because they failed to have a strategic long-range vision that ensured their survival. Other companies with well-considered long-range plans have flourished.

Another reason why long-range planning is not more popular is that it is hard to do. It is hard to forecast the future. While large movements and mass trends can be foreseen, the individual movements that we are most interested in cannot be predicted accurately. Moreover, the validity of predictions varies according to the time span from the present. We may very well be able to forecast a stock price, population growth, or crime rate for tomorrow or maybe even next month, but forecasting for next year and particularly for ten years is entering into the realm of wild speculation. The basic scientific principle of prediction is stated succinctly and understandably by Steven W. Hawking, author of *A Brief History of Time*, as follows:

> Scientists believe that the universe is governed by well-defined laws that in principle allow one to predict the future. But the motion given by the laws is often chaotic. This means that a tiny change in the initial situation can lead to change in the subsequent behavior, a change that rapidly grows larger. Thus, in practice one can often predict accurately only a fairly short time into the future.*

Despite these problems—or perhaps because of them—a long-range estimate or plan is a good thing to have.

One reason to have long-range plans is simply to move out beyond the pressing needs of the moment and think about where you are going and what it is you are going to do when you arrive.

Long-range planning can also provide good feedback that can shape the short- and mid-range plans you are using to guide the work at hand and project resources for a year or two. Even if you cannot predict the future, you can still project your own actions that tend to shape your future. It is this aspect of long-range planning that is most valuable: what you are going to do.

By making broad projections of a possible future, you can cover the most likely conditions and then plan to be able to cope with them when you get there. Certainly, it is better to reach out and be roughly right than to fail to look and be utterly wrong.

Long-range plans need be neither exact nor detailed, for a broad outline can suffice for your purposes. You can state the estimated future situation, examine your purposes, and draw some general conclusions about the kinds of actions that would achieve your goals in that situation. It is the same kind of planning you will be doing on the tactical level for next month, but farther out and less definite.

---

* Stephen W. Hawking, "The Future of the Universe," *Engineering and Science,* California Institute of Technology, Vol. LV, No. 1, Fall 1991, p. 21.

One of my first jobs when I arrived in the Pentagon in 1964 was to work on a team preparing the Army's input to the Joint Long-Range Strategic Survey—the Joint Chiefs of Staff long-range planning effort of that time. We had to stretch our minds to envision what we thought was going to happen twenty-five years in the future, based on what we thought was happening in 1964. It was great fun, and the members of that long-range planning team learned a lot that helped us later. As I look back on that experience twenty-nine years later, the amazing thing is that so much of what we predicted actually did come to pass in general terms. Well, we missed a few biggies—like the collapse of the Soviet Union—but we hit the mark on a lot of other items, and maybe our long-range plan had some good influence on the policies, plans, and programs that shaped events in the intervening period of time.

It is never too late to contemplate the future in an organized manner and think about what and where you want to be in five or ten or twenty years. My advice is to try to make some long-range estimates and broad strategic plans that will provide a better basis for your current tactical plans.

Rule 85: Document the Plan

One important thing that is often forgotten during the planning process is documenting the plan. Documenting means keeping a record of the contents of the plan for future reference, in writing, with pictures, or both. The plan may be written down on pieces of paper (hard copy, as we say), or it may be inscribed electronically on a memory disk. The plan needs to be recorded somehow so that a person can take it out or call it up and look at it.

I once had to take over a large computer program from the contractor who had developed it and had to install it on a large government computer. The contractor had operated the program long enough to demonstrate that it worked all right, and in accordance with the overall plan, the government was now going to operate the program on its own computer. The program was a complex theater-level combat simulation with thousands of lines of code (the measure of the size of a software program is lines of code). It seemed as if it would be a piece of cake until we found that the program was not documented. Now this was in the primitive days of computer programs—about twenty years ago—and all of the rules and standards had not been solidified or in many cases conceived. Theater-level combat simulations were created by a single genius or a small group of eccentric geniuses and then made available to the mere mortals who were charged with running them. The genius who had created this particular model was so busy writing code that he was unable to find the time to write down what he had done. That was in itself excusable perhaps, but he told no one else what he had done, and when we asked him to explain what he had done, he was unable to do even that. So there we were with a big, big program, a deadline, and no documentation. We mucked through it bit by bit and finally got it to run, although we were not certain that we actually did what he had originally done. The impression it made on me was indelible, and I have been a great fan of documentation ever afterward.

It is easy to omit documenting what you are doing. You are so busy creating, which is fun, that it seems a bit sinful to take time to record events, which is tedious. There are some true diarists in the world—people who record what happens around them—and we are forever indebted to them for furnishing us a glimpse of life. But diarists do not ordinarily create plans—the function of observing tends to be antithetical to the function of creating. This is only my opinion, however, and the upshot is that you creators have to devote some time to documentation.

But when there is a choice between doing something or documenting something, doing wins almost every time. When I was in the emergency management business, we all knew that we had to be ready for the catastrophic earthquake in California. The indications were that there would be a large earthquake that would cause a lot of damage, so we spent a lot of time and money preparing for that eventuality. I urged that we also set up a special team to go to the location of the earthquake when it occurred to observe and document what happened. These people would be designated and specially trained to do this, and they would not have any duties to respond to the emergency or help in the recovery effort. Their sole function would be to observe and report. Well, as we all know, the Loma Prieta earthquake did occur in 1989, and thanks in great measure to all of the preparation by the federal government, the state of California, the city of San Francisco, and other government and private agencies, the response was good and the loss of life and damage were limited. So the preparedness paid off. But the observer team never got to observe, because every available person was put to work helping manage the emergency.

A major exception to the lack of appreciation for documentation was during World War II, when the U.S. Army and Navy had the wisdom to place numerous historical teams in the field to report, photograph, and document what happened. This foresight paid off, because it enabled the production of a superb set of histories that have become treasure troves of data for analysis and reflection.

Documenting is so much better than having to go back later and figure out what took place. I have done some historical work, and I have gained a deep appreciation for those who have to try to figure out what happened years ago based on limited data and faulty memories.

You can obviate having to hire some historian to go into the archives and puzzle out what your plan said, and what it meant, and how you did it, and what your thinking was simply by documenting it as you do it. Write it down. Keep copies of all versions so you can track changes. Retain the backup data you aggregated into your tables and charts. Then when you need to understand something, the information will be available in organized form ready to use.

My advice is to include the task of documentation as one of the bites of the elephant. That might give it enough status so that it actually will be done.

15

Preparing

Once you have completed your plan—or even before—you are likely to have identified some actions that can be taken to help implement it. Actions taken in advance of full-scale implementation but in anticipation of going ahead with the plan are preparation.

When I was a kid, we used to start foot races with three commands: "Take your marks," at which we stood on the starting line; "Get set," at which we got down in our starting crouch; and "Go," at which we started running with blinding speed. Well, if planning is moving to the starting line, and implementing is going, then preparing is getting set to go. Preparing includes concrete action and costs money—real money—in comparison with the costs of just planning, which are usually quite small compared with the costs of implementation.* The costs of preparing are not extra costs, however, for they come out of implementation if that occurs.

---

* That is not to say, however, that planning is free, for it does cost money, and sometimes lots of money.

Preparing seeks to accomplish three things: make it easier to implement the plan when the decision is made to do so; speed up the implementation of the plan—particularly the initial steps; and lower the cost of implementing the plan.

Preparing can be very helpful for plans that are certain to be implemented but that cannot for some reason be started immediately. Preparatory actions bridge the time delay between the completion of the plan and the start of the project and seek to minimize the adverse impact of that delay on the ultimate implementation.

Preparing can also be done for contingency plans that may or may not ever be implemented. In this case, the preparatory actions are wasted if the plans are never implemented, but they are invaluable if the time comes to implement the contingency plans.

Identification of useful preparations is usually a by-product of the planning process. As you go through the planning steps, earmark the actions that make sense in terms of making it easier, faster, or cheaper to implement the plan and make your thing happen when you start the clock running. The six rules in this chapter are designed to give you some idea of the kinds of things that can be done to prepare to make something happen.

Rule 86: Identify the Long Poles

One of the purposes of preparation is to get a head start on the plan. By accomplishing some of the key actions in advance, you can enter full-scale implementation with an advantage.

One way to prepare is to identify the "long poles in the tent." In the good old days, before more modern types of tents, erecting a large tent involved pegs, short poles, and long poles. Pegs go in the ground to hold the flaps of the tent securely; short poles go around the perimeter of the tent to hold up the sides; long poles go in the center of the tent and hold the canvas up higher than the sides. While all of the pegs and poles are important, the long poles presumably are the most important because they hold the tent up. Got it?

So the idea of identifying the long poles is to get a firm understanding of what is important and what is less important in making your goals happen. Based on this understanding, you can determine what actions can be taken in advance to make it easier to implement the plan.

Once you have identified the long poles, you will need to consider doing three things:

1. If some of the long poles are weak, revise the plan to diminish their importance. If you find that your plan rests on one or more long poles that are hard to do or will take a long time, you may want to get rid of those long poles and erect others.

2. Pay special attention to getting the long poles ready to go without undue delay for administrative processing or permissions. As you go about preparing to implement your plan, ensure that the long poles are ready to go even if some of the shorter poles are not.

3. Spend money now to increase the likelihood that long-pole tasks can be accomplished certainly and swiftly. This may involve doing some of the work in advance, signing up some key personnel, buying long lead-time items, or taking other measures that will provide you some degree of confidence that your long poles will be there when it is time to erect the tent.

Rule 87: Get the Long Lead-Time Items

One of the traditional steps in preparation is to buy in advance and have on hand the long lead-time items.

Long lead-time items are characterized by a lengthy period from the time you place the order until the item arrives at the place you need it. If you are planning to build a house with some special equipment—for instance, a sauna or an elevator—these items might take longer to obtain than the other, more common materials used in house construction. If you want to avoid undue delay, you can order such components well in advance of the other items.

Buying the long lead-time items in advance is essential for plans that must be implemented fully within a constrained time period or that have to be done urgently once they are started. A plan for cutting timber in a region that experiences heavy rains for six months of the year would mean that the work has to be done during the dry season, and all of the supplies that cannot be delivered within a few months should be bought in advance during the rainy season and stockpiled.

For a manufacturer, buying and stocking long lead-time items is important in case of greater-than-expected sales. Only one thing is worse to a manufacturer than losing sales because of an inability to produce enough goods, and that is not having enough sales. If most of the parts for a manufactured item can be obtained from suppliers within a month after the orders are placed, but two items take six months for delivery, it would make good sense to buy a six-month supply of those two long lead-time items so that the output could be increased in just a month if there were a successful sales campaign.

Buying long lead-time items is also useful for defense manufacturers who want to be able to increase production rapidly in case of a national mobilization for military operations. During Operation Desert Storm it was necessary to increase production of some military items severalfold in order to supply the troops for even that short and highly successful war. In the event of another war, similar rapid production increases would be needed, and advance procurement of long lead-time items would save valuable time.

Identification of long lead-time items can be done by referring to your Gantt Chart (Rule 37) and PERT network (Rule 62). The long lead-time items will show up on these time-line charts as tasks that need more time to be accomplished than other tasks. The first place to look for long lead-time items is the critical path you have identified as per Rule 62. In order to get results faster, you have to shorten the critical path, recognizing that you then will have defined a new critical path.

A planning path is composed of three basic elements: time to do the work, time to procure resources, and time waiting for other paths. To shorten the critical path, you need to look at the first two of these elements. Sometimes the time it takes to perform a task cannot be shortened by advance procurement. Some processes just take a certain amount of time and cannot be hastened by having parts and components on hand. Many times, however, the reason a task takes a certain amount of time is that the workers are waiting for raw materials, parts, and components to process into a higher level of product. In these cases, there will always be an input that is the primary reason for delay, and these inputs are candidate long lead-time items. They can be identified by working through the plan systematically, and most of the time they will be obvious to you.

Once you have identified the long lead-time items, you will have to consider costs of procurement, storage, and maintenance for these items. Finally, the overall cost of buying early has to be balanced against the benefits of faster implementation for each long lead-time item identified.

Rule 88: Buy When It Is Cheap

Another reason to take some preparatory actions in advance is to save money by buying things when they are cheap or when a sudden opportunity arises. One basic reason for buying in advance is to save the additional costs resulting from inflation (Rule 52) or scarcity. Inflation adds to the future costs of almost everything, but scarcity applies only to things that are available in a fixed quantity. If you know that prices are going to increase between now and next year when you will be ready to implement your plan, you might want to go ahead and buy some of the items you will need. This depends on both your financial situation and the certainty that you will indeed need the items in the future.

Beachfront property has tended to increase in price because there is only a fixed amount of it—most of it is already developed, and a lot of it is unavailable for private ownership because it is reserved for parks and wildlife preserves. Thus, if your goal is to have a beachfront house, it might make a great deal of sense to go ahead and purchase some land now and hold on to it even if you don't build the house for five years.

One of the classic opportunities for buying cheap is taking advantage of periodic price wars in the airline industry. For reasons unknown to mere mortal man, one airline company announces suddenly that it is lowering fares by a significant percentage for a stated period of time. Other airline companies soon follow suit, and the rush is on. You can save a lot of money by buying these discount airline tickets, but there is a down side to it: There are usually restrictions on these tickets so that your flexibility if you change your plans is reduced or made costly. If, however, the available dates fit into your plan, or even if they require slight changes to it, buying in advance pays off. In fact, the opportunity to buy these tickets cheaply may be what initiates your planning process by giving you the urge to take a trip.

There are plenty of bargains out there that can save you money if you are willing to take the time and trouble. Your plan bill of materials (Rule 41) constitutes a shopping list for reference when you notice sales, bankruptcies, and other unexpected opportunities to get needed items at less than the normal price. This will allow you to approach saving money in an organized manner.

There may be some costs associated with buying early, such as renting a storage bin or warehouse space, and you should calculate whether the savings from buying early are greater than these additional costs. But do what you can to save money by judicious advance purchases when you are able to do so.

Rule 89: Line Up the Team

Another thing you can do as part of your preparations is to identify, contact, and sign up the people you are going to need to make something happen. You have previously identified the skills and experience you need on your team (Rule 46); now it is time to line up the people.

People with the appropriate skills and good attitudes are the most critical resource you need. You can get along without some of the other kinds of resources, but you cannot get along without people. People, however, do not grow on trees, so you will have to exert some effort to find them. This will require a certain amount of skill and a lot of luck.

Looking back on my own checkered experience as a manager and project leader, I can say that my greatest successes and my biggest failures were due to my selections of people to work for me. Happily, almost all of the people I have supervised have been great. They worked hard, contributed to the achievement of our goals, and were real members of the team.

When I was in the Army, I seldom had the luxury of choosing the people who would work for me, or the people I worked for, either. People were assigned and reassigned in accordance with the dictates of the personnel management system and came and went with dismaying frequency. But we learned not to worry about the fact that we could not choose our people and concerned ourselves with getting the most out of the ones we had.

When I went into civilian life, first in the government and then in the private sector, that all changed. I found that as a supervisor or manager, I did have a say in the people working for me. I could hire and (with some limitations in government) I could fire. This turned out to be a mixed blessing, because when I made a mistake on a person, it turned out to be a whopper. In several instances, I selected people for important jobs that they simply did not do very well. Having made the original selection, there is a tendency to overlook accumulating evidence of incompetence and put off the decision to move or get rid of the poor employee. This, I found, was a mistake, for an incompetent or disloyal employee can do profound damage to an organization in a short time.

One of my worst experiences in staffing was to encourage, mentor, and even promote to senior grade an employee who—for reasons that still escape me—was busy criticizing me behind my back and actively subverting our team's plan. When I learned about this I was stunned, for I had no hint from this person's overt behavior that this treachery was under way. I finally had the person moved, but the damage was lingering and devastating.

The point of this anecdote is that it is important to assure that you don't get a bad apple in the barrel. You should take extra precautions to make certain your team is composed of people with integrity and loyalty. I would rather have on my team people who are less capable but honest than to have highly skilled crooks.

You don't have to hire the whole team in advance of implementation; there is no use paying wages for people to sit around and wait. You can, however, identify key people, approach them, and reach an understanding on their availability to join you.

Key people are those who are important for the success of your plan. They could include your group leaders—people who can themselves take on the task of making part of your plan happen. Your key person list could include someone with a critical skill, such as a particular chef for a fine restaurant, a particular jockey for a horse race, or a particular mason who knows how to finish concrete the way you want it.

Once you have identified the key people as one of your preparatory actions, you can get in touch with them, inform them of your plan, and tell them that you would like them to be on your team when the project starts. If they turn you down, you will at least have already found that out and can look for another person qualified to fill that key job, saving you a problem when you want to start implementing. Most of the time, however, people will not turn you down flat unless they are already committed or have a conflict in available time. If your prospect is willing to become a member of your team, you can go ahead and make an arrangement to ensure that this key person will be there when you want him or her. These arrangements vary from informal oral agreements made in person or over the phone to contingent employment contracts with some advance bonus money paid out to seal the deal. The extent to which you wish to make a firm arrangement in advance with your key people depends on their criticality to your success and on your own situation at the time.

Once you start implementing, you can go ahead and staff up to do the work, and there are agencies to help you do this. Private employment agencies and government employment commissions will find people for you. Or you can simply put ads in the papers and interview the applicants that respond. Whatever method you select, take care to perform this important step properly.

One way to get around part of the staffing problem is to use subcontractors to do some of the work. This puts the job of hiring, firing, training, and motivating on the backs of the subcontractors and relieves you of that burden. But at the same time, it requires you to select for your team the subcontractors that will do the job well, on time, and under cost.

Selecting subcontractors is not easy either. My own experience in using contractors to work around my house has been less than great. My usual selection method for hiring a contractor relies on the telephone business directory and various handouts that are inserted into my mailbox. Using this haphazard approach, I have managed to use a large number of contractors who did poor work for excessive prices and failed even to clean up after themselves. My revenge is not to hire these poor contractors for further work and to tell my neighbors not to hire them either. I have also stumbled onto a few good contractors whose names I keep in my special file to be called back for more work. I have gotten smarter lately and have taken to requesting references from prospective contractors and checking them out. This method works very well. So selecting a contractor is also going to be hard, and most of this can and should be done in the preparation stage before you have to use the contractors to do real work.

Rule 90: Get All of the Permissions

One of the most useful elements of preparing is to go ahead and get all of the necessary permits, licenses, and permissions before you start implementing. We live in a busy, bureaucratic world. In order to liberate us from care, provide freedom, and promote equality, the various local, state, and federal government legislatures, departments, and agencies have enacted a multitude of ordinances, statutes, and laws, which in turn are explained, expanded, and exploited by rules, regulations, and requirements. Governments and governmental agencies or quasi-government agencies such as water districts, sewage districts, and metropolitan transit authorities have proliferated, each writing and promulgating still more rules and restrictions. There are also nongovernmental organizations of homeowners, residents, and just feather merchants (Rule 98) who will get involved in your act too and tell you such things as what color you may paint your house. Even the trash haulers tell you when and how to put the trash out. Modern life is complicated and requires that you clear many, many hurdles in order to make something happen.

As you wended your way through the planning process, you should have looked for potential constraints on your freedom of action. Finding yourself in this kind of situation at this late stage when you have already done the planning is indicative of bad planning. You should already have checked these kinds of things when you considered what you needed to know (Rule 9) and when you gathered data (chapter 4).

If you haven't yet discovered and made a list of all of the permissions you will need, do so now. Consider all of the offices that could affect your plan and assume the worst. Call all of your points of contact and people who have been through the same kind of thing in the past to learn which gods need to be propitiated by some kind of sacrifice either of time, money, or dignity. The table below lists some of the places from which you will have to obtain permission for a few very simple activities. If what you want to do is very complicated, like developing a cure for AIDS, the process also gets very complicated.

Where to Obtain Permissions

What Your Plan Involves	Permission Grantors
Your residence	Condominium association
Your residence	Homeowners' association
Construction	County building permits
Construction	Environmental offices
Home business	County license & zoning
Food service	Health department
Automobiles or trucks	County & state registration
Automobiles or trucks	County & state inspection
Boats	Coast Guard inspection
Boats	Local or state registration
Airplanes	Federal Aviation Administration

The above list is certainly not exhaustive, but it should be enough to get you thinking about this aspect of your planning and preparing processes in case you thought you could do what you wanted without checking with someone.

Now that you have discovered all of the hurdles over which you must jump, one thing you can do in preparing to implement the plan is to clear some or all of them by obtaining permissions in advance.

As you go through the process of obtaining permissions, you will run into situations in which the imperatives of the permission process will cause you to change your plans. You may find that the house you have already laid out does not meet the minimum set-back requirements of your county, so you have to move the house back from the street another two feet. You may find that your plan to add a deck does not meet the restrictions for such structures as laid out by the homeowners' association or the covenants of your deed. You may find that you cannot operate a small business out of your house if customers have to visit you to receive your services. You may find that your plan for a grand family reunion picnic at the park needs to be approved sixty days in advance in triplicate.

I am certain that one of your instincts will be to fight these various limitations on your freedom of choice. That is natural, and that is the American way. I support that option in theory, but you have to realize that fighting city hall or the county engineer is going to be time-consuming, costly, and unlikely to succeed. My advice is to go along with the flow, wait in the lines, fill out the forms, and get the permissions—before you commit big bucks to a plan that turns out to be "Mission: Impossible."

Rule 91: Sell the Plan

Another thing that can and should be done during the preparation stage is to sell your plan. Some people consider this as part of the planning process itself, and I won't quarrel with that. The point is that sometime you should sell your plan, coordinate with all of the actors, and make certain it is ready to go when implementation starts.

If you are the customer for your plan, as is the case for most day-to-day planning, you are probably going to end up with a plan that will please yourself without having to be sold. If, however, you are preparing a plan for someone else—spouse, child, boss, partner, client, or customer—you will most likely have to sell the plan. Remember, a plan that is not accepted will not be used and is therefore useless.

A well-known story in the operations research business is about a prestigious consulting firm that prepared a big plan to revamp the police department of a major city. Everything was done scrupulously, and the data were compiled, costs estimated, benefits counted, and resources marshaled. The plan was great, and the analysis showed that it would cut both crime and costs while providing great benefits to the metropolis in terms of social redemption and renewed moral fiber. Only one problem: The police chief did not like it at all! The planners had failed a simple reality check to see if what they planned to do was acceptable, and in this case—like probably thousands of others—it was not. This plan was not a good one because it failed the primary test of acceptability.*

The point is that when you plan for someone else, you need to sell your plan along the way. Otherwise you can end up with a big white elephant on your hands that will end up in a wastebasket. The selling process should take place throughout the planning process. Don't wait until you have completed your plan to tell your sponsor what you are asking him to implement. Keep the sponsor informed and obtain feedback in the form of corrections, disapprovals, and approvals at every stage in the planning process. Check the goals with the sponsor. Check the assumptions with the sponsor. Let the sponsor know where you have guessed to fill in weak data. Inform the sponsor of the resources you will need and how much this is going to cost him or her. If you do this at each stage, you can proceed more confidently than if you don't, although interim approvals do not always result in final approval. In any case, it is foolish to gamble all of your work on a final, single cast of the dice.

---

* Another equally famous story of what not to do in the operations research business is of another firm that bid on a very large contract to install a new communications and data system for a major metropolitan fire department and won, only to find that it had miscalculated the cost and in order to get the job done would be losing a thousand dollars a day each day of the two-year contract. I would rather have my plan rejected than have to pay for the privilege of doing the work.

It will be more trouble in the short term to accommodate your sponsor as you do the planning, but it will pay off in the long term when it comes time to actually do what you have planned. The process of consultation with the sponsor will have two effects: You will modify the plan to please the sponsor, and at the same time the sponsor will be co-opted into support for the plan.

In the process of selling the plan, my advice is always tell the truth. Do not fake the numbers or conceal the weaknesses. On the contrary, highlight the weaknesses in your plan. This is both honest and prudent, for it means that the sponsor will (may) share responsibility in the not uncommon event of failure. Glory in the truth, for it really does set you free.

Oh yes, make sure that your presentation of the plan is clear, simple, and concise. The art of selling is to allow the buyer to persuade himself or herself to purchase the article you are selling. When your wares are plans, you cannot apply high-pressure tactics; you have to rely on the plan itself to make the sale. Your job is to assure that you present the plan well enough that it can sell itself. I could give you many other tips about selling the plan, including how to prepare a briefing, make slides, use slides, get your points across, and so on, but this is a book about making things happen, not making presentations, so I will just leave it at that.

16   **Implementing**

The plan is done. You have dotted the *i*'s and crossed the *t*'s and re-produced twenty-five copies. All has been measured, costed, sched-uled, and synchronized. The plan is approved, and all parties have signed it. You have prepared carefully, and all is ready. What is left? Only the hard part and the reason for planning in the first place—implementing the plan.

Planning is so much fun for some people that they lose sight of the purpose of the exercise, which is to achieve the goals that initiated the planning process in the first place.

Implementation, of course, is more than simply a matter of sending those copies of the plan to the participants. It requires con-scious, consistent effort to do what the plan calls for and to progress in accordance with the various schedules.

Moreover, implementation deals more with the real world than does the planning itself. A case in point is afforded by the assump-tions that may be acceptable for planning but are quite likely to prove wrong for implementation. As implementation progresses, the effects of a small error initially may grow and grow and grow—

sometimes even enough to invalidate the original plan. So implementation can be messy and requires some attention.

The next five rules are designed to help you do a good job when the time comes to do what you have planned to do. They should give you some idea of what implementation involves and what you should be doing about it. Part of your work in the implementing mode is to follow up to see that some good comes out of the whole mess. You will find it necessary to replan as you adjust your plan to see that what you want to happen is going to happen. You want to learn from all of this, and that is another benefit of the implementation stage. Even if you finish this project, there will always be another one. You will find that you will be planning several things at a time and doing more and more.

Rule 92: Follow Up: Don't Walk Away

One of the worst mistakes you can make is to ignore the plan during implementation. Some people who consider themselves planners believe that it is beneath them to become operators in order to do what the plan says or see that it is done. This is a mistake, and this kind of attitude gives a bad name to planners as a whole.

When planners abdicate a role in implementation, they may also abdicate a role in the planning itself. Operators—those who actually do the work—are offended by people who are afraid to get their feet wet, their boots muddy, or their brows sweaty. Operators want planners who are engaged, and if the planner simply hands over the plan and steps away, the odds are high that the plan will be thrown out and that a new plan devised hurriedly by the operators will be implemented instead.

So my advice is to stick with your plan during implementation if you really want it done. You will not only have to deal with replanning to keep the plan relevant, but you will also have to steer a straight course to assure that changes do not cripple the plan or achieve the wrong goals. You will also have to keep checking to assure that you are on the proper schedule, that costs are consistent with the plan, that resources are on hand, and that progress is being made. In short, you will have to assure that all is going according to plan.

This will be relatively easy if you are both the planner and the doer. All you have to do is check on your own implementation to see that you are on track. That means referring back once in a while to your original intentions to see if you have veered away. Remember that changing course is probably good if you do it intentionally—that is, if you change both the plan and the implementation. Problems occur when you change the implementation without changing the plan. Moving the wedding reception to a different location may be brilliant implementation if it saves money, but unless you also notify the guests and change all of the other aspects of the plan to suit the new location, you are likely to be embarrassed. Similarly, staying in an unplanned location on your trip can be fun, but unless you modify the rest of the itinerary accordingly, it can be expensive and inconvenient later on. You are the boss—both planner and doer—and you have to communicate with both of you.

If you as a planner are reporting to someone else who is responsible for overall implementation, the problem of overseeing the implementation becomes far more difficult. There are three dangers: ignorance, impotence, and indifference.

Ignorance is common. Quite often, the planners are in a different office than the operators. This is done purposely by some top executives because they believe correctly that day-to-day operations tend to drive out planning, and because they have more confidence in "real world" operators than in "fuzzy-headed" planners. In fact, planners are often looked down upon in organizations as people who think a lot but don't do much. While this may appear to be a strange attitude, it exists nevertheless. So it is entirely possible that you, the planner, may not be permitted even to know what is going on when your precious baby is being implemented. You may have to hand over the documents, schedules, and charts to some burly, beetle-browed bumblebee who will actually transform your ideas into reality. This is common in the architectural and engineering businesses, where those who draw the plans are not the ones who build the structures. The results of this unwise distinction are buildings not conforming to the plans, with sometimes even failures. The division between planners and builders also provides a lot of business for those who come around later and prepare plans to describe what actually was constructed. You should take every opportunity to check up on your plan during its implementation phase to assure that the goals and approaches so carefully crafted by you and your team are not butchered by those who do the work.

Ignorance can be allayed a great deal by building into the plan some reports that will provide you the essential information needed to ascertain who has been doing what with which to your plan. If you detect problems in adhering to the plan or making changes whose consequences are not reflected throughout the entire plan, you can at least make some noise about it—which may or may not be of some use.

Impotence is another problem that planners have. That means that even if they detect something wrong, they can't do anything about it. The planners have been stripped of their role in implementation by higher headquarters either purposely or inadvertently. This is usually a mistake, and some organizations have learned that it is highly effective to let the planners know ahead of time that they will be implementing their own plan. This is widely thought to inspire the planners to do a better than usual job since any mistakes will have to be faced later on. Without addressing this slur to the integrity of planners, suffice it to say that the scheme works. If you know you are going to go on the trip, pay for the wedding, operate the business, or pay for the losses incurred, you will tend to be somewhat more careful than if some other poor slob is going to have to live with your mistakes. If, however, you are divorced from implementation and have no say, my advice is to keep careful records; these will be of great use in the lawsuits to come. Even though the top management may allow you no say about implementation of the plan you prepared, they will blame you and your inadequate plan if the project fails.

Indifference is the greatest problem. Unless you are also in charge of implementation, it is possible that you simply will not care very much about how the plan comes out in real life. After all, you have done your part and prepared the perfect plan. It is certainly not your fault if some boob botches it. I have great sympathy for this view, as do all who live by providing advice that others can accept or reject. It is part of our defense against rejection to divorce ourselves from our plans once they are completed. This saves pain when the key points are twisted and the subtleties unappreciated, and when the product fails to live up to the promise. Indifference, however, no matter how consoling, is just a form of self-denial that will turn out to be more bad than good. My advice is to remain on the job with your plan, evidencing interest despite the slings and arrows of outside critics and the attitudes of those responsible. Hang in there and see that the implementation is done as well as possible given the circumstances that apply.

Rule 93: Be Flexible: Revise the Plan

It is foolish to expect that your plan can be implemented exactly as you have planned it. Some assumptions will be wrong, and even some facts will turn out to be wrong. Your costs will be off, or the funding will be just a bit too little or too late or both. The time schedule will slip. The resources you want will be unavailable, and your key worker will become gravely ill or get married or move to another town. Something will go wrong. You have to expect it, and you should have allowed for it.

This means that you will have to revise your plan, and you will have to revise it continuously from the time that you complete it. The only thing certain about your plan is that it will be obsolete the minute you finish it. This is not a criticism of your plan; it is simply the way things are, because time flows and the data become out of date, the costs become old, and the entire thing sort of starts coming unglued the minute you sign your name to it.

Experienced planners are used to this and can cope with it, but it is terribly distressing to neophytes to realize that all of their hard work during the planning process has created a plan that is slightly off at the end of that process. Sometimes the corrections that have to be made for implementation are so obvious that massive adjustments have to be made even before work can start. This is often the case with military contingency plans, which are completed and placed on a shelf until needed, then taken down, dusted off, revised, and implemented. The idea that a plan of this nature has to be revised before implementation has given rise to the notion among nonplanners that it is no use to prepare plans in advance because they simply have to be redone for each actual event. This new planning fad goes under the name of "reactive planning," and it misses the point of planning in the first place. Planners for years have said that it isn't the plan that is the product but the process itself. This is not quite correct in my view, however. The planning process is a valuable experience and much is learned by the planners in the course of preparing the plan, but I say that more is learned about planning than about the particular plan being prepared. I believe that a plan is the true and legitimate product of a planning process. It is a lot easier to prepare a plan carefully and then dust it off, make a few minor revisions, and then implement it than it is to start a wholly new plan from scratch. To distinguish old-line, classical planning from the new variety of reactive planning, we planners sometimes use that great redundancy "preplanning" to denote what we do.

Once the plan is in the process of implementation, another kind of modification occurs—this time because of realities not covered or expected in the plan or because of errors in the plan. This also is a common feature of every plan, and it is common sense to modify the plan to meet the realities, if for no other reason than the simple fact that realities tend to resist change at our whim.

My advice is to be flexible when implementing the plan. One major problem in implementation is people who refuse to change the plan even in the face of evident need. This includes the fellow who insists on going ahead with the picnic when it is raining cats and dogs, or the one who refuses to countenance a substitute item for material that cannot be had for love nor money. When the circumstances no longer fit the assumptions of the plan, it is best to alter the plan to fit the circumstances.

Implementation, therefore, requires constant attention not only to the project or program but to the plan itself.

The process of correcting the plan during implementation is called "replanning" in military circles, and it is a legitimate function. Each level of command prepares a plan and implements it with an operations order. Simultaneously, each level begins the process of replanning because, particularly in war, circumstances change because of enemy action and also because of the initial effects of the original plan. This means that all plans need to be corrected periodically, and this is done by issuing fragmentary orders modifying the original operations order. When enough fragmentary orders have accumulated that the original operations order is substantially changed, a complete new plan is created and a new operations order issued, to be modified by replanning and fragmentary orders as before, and the cycle goes on.

Simply accept the fact that you should modify your plan the minute you start implementing it and you will save yourself and your colleagues a great deal of headaches. Once you have done this a few times, you will learn how to prepare plans that require a minimum of modification upon implementation.

Rule 94: Don't Despair: Stick to the Plan

Another grave problem you will face during the implementation of your plan is the tendency to want to throw it out and start all over again. Resist this temptation, however, and stick to the plan.

As covered in Rule 93, it is certain that some of the elements of your plan—perhaps even important basic elements—will be different in real life than you had thought they would be. While this is grounds for modification and flexibility in implementation, it is seldom grounds for starting all over.

You will find in life many people who will be willing to criticize what they had little heart for doing themselves. These will be the most vocal in pointing out how you have screwed up. They will be the Chihuahuas who will try to tree you. Don't let them.

Remember that you and your colleagues have put a lot of thought and effort into the plan, and that you have the momentum of truth and beauty on your side. While circumstances may differ in detail, it is quite seldom that circumstances change enough to justify discarding all of the prior work and starting over again from scratch.

Sometimes the group that wants to throw out the plan is simply panicking or suffering from a lack of nerve. Not knowing what to do, they advocate doing something else—anything else other than what was being done. Sometimes this works; sometimes it doesn't. The trick is in knowing when to start over and when to persevere.

One of the greatest examples I have observed of loss of nerve resulting in panic was when the Tet Offensive took place in January and February 1968. The North Vietnamese and Vietcong surprised the leadership of the Pentagon (although not the troops in Vietnam) by mounting a large attack throughout South Vietnam that succeeded in seizing and holding momentarily some cities and other key points— notably the American Embassy in Saigon. Although the attack brought the covert cadres of the Vietcong out where they could be—and were—killed, and the military victory of the U.S. and South Vietnamese forces was complete, it was not perceived this way at the Pentagon. High civilian officials—not one a military person—ran up and down the halls of the Pentagon shouting the equivalent of, "The sky is falling!" Without the nerve to see the original plan through, the panickers tossed out the current plan and changed the strategy to one that ultimately led to the abandonment by the United States of the South Vietnamese and their surrender to North Vietnam.

Contrast this unsteady implementation to that of a champion football team that has its game plan and sticks to it through bad breaks, penalties, and outstanding opposition to persevere and win in the end. I can think of no athletic team that epitomizes the virtue of sticking to the plan so much as the world champion Washington Redskins of 1991. They lost only two games and won seventeen, including Super Bowl XXVI, and did so in a convincing manner. They did this in large measure by sticking to the plan—persevering until the plan worked. No panic ensued, and in some cases the "Skins" had to come from behind, but in each game they played the plan calmly, confidently, and in most cases victoriously.

My advice is to stick to the plan even if the going gets rough. The goals and ideas you put into the plan are probably as good now as ever, for much of the trouble you are going to run into during implementation will originate in those who did not participate in the planning. It takes great character to keep your head when those about you are losing theirs, but in the somewhat abridged words of Rudyard Kipling:

> If you can keep your head when all about you
> Are losing theirs and blaming it on you,
> If you can trust yourself when all men doubt you . . .
> Yours is the Earth and everything that's in it,
> And—which is more—you'll be a Man, my son!*

Rule 95: Implement Incrementally

You don't have to implement your plan all at once in a massive spasm of doing. Now, you might want to implement it that way, and if so, fine. But in some circumstances it would be better to implement your plan incrementally—in stages.

Many plans should be implemented in a continuous manner flowing without pause from the start until the goal is achieved. Small plans that cover a short period of time and cost relatively little are probably best done this way. Other plans are not amenable to being done in stages because the flow is so dependent on previous actions and there is no convenient place to stop. Traveling is often like that: Because you have already made arrangements for future legs of the journey, just staying in one place longer than planned—no matter how desirable that might be—is simply not worth the extra trouble it would take to change all of the future plans. In general, if time is of the essence and you have to rush to make happen what you want, then you are likely to want to implement in one massive, wonderful swoosh of frenzied but purposeful activity.

There are, however, a great many plans for which incremental implementation could be very appropriate.

Incremental implementation might, for example, be useful when you lack the funds to do the whole thing all at once. If you

---

* Rudyard Kipling, "If," *The Oxford Dictionary of Quotations,* (London: Oxford University Press, 1955), p. 297.

are building your own house, you might want to do it room by room, providing for enough space for just bare living in the first stage, and then adding rooms as you need and can afford them. You might do the same thing with a business, opening one retail outlet initially and then adding others as business improves. You might want to end up with a manufacturing capability for 20,000 units per month but start with a capability for only 5,000 per month and then add increments of production capacity as sales increase beyond current production.

Incremental implementation is also used for plans that by their nature are reactive to outside events. You might want to avoid going beyond the actions that are actually required to respond appropriately to the cause. This condition would apply if you are planning a marketing campaign designed to counter a competitor, and you want to implement just enough of your own counter-campaign to stay slightly ahead. This means that instead of going all the way with everything you have at the outset, you pace your own releases of advertising and promotions by the actions of your competitor. In this case you are trying to match the competitor and, if your information is good enough, keep ahead of him at each stage.

Incremental implementation would be prudent if there is uncertainty about what will result from implementing the plan. You could implement in stages to give you time to wait for reactions from others, and then adjust your plan so that subsequent stages take those reactions into account. This is the reverse of the situation posed in the paragraph above. If you are planning a large subdivision development, for example, you may want to finish phase 1 and obtain customer reaction before you start phase 2 or phase 3 to see what worked and what didn't, and adjust the plans on that basis.

So there are several reasons why you might find it handy to implement incrementally. In these cases, it is usually possible simply to take your plan and do part but not all of it. This is not always true, however, and a clear distinction needs to be made between implementing ordinary plans incrementally and planning for incremental implementation. In the former situation, the incremental nature of the implementation has not been provided in the planning process itself, but is merely a way that you have chosen to subdivide your plan when you are implementing it. That approach will work most of the time, but you may run into great difficulties in separating tasks, events, and processes that you originally did not plan to separate.

If incremental implementation is a consideration, it is far better to plan for it during the original planning process. Let me illustrate the difference using a plan for building a house.

When planning to build the entire house in one continuous process, the project schedule is laid out to achieve the lowest cost by using each special crew efficiently. The foundation is laid, the floors are placed, the walls are framed, the plumbing and electrical and telephone wiring are put in, the roof is put on, the walls are covered, the painting is done, and the finishing is done in an intricate schedule—but the work of each crew is for the entire house. That is, the plumbers put in all of the plumbing for the kitchen, bathrooms, laundry, and whatever else uses water for the entire house. Electrical circuits are put in for the entire house. The foundation supports the entire house, the walls enclose the entire house, and the roof is put over the entire house. You get the picture: It is an entire house.

Now, if we plan to build that house incrementally, the planning has to be fundamentally different. There are three major differences: We have to provide adequate living capacity in all respects at each stage in the construction, so that the house is at all times furnished with all of the necessary systems. We have to forgo installing complete systems for the entire house, because we are not certain that we will be doing the entire house. And we have to leave connections for each of the house systems to accommodate construction at a later date of additional rooms to the existing house.

So if we are planning to build a house in stages, we would schedule our work crews differently and give them different instructions. We might build the foundation for the entire house (since that is such a basic job) and cover up the unused part for later use, or we could build only the foundation we intend to use at that time while leaving connections for an add-on. We could install only the plumbing for the part we are actually building, but we would have to put in pipes and connections for the new plumbing that would go with the additional stages of construction. For the electrical circuits, we would wire just the part of the house we were building, while assuring that sufficient capacity is brought into the house to support the electricity demands for the ultimate house. At each stage, the house would have to provide a kitchen, at least one bathroom, a complete electrical system, a complete heating and cooling system, and enough of all of the other things that go into a modern house to make it livable. So planning to build a house in several stages is more complicated than simply taking an ordinary house plan and construction schedule and spreading it out over time. Building a house by stages tends to be more expensive, because you have to make provisions at each stage for tying in the next stage. The additional overall cost may not be the major consideration, however, since by building the house in cleverly planned stages you presumably will have matched each construction stage to your current financial condition.

It would be a major problem, of course, if you built the first stage as a self-contained unit and then found that the second stage would also have to be self-contained because you forgot to provide the necessary connections in your construction planning. Therefore, if you intend to implement incrementally, you should provide for that in your original planning process.

Rule 96: Apply Quality Control

One of the major aspects of implementing your plan is quality control. If you are in business, you have to ensure that the product you make or the service you offer is of sufficiently high quality to attract customers at the price you are charging. If you work for the government, you will have to meet the expectations of your supervisor and his or her boss. If you are doing something for yourself, you have to measure up to your own standards of what is acceptable.

Quality is the attribute of a product or service that describes its distance from the standard for that product or service specified in the plan. The word *quality* is normally used to describe something that is excellent or above the norm, but in business quality is relative to your own standards. There can be low quality, high quality, or average quality. Low quality denotes that the product deviates a great deal from the planned standards, and high quality that the product adheres to those standards.

Quality depends on price, so acceptable quality is not always high quality. It is acceptable to produce inexpensive items that are of lower quality than expensive items. What is not acceptable is to provide lower quality than is expected or customary for the price.

In a manufacturing process, quality control means producing items that meet the minimum standards and tolerances called for in the engineering specifications. If a tube is to have an outside diameter of 5 centimeters, plus or minus 5 millimeters, the quality standard is met by those items whose outside diameter measures between 4.5 and 5.5 centimeters. Any item whose measurements fall outside this range should be discarded as failing to meet the quality standards.

Quality is determined by inspection and measurement. For the manufacturing case discussed above, once the items are made, they are inspected and measured to see if they fit within the specified range of acceptable diameters. This can be done by inspecting every item (enumeration), or it can be done by collecting a representative sample of items and applying statistical methods to estimate the quality of the entire batch of items. If the number of bad parts is higher than you want to accept, it is necessary to adjust the manufacturing process to provide fewer bad parts—higher quality.

Your products can be inspected while they are being made or afterward. Obviously, it is a good idea to apply as much quality control as you can before the product is finished. If you have to wait until the items are made before you can check them—as is the case in many manufacturing processes—you may have to reject a lot of bad items until you get it right. When you are building a house or some other product that proceeds in stages, it is wise to inspect and measure frequently at each stage and correct mistakes before proceeding to the next stage. If the foundation of your house is defective, it would not make sense to go ahead and frame the walls and build the floors. If you are in a service business, you can check up on the manner in which that service is being provided by simply stepping back to gain perspective and notice what is happening. Fast-food restaurant chains use inspectors who eat anonymously in their outlets to observe and report on how ordinary customers are treated and whether the food measures up to the standards set by the management. Courtesy and cleanliness are part of the service for any business dealing with the general public, and they have to be subject to quality control just like the tube discussed earlier.

Quality control has been important in business from the beginning. Customers expect to be treated well and to receive value appropriate for the price. Many successful entrepreneurs have built business empires by training their work forces to treat customers well, by adhering to high quality standards, and by applying quality control continuously to assure that the customers got their money's worth.

One of the new buzz phrases is "total quality management" (TQM). This is a system of quality control that was invented in America but taken seriously by the Japanese, who used it to beat the socks off our automobile industry in the 1960s and 1970s. While cars made in the United States required a lot of maintenance, had doors that closed poorly, and had fittings that were shoddy, cars made in Japan worked properly and looked good. U.S. consumers bought the higher-quality products—even at higher prices, in many cases. In response to dwindling sales, U.S. car makers also placed greater stress on quality control and today are making cars of equal or higher quality than the Japanese. The major elements of TQM are as follows:

1. Continuous improvement of the product by making many small adjustments instead of accumulating changes and making infrequent large adjustments. This means that errors are corrected as soon as they are noticed.

2. Incorporation of the work force into the quality control system by encouraging and accepting suggestions from the workers on how to make a better product. Instead of a plant where workers are indifferent to quality, work only for their wages, and do poor work, TQM seeks to foster a climate in which workers take pride in putting out a high-quality product or service.

3. Consideration of quality and quality control from the start of the design or plan through the process of making the product. Under TQM, quality control is not something done incidentally after the fact but a major consideration from the start.

I have discussed quality control in the chapter about implementing because it had to go somewhere, and it is a part of implementation. But quality control really starts in chapter 1 when you think about what it is you want to make happen. As you formulate your goals, implicitly or (preferably) explicitly, you establish for those goals quality standards that serve as the benchmarks against which you will control quality. So the level of quality you want and the ways you are going to ensure getting that quality should be considered from the start.

17 Making Things Happen

It is not easy to make something happen. It takes inspiration, ambition, perspiration, and grit to get anything to happen purposefully in this world of ours. For one thing, the laws of nature work against making something happen. The Second Law of Thermodynamics implies that entropy—the condition of disorganization—increases naturally and that it takes energy to prevent disorganization from spreading until all activity ceases. Left to its own devices, nature would simply wind down into undifferentiated inactivity. It is man who applies energy purposefully to foil the encroachment of entropy, but it is also man who is the biggest problem in making things happen.

In this final chapter, I am providing some advice on how to deal with your fellow humans, who for various reasons good or ill will try to impede your progress. Some of these problem people are outsiders; many are close associates; and one of them is you.

Despite the difficulties, there is merit in planning, preparing, and implementing to get things done and make things happen. These final five rules take a philosophical look at the practical advice presented in the first ninety-six rules.

Rule 97: Don't Get Mad at Nitpickers or Wordsmiths

Just as soon as you have completed your plan, and perhaps even during the planning process, you will be annoyed by small-minded people who will criticize what you have done. There are three general classes of critics: nitpickers, wordsmiths, and feather merchants. The third group is so prevalent that a separate rule will deal with them.

Nitpickers are people who find tiny flaws in your otherwise impeccable plan. They take great delight in finding a typographical error, a numerical mistake, or a misspelling. Then they trumpet the blemish to high heaven, proclaiming that these errors are proof that your basic concept, your goals, your schedule, and even your morals are faulty. Tiny errata are advanced as evidence of evil incarnate.

Wordsmiths, on the other hand, are people who perceive themselves to be great authors—unpublished, but great nonetheless. Wordsmiths act as masters of the English language and take great delight in changing the words, word order, punctuation, and syntax of your sacred writings. They delight, in other words, in smithing words. Wordsmithing is particularly insidious in hierarchical organizations where each layer in turn changes the changes just changed by the previous layer. The acme of wordsmithing is the chief executive officer who personally rewrites the letters sent to him by underlings for his signature. We used to refer to this custom as changing "would" to "could" and back again.

This is a book on planning, not personal relations, so I am going to gloss over the more delicate aspects of this kind of interference and simply deal with the effects on the planning process.

My advice is to take all nitpicking and wordsmithing seriously. These interventions are annoying, but they can also be helpful. In keeping with the general application of the Tom Sawyer Whitewash Principle, try your best to convert nitpicking and wordsmithing into positive experiences that strengthen your plan. You may recall how Tom Sawyer managed to turn his chore of whitewashing Aunt Polly's fence into a masterpiece of fun for profit. By pretending that white-washing a fence was a wonderful experience only to be accomplished by the very best, he was able to persuade his fellows not only to do the work for him, but to pay for the privilege with important and valuable possessions. This episode by Mark Twain captures the spirit of American entrepreneurial endeavor—and it also can be applied to the planning process.

Simply accept the nits and the word changes at face value, ignoring the source. Swallow your pride. The suggested corrections to your spelling, arithmetic, and grammar will help you make the plan error-free, so just accommodate them, provided of course they are correct. The same thing goes for suggested changes in your Pulitzer Prize—winning prose. Take the changes you like and discard those you don't like. That will make for a better paper and a better plan.

When I worked on the Army staff, we all used to wordsmith each other. I started as an "action officer" at the bottom of the chain and would prepare a draft, which I submitted to my branch chief, who would rewrite it and send it back to me for revision. I then prepared another draft that went through the branch chief to the division chief, who also rewrote it and sent it back. Once the paper was approved by the division chief, it had to go through the "planners," a group of senior colonels whose job it was to question every nit and smith every word, and these guys were really tough. We action officers really hated having to go through the planners, but there was no way around it, and we invariably had to have the paper retyped after that for yet another submission to the general, which often resulted in additional word changes. Finally, after much explaining, justifying, and rewriting, we action officers took our (??) papers to the Chief of Staff of the Army for his review and action. This was in the days before computers, when everything had to be retyped in its entirety, so the process was arduous.

At first I hated the wordsmithing process since, like everyone else, I thought I was a great writer. Once I got used to the idea, however, I found that two heads or five heads or fifteen heads often were better than one, and that it all went to make the paper better. So the process has merit, and you can benefit from the help, with just two important provisos:

First, stay in charge of your plan. If you simply accept all changes willy-nilly, it is highly possible that the plan will be distorted so much as to be quite different and probably not as good as the original. So you have to be the judge of what you accept and what you don't.

Second, accept unimportant changes eagerly, but reject those that alter the fundamental nature of the plan. This is particularly important when changes come from those above you in the hierarchy. Give in on the little things. Hold fast on the important things. You will find that others often are so grateful for an opportunity to insert a word or even a comma that you can placate them without major change to the thrust of the plan. Of course, this is not always the case, and sometimes major changes—even disabling changes—come in the guise of a modest wordsmithing proposal, but you will have to be alert to this possibility. Simply remember that everyone whose suggestions are incorporated into the plan now has a vested interest in its success.

This all goes under the heading of making a virtue of necessity, which is really difficult when you have to deal with that special brand of helpers called feather merchants.

Rule 98: Beware of Feather Merchants

One of the biggest problems that planners and doers have is the appearance of feather merchants.* A feather merchant is a fellow who knows nothing about what you are doing and has no responsibility for it, but who does not hesitate to give you strong advice on how to do it. The very ignorance of a feather merchant is—in his eyes at least—his greatest stock in trade. He will come in out of left field and tell you not only what is wrong with what you want to do but very often what is wrong with you yourself.

Feather merchants are found everywhere, and anyone who has tried to accomplish something will find them emerging from the woodwork with (sometimes) well-meant advice. You must recognize that

---

* This slang expression originally was applied to people who failed to do their duties during time of war. Somehow the meaning was broadened to include those who did little but talked a lot and then to those who got into everyone else's business. I have done a lot of research on the origin of the term, but to no avail. Perhaps one of you readers could enlighten me.

feather merchants take themselves seriously and resent being informed that they are objects of ridicule. In fact, according to the Law of Inverse Insight, the less a feather merchant knows about a subject, the more he or she is convinced of being right. Ignorance breeds arrogance.

Although they have a frivolous name befitting their intellectual worth, you cannot afford to ignore feather merchants, many of whom are persons of wealth, influence, and reputation. In fact, the bigger the reputation, the greater the temptation for some people to meddle in what they know not.

Neither your client nor your boss is a feather merchant, no matter how little they know about the topic at hand. Clients and bosses are entitled to opine on your work and nitpick or wordsmith as they deem necessary. In particular, the act of paying for a product or service entitles a person to give opinions, good or bad.

My advice is to beware of feather merchants. Do not sass them, or they might turn mean. Do not ignore them, for you might find them circumventing you in adverse ways. Do not argue with them, for it does little good. Fend them off without taking their advice or antagonizing them. This may mean giving in on style while holding fast on the substance. It may mean giving in on the little things while holding fast on the big things. The degree to which you accommodate a feather merchant should depend on his or her influence and the extent to which he or she can do you dirt. The best approach is to humor these individuals while sticking to your plan and moving smartly to your goals.

Rule 99: Look Out for Planning Pitfalls

Planning can be treacherous, for there are many pitfalls along the path to success. Just when you believe you have reached the goal, something happens to convert your success to failure. In a real sense, this entire book about planning is a guide to help you avoid pitfalls, but I want to take just one last opportunity to point out again some common pitfalls that can make your plans invalid. These are insufficient information, failure to consult others, a poor plan, and hope.

A common planning pitfall is insufficient information. We will never have complete information, and we have to face life without knowing what is going to happen in the future. But we ought to face that future with some knowledge of what might happen and some ideas on how to make what we want to happen happen. This actually puts a premium on planning, which allows us to influence the future in some measure. Making decisions in the face of incomplete information is our lot, and many of the rules in this book are intended to help you deal with that.

Sometimes we are compelled to act with less information than we are really comfortable with, and we just have to accept those times. On the other hand, it is also legitimate to delay implementation until you can get enough additional information to give you some measure of comfort. My advice is to defer acting until you have enough information to accomplish the plan.

Remember that a decision not to act or even a decision not to decide is itself a decision—and a legitimate choice. In fact, the existing situation, or base case, should be considered in all planning as an alternative from which to measure marginal costs and benefits.

Another common pitfall of planning is failure to consider the reactions of others to the plan and how those reactions will affect the plan in implementation. Planning tends to be a very emotional matter, because it necessitates choices based to a great extent on personal preference of the person or group doing the planning. This means that the reaction of people outside the planning group may be quite different than the reaction anticipated by the planners. I have seen planners quite crestfallen when their best efforts have been rejected firmly by those quite close to them. This happens fairly often, I suppose, with plans for trips, funerals, parties, and weddings, all of which are events that can bring deep emotions to the surface. Weddings are particularly hazardous, because they tend to pit the bride's ideas against the mother of the bride's ideas. This pitfall may also be a problem with plans for buildings, battles, and election campaigns. The solution to this pitfall is to consult with interested outsiders or involved bystanders during the planning process. If the bride rebels at the plan for the wedding reception, the planners are at fault for not having taken into account her preferences in the first place. As in any other case of this kind, the best way to find out what people think about your plan is simply to ask them.

Another pitfall, of course, is a poor plan. You may realize after you have done the work or upon receipt of new information that the plan is just not very good. If there is time to do it over, that is advised, but in some cases you cannot delay the implementation. In this situation, it may be better to implement a poor plan energetically than a good plan half-heartedly. This thought is captured in the famous exhortation common in the halls of the Pentagon: "Do something, even if it's wrong!"

The most common pitfall, however, is what I call the triumph of hope over reality. Sometimes the desire to do something is so great that it causes planners to assume away the problems and difficulties, lower the cost estimates, increase the sales projections, or say whatever else is necessary to justify the plan. Sometimes an overly optimistic plan will succeed despite a rosy approach, and sometimes perhaps plans succeed because of an overly rosy approach. In this life, it is difficult to generalize, but ordinarily the best plans are those that meet the harsh realities head-on and are neither overly optimistic nor overly pessimistic.

I am certain that there are many other things that can go wrong with plans, some of which may indeed also merit the designation of pitfall, but these are the ones that seem to occur most commonly.

Rule 100: Learn from Your Mistakes

Planning is a continuous process, and so it gives you plenty of opportunity to learn from your mistakes. Having the opportunity, however, does not necessarily mean you will learn from your mistakes, because that requires an ability to admit that mistakes were made.

Learning can apply to the same plan, as you improve the plan through successive iterations. It can also apply to the next plan, and the next plan, and the next plan after that. But merely applying marginal corrections either in successive versions of one plan or to successive

plans is not sufficient. You have to learn from your mistakes systematically in order to avoid making the same ones over and over again.
It usually is easy to ascertain when a mistake was made. When
the business goes bankrupt, you lose the election, the guests go away
mad, the bridge collapses, the bride gets hysterical, or you find yourself stranded in a dingy pension in a remote Himalayan village with
no food or drink, it is going to be somewhat obvious that a mistake
was made.

The politically correct response to these kinds of mistakes is to
remain calm and take copious notes so that you can analyze objec-
tively what went wrong. The usual response is to get hysterical
yourself and either hit someone, drink too much booze, or both.
Actually, my advice is to try a reaction somewhere in the middle of
these two extremes. That is, allow your emotions to lead you to a
serious examination of what went wrong. In military terminology,
this kind of reflection produces "lessons learned."

After the war with Iraq in 1990 and 1991, the entire Department
of Defense went into the lessons-learned business in a big way. The
combat phase of the war lasted only forty-three days from start to
ceasefire, but already it is the most researched, studied, analyzed, and
generally poked-into military campaign in history. The guns had hardly
cooled off when teams of active and retired military personnel and
civilians were convened to figure out what went wrong. Despite the
fact that this was probably the shortest, most overwhelming victory
in modern military history, a lot of things did go wrong. So there are
a lot of lessons to be learned even after a tremendous victory.

Consider how much easier it is to learn from defeat. Throughout
history, it has been the losers who learned while the victors rested on
their laurels, the idea being that if we won, we must have been doing
something right, so why worry? Losers are still smarting from defeat
and want to change something so they will win next time, and so they
are more prone to introspection and innovation than the complacent winners.

I am not advising you to avoid learning from your victories, for
it is good to learn even while you are doing well. That is wisdom.
But I really am urging you to take the time to figure out what went

wrong and why when you lose. That is the only way you are going to be able eventually to win.

It hurts to face up to failure, but we all admire people who fail at first but eventually triumph. My advice is to remember the little engine that could, and revise your plan until you can.

Rule 101: Keep On Making Things Happen

There is a choice in life between purposeful activity and aimless existence. I suppose we all imagine at one time or another that we would be happy if only we had nothing to do and could be spared thereby the necessity to plan and prepare. In fact, we seldom accept opportunities to do nothing in favor of some kind of activity that does involve planning and preparing. We divide our lives into work and leisure, and though we acknowledge the necessity of planning for work, we sometimes pretend that we don't plan for leisure.

Yet much of our leisure time is not truly leisure, but consists largely of events that are just different from our normal events and are often complicated, sometimes dangerous, frequently arduous, and always costly. These so-called leisure activities all require planning and preparing so that we can accomplish them in some kind of systematic and efficient manner. Perhaps our greatest luxury of this kind is to pay for a vacation during which most of the planning is done for us by someone else. This is an attractive feature of cruises, guided tours, summer camps, and resort hotels, where the staff does the planning and all we have to do is do as we are told.

Those cases, as far as I am concerned, are about the only ways we can get relief from the incessant need to plan, prepare, and implement. Having servants or employees to help do the work eliminates or reduces one level of doing but establishes a need to plan, prepare, and oversee the work of the servants or employees. So there is nothing for it but to keep on making things happen.

I for one cannot speculate on an existence in which planning is not necessary in its most basic form. Living on the fabled idyllic South Seas island, where food can be picked from the trees and clothing is not needed for protection from the elements, appears at first glance to offer a respite from always having to think ahead, but even in this hospitable environment there will be a need to consider the future—when the best time is for picking the bananas, perhaps, or what to do when illness strikes or a storm appears. Even Eden could have benefitted from some planning. What if Adam had given a little thought to the unintended adverse consequences of eating apples?

My final advice to you with respect to planning is to keep on doing it. It is a natural thing to do, and it helps all of us cope with the uncertainty of the future. It also helps us be the masters of our fate instead of mere puppets dangling on strings manipulated by larger forces.

I don't know for sure if planning is innate or learned. Certainly the premise of this book is that people can learn to do it better, but it is quite possible that we have a planning gene in our makeup. I thought about this particularly when I observed my then almost two-year-old granddaughter, Bunnie, barely walking, deliberately formulate a plan, make preparations, and implement it purposefully. She wanted to get a toy that was on top of her changing table (the goal), she appeared to think about it awhile (the concept), then she looked around her nursery (data compilation), pulled a chair over to the changing table (preparation), climbed up on the stool (implementation), and got the toy. While not a particularly complicated or ambitious plan, it worked!

So I believe that planning is a normal and natural activity for humans that, like other human activities, can be improved with a bit of instruction and lots of practice. I have provided the instruction; now it's up to you to do the planning and make things happen.